D1625136

DIGITALLY YOURS,

MRWade

Praise for *Hacking Digital*

Finally! A pragmatic guide focused on the "how" that considers that every transformation journey is unique. Whether you are at the beginning or in a more advanced phase, this book is an essential resource to use every day to find your way for a successful digital transformation.

—**Luca Cavalli**, Chief Digital Officer, Cornèr Bank

Digital innovation is all about execution. *Hacking Digital* is a must-read book for all innovators. It provides a rich and practical toolbox of best practices that strongly resonated with me, as they are at the heart of my day-to-day execution challenges. The frameworks helped me to think differently about solving my implementation problems. And most importantly: I had fun reading it, with many executives' testimonies and practical cases.

—**Claire Calmejane**, Chief Innovation Officer, Société Générale Groupe

No matter how faddish the technology or grand the vision, excelling at the basics is essential. The authors illustrate how to adroitly sequence business fundamentals to execute a successful digital transformation.

—**Richard Watson**, Regents Professor and J. Rex Fuqua
    Distinguished Chair for Internet Strategy, University of Georgia,
    and author, *Capital, Systems, and Objects*

Companies don't lack ideas for digitalization. They lack success in having these initiatives contribute to the bottom line. Examples of failures are aplenty because not all aspects were considered. The team behind *Hacking Digital* guides you, in a practical way, through successfully implementing and executing a digital strategy. A must-read to harvest results from your investments in digitalization.

—**Ursula Soritsch-Renier**, Group Chief Digital and
    Information Officer, Saint-Gobain

Hacking Digital shows the pieces of the complex puzzle that need to be in place to run a successful digital transformation. A very interesting read about the trickiest digital transformation challenges accompanied by many best practices from different organizations. Useful insights for digital transformation executives and also very relevant for those in related work fields.

—**Bart Leurs**, Chief Digital Transformation Officer, Rabobank

The digital transformation challenge is truly a trek up a tall mountain. This book is like a Sherpa guide for that journey.

—**Hiroshi Nishino**, Co-Founder, Digital Business Innovation Centre, Tokyo, Japan

Hacking Digital delivers on its promise by taking problems straight out of real life and providing honest analysis and practical solutions to solve them.

—**Tom Voskes**, Managing Partner, SparkOptimus

The purpose of any digital transformation is about your consumers and your future relevance as a social entity. Transformation starts with people, organization, and culture. It also requires many technical and financial enablers. The challenge is to create the relevant ecosystems to effectively and sustainably adapt to fast-changing and complex environments that are now the norm. This is nicely said, but how do we start/accelerate, how do we operationalize this transformation and adapt to different context if there is not a unique path to follow? Doing is everything, and *Hacking Digital*, as a practical compilation of insights and best practices, will inspire and help many leaders accelerate their transformational journey whatever the step they are in.

—**Cyril Lamblard**, Global Head of eBusiness, Nestlé Nespresso S.A.

Hacking Digital is a must-read for practitioners looking to successfully scale digital transformations in the COVID era. The authors thoughtfully analyze the key organizational and operational challenges that must be overcome to make digital transformations successful by leveraging the real world-experiences of digital leaders at every stage of the transformation process. Whether you are just starting your journey or are well along the maturity curve, this book will give you practical insights, frameworks, and tactics to help you achieve your organizational objectives.

—**Stephen Bailey**, Founder and Chief Executive Officer, ExecOnline

A state-of-the-art field manual for navigating the twists and turns of digital transformation successfully. Required reading for anyone embarking upon the journey.

—**Tim Ellis**, Founder and CEO, The Digital Transformation People

HACKING DIGITAL

BEST PRACTICES TO IMPLEMENT AND ACCELERATE YOUR BUSINESS TRANSFORMATION

MICHAEL WADE · DIDIER BONNET
TOMOKO YOKOI · NIKOLAUS OBWEGESER

New York   Chicago   San Francisco   Athens   London
Madrid   Mexico City   Milan   New Delhi
Singapore   Sydney   Toronto

Copyright © 2022 by McGraw Hill. All rights reserved. Printed in the United States of America. Except as permitted under the United States Copyright Act of 1976, no part of this publication may be reproduced or distributed in any form or by any means, or stored in a database or retrieval system, without the prior written permission of the publisher.

1 2 3 4 5 6 7 8 9   LCR   26 25 24 23 22 21

ISBN   978-1-264-26962-4
MHID   1-264-26962-5

e-ISBN   978-1-264-26963-1
e-MHID   1-264-26963-3

Library of Congress Cataloging-in-Publication Data

Names: Wade, Michael, 1968- author. | Bonnet, Didier, author. | Yokoi, Tomoko, author. | Obwegeser, Nikolaus, author.
Title: Hacking digital : best practices to implement and accelerate your business transformation / Michael Wade, Didier Bonnet, Tomoko Yokoi and Nikolaus Obwegeser.
Description: 1 Edition. | New York City : McGraw Hill, 2021. | Includes bibliographical references and index.
Identifiers: LCCN 2021011947 (print) | LCCN 2021011948 (ebook) | ISBN 9781264269624 (hardcover) | ISBN 9781264269631 (ebook)
Subjects: LCSH: Business enterprises—Technological innovations. | Information technology—Management. | Organizational change. | Organizational effectiveness.
Classification: LCC HD45 .W233 2021 (print) | LCC HD45 (ebook) | DDC 658.4/06—dc23
LC record available at https://lccn.loc.gov/2021011947
LC ebook record available at https://lccn.loc.gov/2021011948

McGraw Hill books are available at special quantity discounts to use as premiums and sales promotions or for use in corporate training programs. To contact a representative, please visit the Contact Us pages at www.mhprofessional.com.

To Heidi, with gratitude that
not everything important is digital
MW

To my coauthors who have taught me much
about scholarship, collaboration, and good fun
DB

To my parents, who finally figured out how to Skype
TY

To Noémie and Isabel, my never-ending sources of inspiration
NO

CONTENTS

Part Five
Hacking Digital Transformation Leadership
Leading People and Organizations

Part Six
Hacking Digital Momentum
Anchoring and Sustaining Performance

INTRODUCTION

My destination is no longer a place,
rather a new way of seeing.
—Marcel Proust

The lights dimmed as the participants attending the Next Wave of Digital Transformation Conference filed out of the auditorium. The first day of the conference had drawn to a close, and the networking reception was about to begin.

"If I could just find some people to talk to," thought Ian as he scanned the room. He was an engineer by training, and his career had recently taken an interesting turn. He'd been tapped to look after digital for his employer, a global engineering company where he had worked for the past 20 years. His company had agreed to let him attend the conference so he could figure out how to get started.

Ian caught sight of Elena, who had made a presentation earlier that day. Elena was one year into the chief digital officer (CDO) role at a Dutch bank, and she had indicated that she was open to sharing her experiences. She was already speaking with another participant, who introduced himself as Andrej. Andrej had been recently promoted to the role of chief information officer (CIO) of a consumer goods company, before which he had been the company's CDO.

Ian was keen to learn from both Elena and Andrej about managing large, complex digital transformation projects. After a round of introductions, they asked him about his new role.

"It's strange," Ian began. "All the signs are positive, but I have an uneasy feeling."

"What do you mean?" asked Andrej.

"Well," Ian continued, "I was asked a month ago by the chief operating officer, my boss, to look into digital. He wasn't very specific about it—only that we needed to do something digital quickly. Sounds good, right? He also told me that he'd make whatever resources available, within reason, to 'transform the company into a digital business.'"

"So far, so good," said Elena. "What's the problem?"

"The problem is, I don't think my boss, or any of the management team, really understands what digital transformation is. I've talked to the CIO, the head of finance, and the key executives who actually run the business, and they're all supportive, but they don't really engage with me. When I press for details, not much comes back.

"I sense there's a lot more going on in digital than I'm aware of. I don't have a good sense of all the projects that exist across the company. We have a website and an app—actually we have multiple sites and apps—but no one seems to know how much business they generate or if they're profitable.

"Overall, I feel that everyone is tolerating me, but not really committing to the transformation. They nod their heads when I talk about disruption and transformation, but I sense that the message is not really landing. I don't know if it's because they don't believe in it or they don't believe in me to deliver it."

"Basically," Ian continued, "I think they would be happy to just keep doing what they're doing without any interference from me. It's OK for me to be around, as long as I don't get in their way."

"How big is your team?" asked Andrej.

"That's another thing," replied Ian. "It's really small. I inherited a small team of five people with a wide range of skill sets—a project manager, a communications person, an agile coach, and a couple of IT people. My boss tells me that I can hire anyone I want, but I'm not sure what skills we need. Plus, there's no governance structure around digital to build around. To be honest, I'm not really sure what I am supposed to do next."

"That sounds familiar," said Elena. "When I joined the bank a year ago, we were going through a major business transformation. The company was change-weary, and it was hard to motivate people to embrace digital. It took me a while to get a handle on things, like you mentioned, Ian. I had to conduct an audit to figure out where we were on digital. So I built a team and identified a set of projects to work on. I was starting to get some traction when COVID hit."

"What was that like?" asked Ian.

"Well, from being a bit player in the corporate landscape, suddenly everyone was looking to me for answers. Luckily, I had built a good relationship with our IT folks, and we worked closely together to accelerate our video banking project, which really saved us. I also took the lead on our work-from-home project, which took a lot of time and energy. Thankfully, it went well. We got 7,000 people up and running from home offices in about two weeks. Video banking and working from home really helped to build my credibility within the bank."

"Sounds like COVID worked out well for you, at least professionally," said Andrej.

"Yes, it probably did," replied Elena, "but at the same time, it raised unrealistic expectations about how digital projects typically go. More recently, some of our digital initiatives have failed, and the old resistance is back. We've sort of stalled. I spend most of my time these days on the organizational side rather than technology, like building momentum for change, redesigning processes, working with the business and HR on incentives, training employees on digital skills, and trying to build the case for new business models. I'm also spending a lot of time with customers, trying to understand what they need and, most importantly, what they're willing to pay for.

"My biggest challenge these days is actually taking digital pilots to scale. We have lots of great digital projects in some kind of incubation stage, but I can't seem to get them to scale, which is driving me nuts! In some ways, it gets easier, Ian. But in other ways, it's a lot harder. Even with some successes over the past year, I don't feel as if I am completely on top of things."

Andrej chimed in, "It gets better—at least it did for me. We've gone through a lot over the past three years, and it wasn't always successful. In fact, we made a lot of mistakes. But I think we're finally on the right track. I spent a lot of time, early on, convincing my colleagues of the need to transform. First, they didn't really see the threat—it wasn't in their nature to deal with disruption. Second, they weren't convinced that digital could provide the answers. Most of them thought of digital as fancy IT tools, including the IT department by the way!

"It took a couple of shocks to the business to convince them that all was not well with the status quo. And that was before COVID. For us, in the consumer goods space, COVID was actually positive for our business. Our challenge was how to scale up quickly to meet the additional demand. Digital really helped us a lot. Thankfully, we had set up a strong digital team with clear governance and well-defined relationships with other departments, like operations and IT. We're now able to develop new digital tools, evaluate them, and integrate them into our business at scale. Well, most of the time.

"My biggest challenge at the moment is how to transition digital transformation from a program, which is what it's been for a few years now, into the regular way of doing business. I don't think it makes sense any more to separate digital. Pretty much everything we do nowadays in our industry is digital. We need to make ourselves much more agile, more collaborative, and more data-driven than we are today. Digital tools and technologies are necessary for this, so we need to integrate them into the core of our business. But if we want to become a digital business, we also need to redesign our organization and operating model, so we've still got some way to go."

THERE IS NO ONE-SIZE-FITS-ALL SOLUTION

Ian, Elena, and Andrej are not real people. They are composites of many people. But in our consulting work, our executive education activities, and our research, we have interacted with many thousands of executives like them—people struggling with the realities of managing digital projects and transforming their organizations.

If there is one thing we have learned over the years, it's that digital transformation is hard. We wish there were a magic formula, a single methodology, or a road map to follow, but despite what you may hear from consultants or read in other books, there isn't. Trust us.

Digital transformation is a journey with many twists and turns. At each turn, a new challenge presents itself. Some of these challenges are related to technology, but more often than not, the barriers to successful transformation are organizational. They concern people, organizational structure, culture, incentives, governance, vision, and a host of other thorny challenges.

Our analysis of 11 research-based studies of digital transformation performance suggests that 87 percent of programs fail to meet original expectations.[1] Those are not great odds! So our best advice is that if you don't need to transform, don't. Unfortunately, *not* transforming is an option for fewer and fewer organizations. The opportunities (and the threats) are large enough that you are left with little choice but to embark on some form of digital transformation. It's hard and the odds aren't great, but most likely, you won't have a choice.

Although we can't promise success, we believe we can improve the likelihood. In other books we have written, we have broken down the dynamics of digital disruption and recommended useful tools and frameworks to navigate the transformation journey. We were not alone. Academics, consultants, and analysts across the world have provided frameworks and insights to help guide the digital transformation process. Yet many executives are still struggling.

In this book, we take a different approach. After a decade of digital transformation experience, we have captured the best practices from practitioners—best practices that can help others hack their way through these difficult transformations.

HOW TO USE THIS BOOK

Many digital leaders face similar challenges—and we hope to address the most relevant ones here—but each journey has different goals and priorities that heavily influence the digital road map. With this book, we acknowledge that each digital transformation journey is unique and has to follow its own path to success.

Consequently, to make this book most useful, we have structured it in a way that fully supports your individual circumstances. Different readers have different levels of digital maturity and goals, and there is no one silver-bullet digital road map that works for all organizations. As a reader and digital leader, it is your responsibility to accept each challenge and adapt it to your organization's context. Based on our extensive research and countless conversations with digital leaders, we know that each of the challenges described in this book will be more relevant for you at different times. But only you know about the *when* and *how*.

Approach this book as your to-do list. Start by identifying the most pressing to-dos (i.e., challenges) for your organization, and regularly update the list as you progress. There is no universally right order. It all depends on your organization's digital journey.

Let's look at Ian, Elena, and Andrej again. They need practical advice directly linked to the challenges they face. And because they are at different phases of the transformation journey, their challenges are not the same.

Our research and experience have convinced us that digital transformation programs go through three natural phases: initiation, execution, and anchoring. Each phase has its own distinct challenges that business leaders will need to carefully navigate to succeed. (See Figure I.1.)

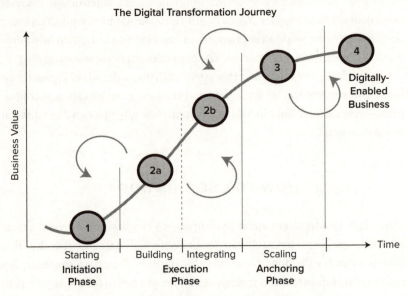

Figure I.1 From initiation to building a digital organization

The initiation phase may not be the largest in terms of activity—we estimate that it takes about 10 percent of the overall effort—but the whole digital transformation program is put at risk if it's not completed properly. The initiation phase is all about building a solid foundation and setting up the digital program for success. There are three principal components within this phase: building momentum, setting objectives, and understanding the landscape.

Building momentum includes creating a sense of urgency for transformation and aligning the key stakeholders on the need for change. In particular, the top team needs to be aligned internally and solidly behind the digital transformation program. It also needs to ensure that appropriate funding and resources are allocated to the program.

Setting clear objectives is a critical step to avoid the common problem of focusing on "digital for the sake of digital" rather than pursuing a larger, business-focused set of objectives.

Finally, understanding the landscape is about forming a clear assessment of the digital maturity of the organization and capturing an accurate picture of the current portfolio of digital technologies and projects.

The execution phase is by far the largest and most challenging part of any digital transformation program. We estimate that it represents approximately 70 percent of the overall efforts. It also creates the most value for the organization. Most digital transformations are won or lost here!

Due to its size, we have divided the execution phase into two parts: building and integrating. Building is about getting the transformation off on the right foot. It includes important elements such as setting up the right digital governance and building a balanced portfolio of digital projects. A successful building phase means that regular experiments are conducted to test what works and what doesn't. It's about establishing quick wins and creating instant, visible impact from digital projects. The building phase can operate in relative isolation from the rest of the organization.

The integration phase is probably the hardest because it requires that digital projects and digital teams be assimilated into the existing organization. Sustainable results can only be achieved when this happens. This phase requires a great deal of stakeholder management and team alignment across different functions, such as operations, HR, marketing, and IT. Many activities are included within this phase, such as setting up clear KPIs (key performance indicators), building digital skills among employees, integrating digital technologies into legacy products and processes, fine-tuning new business models, and working with external partners.

The third phase, anchoring, is the beginning of the end of any digital transformation. We estimate it represents about 20 percent of the overall effort. As digital tools, systems, and processes become embedded within the normal way of doing things, the need for a separate digital program or infrastructure is diminished. Anchoring is about deeply embedding digital tools and technologies within the organizational fabric, and scaling them so that digital business becomes just business. This phase involves building a foundation of digital capabilities within the employee base so that new developments in technologies or business models can be quickly integrated without the need for a separate digital program. It includes embedding an appropriate level of digital governance so that digital becomes a natural part of the organization's work. Anchoring is fundamentally about creating a future-proof organization able to leverage and scale digital tools and technologies to capture opportunities and respond to threats as they arise.

These phases are also not carved in stone. They have porous boundaries, and there is a lot of back-and-forth between them. For instance, a new technology innovation, such as machine learning, can force digital leaders in the execution phase to rethink the governance of their program to ensure they can share a rare, and expensive, skill set. Equally, other conditions might change. The arrival of a new CEO, for example, might lead to a rethink of the digital transformation ambitions and/or the urgency of the change. Again, it's up to you to keep the to-do list up to date and reprioritize continually.

Let's revisit Ian, who's a few weeks into a new position. He is firmly in the initiation phase. Expectations are high, and the future looks bright, but unless he is careful, he could easily fail. The first part of the book, dealing with the digital transformation setup, would be most useful to him. He might be wise to peruse some of the earlier chapters in this book, such as "Creating a Clear and Powerful Transformation Objective" (Chapter 1), "Building Urgency When Your Business Is Doing Well" (Chapter 2), or "Taking an Inventory of Existing Digital Initiatives" (Chapter 5), among others.

Elena's needs are different from Ian's. On the job for almost a year, Elena has navigated many of the challenges that Ian is currently struggling with. There have been some wins, but also losses. She is getting into the core of the execution phase. In addition, Elena is at a very fragile point in her tenure: our research has found that the average "life span" of a CDO is just over 2½ years.[2] She needs to go beyond the technology to embed transformation deep into the organization. Most digital transformation practitioners these days are some version of Elena, and so the challenges she faces make up the bulk of the book. She might be most interested in chapters such as "Accelerating Digital Using Agile Methods" (Chapter 10), "Managing Digital Transformation Responsibly and Sustainably" (Chapter 16), or "Convincing Customers to Pay for Digital Services" (Chapter 18).

Andrej is a digital transformation veteran. But this doesn't mean that he's out of the woods. Unfortunately, we have seen multiple cases of successful digital leaders becoming unhinged by a failure to embed digital initiatives into the wider organization. He is transitioning from the execution to the anchoring phase. Andrej's challenge is how to move from digital transformation programs to a digital organization. These challenges are less tactical than Ian's or Elena's, but they are no less critical. We have written the latter sections of the book for all the Andrejs out there. These later chapters include advice on challenges such as how to build scaling capabilities for your digital initiatives (Chapter 27) and how to set up KPIs to measure progress and success (Chapter 28).

You may see yourself as an Ian, an Elena, or an Andrej, or you may recognize each of them in your current situation. Whatever part of the digital journey you may find yourself on, there are plenty of hacks that are available to maximize your chances of success.

GETTING STARTED

We recommend that you peruse the table of contents and start with a challenge that sounds very relevant to the phase you're in, perhaps one that you're facing right now. Go to that chapter and read through its recommendations. In each chapter, we reference additional chapters that tend to go hand in hand. As you browse through the chapters and challenges, your initial to-do list will grow and priorities will become clearer.

Each chapter has a consistent format to ensure that you can easily extract learnings and insights as you move through the book. After describing the challenge and providing a short summary of the chapter's most important recommendations, we break down the content into these elements:

> **Why It Matters.** We present the justification for including the challenge in the book—in other words, why it's a big deal to the success of digital transformation. This section often includes facts and statistics to illustrate the relevance of the challenge.

> **Best Practices and Key Insights.** This is the largest section in each chapter. It outlines our evidence-based advice on how to address the challenge. We provide recommendations and best practices for typical use cases, supported by examples. We often back up this advice with a tool or framework that you can apply in your organization.

> **Hacker's Toolbox.** In this section, we provide a set of super-practical tools and advice that you can apply to create immediate impact.

> **Self-Reflection Questions.** Here, we provide a set of questions that can be used as a checklist or validation of the recommended approaches.

YES, IT CAN BE DONE

The metaphor of an airplane is often used to describe digital transformation. As long as you load the plane with fuel, get to the runway, and take off in the right direction, you'll be fine. This metaphor does not reflect our experience. For us, digital transformation is more like a trek in the mountains. Preparing well for the journey is necessary, but not sufficient. You can never let your guard down. Successful trekking requires paying constant attention to the environment, as well as avoiding obstacles, adapting to changing conditions, managing the expectations of those around you, and, most importantly, persevering.

Think of this book as a Swiss army knife for digital transformation. Feel free to dive in and out at any time, depending on which phase you're in and the specific challenges of the day. But keep it close, for you never know where the next digital challenge may come from!

The goal of *Hacking Digital* is to decode the *how* of digital transformation. Yes, it's hard, but it's not impossible. We have seen a lot of failures, more than we care to remember, but also many successes. In this book, we offer a suite of best practices, insights, and recommendations to help you tackle your most burning digital transformation challenges, stack the deck in your favor, and move closer to becoming a digital organization.

Part One

Hacking the First Steps

Initiating Your Digital Transformation

The secret of getting ahead is getting started.
—Mark Twain

Laying the foundation is not the most complex part of building a new house. Nor is it the most pleasing to the eye—and over time, it will be forgotten. But if done poorly, you will eventually pay a high price. Rising damp, cracks, and subsidence problems (sinking) may turn your dream home into a crumbling wreck. The same issues apply when initiating a digital transformation program.

Build solid foundations, and your digital program has a good chance of moving smoothly into the execution phase. Skip the important setup elements, and you will constantly find yourself in course-correction mode. Over the last decade of studying digital transformations, we've seen many organizations struggle to make progress, and in many instances, the root cause was a bad initiation. So what does it take?

First and foremost, ask the *why* question. Embarking on a digital transformation has become a corporate quasi-fashion statement. This is dangerous. Doing "digital for the sake of digital" will almost certainly lead to increased costs, but whether it also results in superior performance is less clear. Vision is important, as is a clear set of transformation objectives that encapsulate your aspirations and business goals. Without such clarity, your digital transformation will soon become diffused.

To put your organization in motion, you will need to convince the management team, along with other relevant stakeholders, about the urgency for change. Paradoxically, if you're under intense competitive and financial pressures, this will be an easy sell. But if you're not, you will need to paint an aspirational goal that promises to be worth the effort.

Digital transformation may be top-down driven, but it's not a solo sport. A good vision, clear objectives, and an aligned top team should set the right direction, but an engaged workforce is needed to transform that vision into reality. Building early organizational momentum is critical to success.

Few organizations begin their digital transformations with a blank canvas. Most likely, some digital activity will already be happening. To determine the best starting point and the organization's overall digital maturity, take stock of all ongoing digital initiatives.

Lastly, digital transformation costs money. No matter how good your setup, if you don't have a clear funding commitment, the transformation program will rarely progress beyond a set of pretty PowerPoint slides and a few pilots. Without a commitment to change that is both verbal and financial, you will never make a smooth transition to the execution phase.

So just as you would when building the foundation of a new house, devote time, care, and effort to properly initiating the digital transformation. It is a short-term precondition for success, but a long-term investment that will underpin the proper execution of your digital program.

CREATING A CLEAR AND POWERFUL TRANSFORMATION OBJECTIVE

A transformation objective is a statement that outlines the company's overall digital transformation aspirations and goals. It aggregates the strategic intent of all the guiding objectives that span the company's divisions or businesses. As such, it unifies the aims of the transformation to promote aligned execution. Without a clear objective, the transformation can quickly become fragmented and unmanageable.

WHY IT MATTERS

Many organizations aspire to be vision or mission driven. Although this is an admirable goal, most vision or mission statements—or "North Stars"—lack a clear impetus for digital transformation. The reason? They are too vague and high level to be effective drivers of execution.[1] Without a clear statement of objectives, a digital transformation program can easily become an ungainly confederacy of digital initiatives revolving around new technologies, a few Skunk Works projects, and random acts of digital enablement.[2] Worse, they can fall into the trap of being "digital for the sake of digital." Indeed, poor or missing objectives are a key contributor to the high failure rate of digital transformation programs.[3]

A clear statement of objectives, along with strong governance, can help ensure that digital transformation programs stay on track by focusing on the real drivers of performance.

BEST PRACTICES AND KEY INSIGHTS

We recommend that a digital transformation objective incorporate five key characteristics, which are described with the acronym PRISM—precise, realistic, inclusive, succinct, and measurable[4]—and depicted in Figure 1.1.

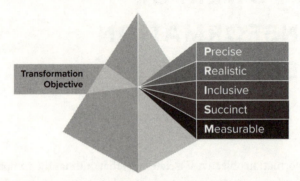

Figure 1.1 Components of effective digital transformation objectives

First, the objective should be *precise*. By precise, we mean clear and unambiguous. For example, Cisco's five-year digital transformation objective from 2015 to 2020 was captured by "50/50/2020."[5] This meant that 50 percent of revenues would come from software rather than hardware, and 50 percent would come from recurring sources rather than one-time sales. These objectives would be achieved by the end of fiscal year 2020. At the time the objectives were set, in 2015, nonrecurring hardware sales accounted for about 80 percent of Cisco's revenue. Because these objectives were so precise, there was very little room for doubt or misinterpretation. Without precision, there is a danger that different parts of the organization will apply their own understanding to the objectives and end up "transforming" in different directions. Often a lack of alignment will risk producing "change for the sake of change" where velocity trumps strategic direction. But *with* a high degree of precision, people tend to pull in the same direction. The precision need not come from a precise number, but numbers are useful as a counterweight to inspiring, but often vague, vision and mission transformation statements.

Second, the objective should be *realistic*. Goals that are possible, but hard to achieve, are fine. Impossible goals are not. The objective should be something that executive leadership, middle management, and individual contributors can all credibly see the company actually pulling off over time. Unrealistic objectives may lead to frustration and lack of motivation. If the objective cannot be realistically achieved, then why bother trying? If Cisco's transformation objective had been 50/50/2016, most people would not have taken it seriously. They would have known that such an objective was unachievable in such a short time.

> We have to come up with figures, KPIs, benchmarks, and so on to show we are not pushing [the transformation] to look modern or because it's trendy but because it's really impacting the business.
>
> —PATRICK HOFFSTETTER, FORMER CDO OF RENAULT [6]

Third, the objective should be *inclusive*. It should be relevant to everyone in the company, from top to bottom and from side to side. Cisco's 50/50/2020 objective was relevant across the organization. R&D teams had to develop new types of products and services, marketing teams had to figure out how to promote them, sales team needed to adjust their customer engagement processes, manufacturing and logistics had to be adjusted to meet the different demands of software rather than hardware, KPIs needed to be adjusted, hiring and retraining programs needed to be set up, and so on. The objective required changes in behaviors across the organization.

Fourth, it must be *succinct*. If a digital transformation objective is not something an employee can digest and easily remember, it isn't an effective objective. Describe a destination instead of creating a laundry list of all the steps required to get there. A succinct, easy-to-recall transformation objective enables people to gauge whether their work is actually supporting the goal. Axel Springer's transformation objective—to achieve 50 percent of its revenues and profits from digital sources in 10 years (set in 2006)—was not only precise, realistic, and inclusive; it was also succinct and easy to remember.

Fifth, the transformation objective must be *measurable*. Some objectives sound wonderful, but they are so "squishy" that people can define progress in their own way. Hilton's vision to "fill the earth with the light and warmth of hospitality" may be inspiring, but it's not a good digital transformation objective. When there is no clear way to measure any of the elements, people within the organization will define them as they wish, making it impossible to know if and when the objective has been achieved. Quantifiable targets such as revenue, profit, market share, net promoter score, employee engagement score, and so on tend to be more effective because they can be measured on an ongoing basis. There should be consistent metrics that allow the organization to pinpoint where it is on its journey and what remains to be accomplished.

Transformation ambitions that embody the PRISM characteristics help steer decision making and execution. Unfortunately, many corporate articulations of purpose amount to little more than window dressing—what the late US president George H. W. Bush famously dismissed as "the vision thing."[7] These messages may work as inspirational posters in the company cafeteria, but they have little relevance for the people who make decisions or are asked to execute a complex change.

Hacker's Toolbox

Avoid overly complex objectives. Digital transformation objectives are often defined and built by teams. Inevitably, what emerges from these discussions is a set of compromises between different interests. This process can result in unambitious or overly complicated objectives. We highly recommend, therefore, that teams undertake a second round of refinement and simplification to test the objectives' compliance with the PRISM factors.

Stop wordsmithing and start thinking in terms of trade-offs. When writing statements, there is a tendency to get stuck on specific wording. Instead, refocus the exercise on making decisions and prioritizing what you want to achieve. Ask yourself, "If we get to choose only one thing, which would it be: X or Y?"

Test, test, test. Testing the objectives with a wide spectrum of stakeholders is also helpful to assess clarity (do they understand them), relevance (do they care about them), and realism (do they think they can achieve them). Revising the objectives after testing them with these stakeholders is highly recommended.

Be specific and commit. Push yourself to add specific targets to the digital transformation objectives. Many stakeholders become uncomfortable when targets are defined in terms of numbers. It means that they will be held to account to deliver. Don't be vague. The most effective objectives are those that commit to specific targets and dates.

Self-Reflection Questions

Is your transformation objective precise enough that the outcome is clear and unambiguous?

Can your transformation objective be realistically achieved in the given time frame?

Is there anyone who is not impacted or is not included in the objective? If so, how can you include these people?

Can you make your transformation objective simpler to assimilate and remember? Can employees three, four, or five layers from the C-suite explain your objectives?

How can you make sure that your transformation objective is measurable?

RELATED CHAPTERS

Aligning the Top Team to Drive Transformation Success (Chapter 3)

How to Get Your Board Onboard (Chapter 7)

Managing Digital Transformation Responsibly and Sustainably (Chapter 16)

Measuring the Performance of Digital Initiatives (Chapter 28)

BUILDING URGENCY
WHEN YOUR BUSINESS
IS DOING WELL

Digital transformation works best when a sense of urgency sparks the organization into action. When a company is facing obvious competitive or financial pressures, most leaders find it easier to communicate the urgent need for change. But what if all is well in the world? When businesses are humming along nicely, building urgency through scaremongering won't work. Instead, you need to paint a compelling picture of the opportunity that digital transformation offers to the organization and its workforce. You need an aspirational model.

WHY IT MATTERS

Research shows that creating an atmosphere of urgency is the first practical step in any large-scale change effort.[1] Digital transformation is no exception.

Some organizations may face a competitive and/or financial crisis that demands urgent action. When financial metrics are going south, or a competitive position is strongly challenged, or a new business model disrupts the industry, creating urgency is less of a problem. Why? Because the risk is obvious, immediate, and easy to communicate. It is the proverbial "burning platform." Momentum is created through instant awareness, at the leadership and employee level, of the urgency to change to protect the future health of the business. It is a "deficit model" in which organizations see digital transformation as a necessary step for survival.

But what if all is well? Commercial performance is fine, competition is stable, and financial results are healthy. The natural impulse is to stay the course because "if it ain't broke, don't fix it." But as a leader, you may be uncomfortable. Your intuition may be warning you that this situation might not last long. You may be convinced that digital transformation is critical to making your business future ready. In this context, how can you create momentum and a sense of urgency?

Enter the "aspirational model." With this model, business leaders build a compelling vision of the opportunity that digital transformation can create for the business in the medium to long term. However, this is one of the most difficult leadership challenges in business transformation.

BEST PRACTICES AND KEY INSIGHTS

Urgency for business change doesn't happen naturally in organizations, particularly when all is going well. As Bill Gates once said, "Success is a lousy teacher. It seduces smart people into thinking they can't lose."[2] So how do you overcome the "business-as-usual" mindset and the inertia it produces?

Sometimes inspiration can be found in unexpected places. For example, the public sector is rarely mentioned as an example of leading with innovation, and yet the government of Estonia managed to create a shining example of aspirational digital leadership. Starting in the 1990s, Estonia embarked on an ambitious "E-Estonia" program that targeted the country's digital infrastructure and citizen services. The program was highly visible, backed by a broad political consensus, and a symbol for opening Estonia's society and economy to the West. The program had very few legislative initiatives. Instead, it was mostly about inspiration—about envisioning a digital future for the country and its citizens. The program has since become part of Estonia's official image and branding, and it's often ranked high on the list of government digital transformation successes.[3]

What are the elements of this aspirational model?

> **Stretch the aspiration with an outside-in perspective.** Urgency is easier to perceive when it originates from the outside. Paint a picture of a better digital future for your organization and its workforce. Describe a way to get there. Define the rationale for the urgency and the outcome (what does *good* look like?). Like big crises, big opportunities can also help create organizational momentum for change. Focusing on positive opportunities, rather than

negative threats, can jump-start momentum and the necessary engagement for change.

Think and manage in multiple time scales. Balance the management of today's successful business with the need to build a future digital business. It's important to focus on both current short-term needs and longer-term aspirations. Too much focus on the short term can lead to urgency "burnout." Too much focus on the future can dampen the pressure to "act now."

Reframe your communication. Build your own personal narrative with positive storytelling, and reinforce and update it over time. There is no bigger urgency-killer than a stale transformation narrative. Sustaining urgency is as important as creating it in the first place.

While trying to build urgency for digital change, many executives emphasize the risk of digital disruption to their business or industry. Others use motivational statements such as "Let's disrupt ourselves before someone else does." Don't bother with these approaches. They won't cut it with your leadership teams or employees. Hypothetical burning platforms don't work.

> The first challenge we have is addressing the 130-year legacy that has been established by a very successful business. . . . The second challenge we have faced is driving change when there is no burning platform. Many companies are forced to transform because of financial duress or an existential threat. Fortunately, neither applies to BHP. We start from a position of strength, not stress. As enviable as that sounds, it does make it harder to lift the activation energy of an organization. While we don't have a burning platform, we do have a burning ambition . . . to be even better than we are today and develop our sector leading capabilities.
>
> —JONATHAN PRICE, CHIEF TRANSFORMATION OFFICER, BHP[4]

Shifting from the "business-as-usual" mindset to a game-changing perspective requires a vision that paints a more attractive picture than current reality. The best way forward is to describe the "nirvana" that the new digital reality will usher in, and convince people that this new reality is where their futures lie. To start the process, focus the organization on the outside world. Where are customers' digital behaviors changing? Which companies have excelled at their own digital transformations? Which brands do digital natives want to join?

Build the vision not from what can be improved from the inside, but from what is aspirational on the outside. Put tangible images into the minds of your employees:

> "What if we had the quality of service of Apple stores' sales agents?"

> "What if we could provide the seamless user experience of an Uber?"

> "What if we could provide the product quality of an Audi?"

> "What if we could sell our products and services on a subscription basis like Netflix?"

Define and refine your digital vision with practical examples that people can see and relate to.

When the business is smoothly sailing forward, you need to think and manage the digital transition in multiple time scales. Exploit the current business to maximize the financial return (exploitation) and, at the same time, build an insurance policy for your digital future (exploration). The trick is to manage the tempo of the digital transition. How fast do you want to see the transition happen, and what organizational changes are you prepared to make?

Start with a positive funding logic: "It's because we're successful today that we can afford to build the organization's digital future," and then share this message with your board. You may need to reassess how innovation works in your organization. You may need to harness more energy and resources to build a new digital leg for your business.

Always remember, however, that change is a team sport. Share your broad digital vision! Invite people to cocreate the digital transformation path. Let your people figure out what needs to change to achieve the vision. Start breaking down the traditional linear approaches to planning—e.g., strategy formulation, budgeting, resource allocation, etc.

To reinforce the urgency of moving into digital banking, DBS Bank, the Singaporean multinational financial services company, created a new organizational unit called "Digibank" to spearhead the launch of stand-alone digital banks into new markets, such as India. The effort was aimed at developing outside the home base so as not to unsettle the successful existing business, but it sent a very strong signal to the whole bank that digital banking was the way of the future.[5]

Reframing communication is about building a new narrative (not a slogan) of the organization's digital future. It should be logical (digital strategy); it should appeal to people's emotions (exciting future); and it should be reinforced by behaviors (new program, new organizational unit, digital champions, etc.). Show how people's jobs can be enriched when the vision is realized. Celebrate the business of today while continuously pointing to the even-better future that awaits.

Occasionally you may face pockets of resistance. When that happens, it's OK to inject a bit of "shock therapy" into your message to push people out of their complacency. But stick to the positive message about a better future, and highlight the threats to the organization if it does not embrace digital transformation. In all cases, engage your internal communications and HR departments to spread the narrative widely and encourage feedback.

Finally, keep reinforcing the message over time. Complacency is the enemy. Highlight progress, but also communicate what remains to be done. And be sure to measure momentum and people's engagement along the way.

When existing businesses are doing well but still need to embark on a digital transformation, you cannot create urgency and momentum through fear of what might go wrong (burning platform). You need to construct an outside-in vision of a better digital future that people can aspire to over time.

Hacker's Toolbox

Build an outside-in vision. Have a small group of people focus outside of the firm to help you build an outside-in digital vision. Make sure the outside-in team represents the complexity of your organization, i.e., cross-functional, geographies, etc., and is diverse in its composition. Focus the group on identifying customer behavior changes, future consumption patterns, emerging digital technologies, emerging markets, and new business models.

Use "digital vision crushes." Identify external role models that exemplify your whole digital vision or elements of what *good* looks like. For example, "We want to have the speed of the supply-chain replenishment of a Zara," or "We need the quality of service of Apple stores' sales agents." Then create workgroups within your organization to help you cocreate how the vision can be implemented by looking into the details of how these organizations deliver.

Signal your intentions. Once the aspirational vision takes shape, signal your intent by making visible moves and investments to support the implementation of the vision—e.g., creating a new digital unit, nominating digital champions, and perhaps realigning departments. These will demonstrate the seriousness of your intent to the organization.

Enlist your communications and HR departments. They will help you build and spread an exciting narrative for the digital vision. Avoid being too grandiose. For example, don't end up with "We're going to be the Uber of the financial services industry." That will not cut it. DBS Bank, for instance, recognized that banking is a small part in an overall customer purchase, and therefore the most customer-centric thing it could do was to make the act of banking fast and invisible. DBS coined its digital vision the "Red Mantra: Respectful, easy to deal with and dependable" and linked its digital transformation initiatives to these objectives.[6] Once you have a good digital transformation narrative, make sure you and others repeat it often.

Self-Reflection Questions

How much time do you spend looking outside your organization for digital best practices?

Can you formulate a digital vision that does not include what needs to change inside your organization, but focuses on what it could aspire to become (outside in)?

Can you identify people in your organization who are excited about, and could help you champion, the digital transformation?

Do you have the organizational construct and resources to break from business as usual? If not, what changes could serve as visible triggers?

Have you developed a clear and compelling narrative that creates both urgency and engagement?

RELATED CHAPTERS

Creating a Clear and Powerful Transformation Objective (Chapter 1)

Building Organizational Momentum and Engagement (Chapter 4)

Building Hyperawareness into Your Organization (Chapter 12)

Staying on Top of New Technologies (Chapter 29)

How to Leverage Digital for Organizational Resilience (Chapter 30)

ALIGNING THE TOP TEAM TO DRIVE TRANSFORMATION SUCCESS

When CEOs decide to launch digital transformation programs, there is usually little dissent in the top team. That makes sense. Customers are becoming more digital, business operations are more and more connected, and most industries are already being disrupted. Thus, finding new sources of digital growth is essential for the firm's long-term prospects. What happens next, however, is often less straightforward. Road maps need to be created, programs funded, resources allocated, talent redirected, projects started and stopped, etc. When the rubber meets the road, the collective nodding stops. Resistance (active or passive) sets in, disagreements about priorities emerge, and people revert to defending their slice of the business. In other words, there's no alignment at the top-team level. And that's a sure way to put a transformation at risk. Collective commitment to digital transformation will only happen through constructive debates among organizational leaders and a fair (and transparent) process.

WHY IT MATTERS

According to a survey of more than 4,000 managers by MIT Sloan School of Management, only 28 percent of respondents could correctly list three of their firm's top strategic priorities.[1] Another survey identified the number one challenge facing digital transformation as "unspoken disagreement among top managers about goals."[2] These are worrying facts because our own research indicates that nearly all successful digital transformations in large firms were led from the top down.[3] What are the chances that a digital transformation will succeed without strong, aligned leadership at the top? How can leaders focus teams on the right digital priorities if other leaders' interpretations of objectives differ? What about clear and coherent allocation of resources and digital investments? How will the organization view leadership in that context?

Aligning digital transformation objectives is hard work, and organizations need to reach a consensus on *why* they are doing it. Is the firm playing defense against changes in consumer behavior, or playing offense to capture new sources of digital value, or both? Then comes the need to align on the *what*. What smart digital investments must be made to reinvent customer experiences, connect and automate operations, or explore new digital business models? Lastly, but most important, there needs to be an alignment on the *how*. How to mobilize and engage the organization. How to hire, train, or redeploy the right capabilities to the right opportunities. How to govern the program across functional, geographical, or other silos. How to empower agile technical and business teams to experiment and deliver scalable successes.

A tall order? Yes. But top-team alignment is the most direct way to reduce the strategy-to-execution gap and to drive value from digital transformation programs.

BEST PRACTICES AND KEY INSIGHTS

Alignment of the top team is a collective effort that must be orchestrated. It rarely happens naturally. Of course, it should be the team leader's role to initiate the soul-searching and uncover areas of misalignment. But that's not all. Because well-functioning teams must exhibit collective responsibility to keep everyone honest, digital leaders must also nurture an environment (one that academic researchers have dubbed "psychological safety"[4]) in which it's safe to take a risky stance and encourage productive disagreements. That's not easy. The journey toward top-team alignment around digital transformation is rife with roadblocks that must be exposed and overcome.

The "HiPPO" Effect

Deferring to the highest paid person's opinion (HiPPO) might be a sign that you have a strong leader—someone who's done homework on the need for digital transformation. But it's not a guarantee of strong alignment. We've seen many "digital days" or other consensus-building events dominated by strong leaders with a clear personal view on the company's digital direction. But when the top team's involvement has been minimal or absent altogether, the events produce, at best, a weak agreement (collective nodding) or, at worst, complete silence. Both situations typically mask differing views and underlying conflicts that will not go away during the transformation.

An executive at a Canadian television company recalls several meetings "where people are brainstorming, throwing around ideas, and ultimately going with what the boss came up with on a whim. You kind of see all the subordinates in the room glancing at each other defeated, [their faces] saying, 'are we really going ahead with this?'"[5]

When you face such a leader, find a moment of relative safety when you can constructively raise the need for a deeper alignment. If you are one of these leaders (meaning self-awareness exists), seek personal coaching or gather a smaller group to help you shape a constructive team intervention.

> No matter how brilliant your mind or strategy,
> if you're playing a solo game, you'll always lose out to a team.
> —REID HOFFMAN, LINKEDIN COFOUNDER[6]

The Curse of "Underlying Assumptions"

What drives a leader's judgment are his or her underlying assumptions about the speed of change, the nature of competition, the benefits that digital technology can bring, and so on. (Some of these assumptions will be shaped by reason; others by emotion.) Unless these assumptions are openly exposed so they can be debated, people won't change their position. When these assumptions are exposed, a constructive debate will follow, enriched by a diversity of views and experiences. This is good practice and a key to alignment. Of course, it requires some level of trust and an environment conducive to productive disagreements. But isn't this what effective teams are about? As Steve Jobs once said, "It's more fun to be a pirate than to join the navy."[7]

The Curse of "Averages"

Too often, important issues about the course of a transformation are decided through some form of assessment or even a team vote. Although this may be comfortably democratic, it's not conducive to good decisions or commitment from the top team. Why? Because people's views rarely represent a small deviation from the average. Focusing on the average obscures the depth of the differences. Instead, take the opposite stance. Look at the digital outliers—the extreme views that will help you build understanding, get voices heard, and (the hope is) sway opinions.

Several techniques have proved effective, such as separating the top team into two groups, each representing the extremes—e.g., digital optimists versus digital pessimists or "disruption at the door" versus "why change a winning formula" supporters. Then detail what would have to happen for each extreme view to be correct. Another effective approach is to launch a scenario-planning exercise to push people into scenarios that are challenging but plausible. Get people to outline their underlying assumptions for each scenario, and use the richness of the debate to reach a common view.

The Curse of "Undiscussables"

In many organizations, certain topics are consciously or unconsciously deemed "out of bounds." This can make it almost impossible for top teams to function. Recent research from IMD colleagues shows that when executive teams struggle with undiscussables, the consequences range from unresolved conflicts among team members, to uneven participation and engagement, to destructive groupthink.[8] Undiscussables come in various forms: Things people think but dare not say (risky)—e.g., "We'll never get the level of funding needed to pull off this transformation." Things people say but don't mean (behavior)—e.g., "Digital is core to our customer-centric focus." What people feel but can't name (negative feelings)—e.g., "We have none of the capability required to achieve this ambition." And finally, things people do without realizing it (unconscious behaviors). The good news, and the paradox, is that teams overestimate the risks of raising undiscussables. In fact, the IMD research found that discussing undiscussables openly brings relief, boosts energy, and bolsters team goodwill. In short, discussing the undiscussables is a no-brainer if you want to avoid aligning around a shared digital illusion.

• • •

Aligning top teams is not about making everyone happy. It is about setting up your digital transformation for success so that actions follow discussions. Commitment will stick only when different voices have been heard and the process has been fair and transparent. The people in your organization will thank you for it.

Hacker's Toolbox

Create space on the agenda for regular top-team "detox sessions." Create space where dissent, contrarian views, and taboos can be openly and constructively discussed, with no consequences. This approach will enrich both the team dynamics and the content of your digital transformation discussions.

Don't look for the average consensus. Reverting to a simple vote doesn't help. Instead, encourage or role-play extreme views and build scenarios to educate and move the team's position.

Go beyond each team member's opinion. Uncover the assumptions that lie beneath the opinions. Consider using a live polling solution during meetings to expose misalignments and underlying assumptions and to avoid falling into the trap of "averages." Focus the ensuing discussions on the outlier responses in order to expose and understand different assumptions.[9] Diagnose your team's undiscussables by asking the right questions.[10]

Bring neutral perspectives. Expose the senior team to cutting-edge thinking from external experts such as researchers, academics, and other business leaders. This will bring outside-in views to the digital transformation discussions.

Consider establishing a shadow committee or advisory board. AccorHotels, for example, as part of its digital transformation strategy, set up a committee staffed by six women and six men aged 25–35 and representing seven nationalities. Meeting every two months, the committee was charged with evaluating new projects and provided a sounding board for strategic decisions.[11]

If some contentious assumptions remain, don't ignore them. Instead, task groups to clarify them through further fact-led research and report back.

Self-Reflection Questions

If you are the team leader, ask yourself whether you are faced with a problem that you have helped create. Self-awareness is a powerful tool for aligning the top team.

Do you sense that several of your top team members overtly "manage upward"?

Do you see top team members agreeing during meetings, but taking different actions or behaving differently when back in their operational roles?

Have you spent enough time analyzing the opinions of your team members to understand their underlying assumptions?

Is the top team's communication on digital transformation objectives, to the rest of the organization or to the outside, clear and aligned?

RELATED CHAPTERS

Creating a Clear and Powerful Transformation Objective (Chapter 1)

Building Organizational Momentum and Engagement (Chapter 4)

How to Get Your Board Onboard (Chapter 7)

How Digital Leaders Can Establish and Maintain Credibility
(Chapter 22)

BUILDING ORGANIZATIONAL MOMENTUM AND ENGAGEMENT

A good vision sets the strategic direction, but an engaged workforce creates the momentum needed to transform the vision into reality. Large, transformative change programs only succeed when leaders earn employees' trust, engage them, and mobilize them for action. Unfortunately, there is no "secret sauce" that will instantly generate organizational momentum for digital transformation: it takes time and resilience. Building organizational momentum and employee engagement is about connecting the organization, giving people a voice, and fostering new ways of working.

WHY IT MATTERS

Building momentum for digital transformation hinges on bringing a company's best assets on board—its employees. But employee engagement cannot be mandated. It must be earned. And that's easier said than done. According to Gallup's "State of the Global Workplace," average employee engagement worldwide is only 15 percent.[1] Hence, successfully motivating the workforce is a key task for digital transformation leaders. The most obvious first step is, of course, good communication. Research shows that 64 percent of employees do not feel that senior leaders have adequately shared a vision for digital transformation with everyone in the organization.[2]

A top goal of digital transformation is evolving the culture and empowering people to work in new ways, particularly frontline employees. Engaged employees become champions of the change effort. But this won't happen naturally. Although many organizations have invested heavily in digital technologies, such as videoconferencing, cocreation platforms, or enterprise social networks to engage employees at scale, none of these tools is useful without user adoption. The ROI of digital collaboration tools occurs *only* if employees actually adopt them and change their work practices, not when the technology is deployed.

The success of a digital transformation rests heavily on whether employees buy in. When employees are not engaged, or when early excitement about the digital ambitions is not sustained, digital transformation programs are unlikely to succeed. Therefore, it's as important to create a plan for continually engaging employees as it is to chart a road map for implementing digital initiatives.

> We think of our employees as we would think of consumers—internal customers but the same principles. For a successful digital transformation, stamina is just as important as speed. Organizations must be steadfast and commit to a marathon rather than a sprint. It's easy to get off the mark and go at top speed initially. However, the real challenge is whether the organization, people and leadership can keep up in terms of stamina and thus keep the momentum.
> —RAHUL WELDE, EVP DIGITAL TRANSFORMATION, UNILEVER[3]

BEST PRACTICES AND KEY INSIGHTS

To stack the digital transformation deck in their favor, we recommend that organizations follow three critical steps to build momentum and engage employees.

Connect the Organization to Engage Employees at Scale

Most organizations have implemented digital tools to facilitate enterprise-wide communication and collaboration. The next step is to conduct an inventory of these existing tools and assess how well each contributes to enhancing the employee experience and/or to effectively serving customers and the business. Because workers have, on average, at least nine different technologies for managing workgroup interactions,[4] it's important to streamline these tools and provide clear, community-specific use cases to make employees' jobs better, easier, and more fulfilling.

General Electric, for example, faced the challenge of accessing fragmented pockets of expertise distributed across the organization. The company decided to leverage analytics to better assess and predict how business expertise could be easily shared across its nine businesses. The company used the analytics to predict which community member would have the right expertise to answer particular questions and, through the implementation of industrial-scale software, to automatically distribute questions to the appropriate community experts. This targeted implementation of digital tools enabled GE to better connect and engage with its people. In one year alone, 1,172 internal collaborators were able to solve 513 customer problems by collaborating at scale.[5]

Give Employees and Communities a Voice

Wiring the enterprise enables engagement, but giving employees a voice and encouraging meaningful dialogues is the real purpose. Digital transformation objectives are often framed in terms of competitive response or demands for increased efficiency or better financial metrics. This makes sense at the company level. But to truly engage employees, such goals must be translated into language that is meaningful to frontline employees—e.g., "Here's how the transformation will make your job better, easier, or more satisfying."

Employees who believe that they have contributed to the transformation, and have been listened to, are more likely to embrace the change. Therefore, managers and executives must focus on training, upskilling, and empowering the frontline workers in business-relevant communities with two-way dialogue, feedback, ideas, insights, and best-practice sharing.

An iconic example of encouraging employee engagement is IBM's "ValuesJam." When Sam Palmisano became CEO in 2003, he initiated a companywide project to reexamine IBM's values for the first time in nearly 100 years. Acknowledging that a command-and-control decree of values would not work for a 300,000-employee organization, Palmisano encouraged employees to contribute to a 72-hour online discussion around four concepts that had been previously discussed with 300 senior executives. In all, 50,000 employees attended the online discussion and contributed more than 10,000 comments, which were fed into IBM's revised corporate values (which are still in place today).[6]

Foster New Ways of Working

It's the leadership's job to engage employees. Serving as a role model for the desired change is a good first step toward earning the right to engage employees, but it's not enough.

When Adobe Systems sought to transition from a product-oriented business to digital new business models and services, CEO Shantanu Narayen took a "flag-planting and roadbuilding approach," which he described as "certainly uncomfortable . . . which is why you have to reinforce the positives."[7] He "flag-planted" by announcing to internal and external stakeholders the proposed digital transition, and then showed how the road was to be built with clear timelines and milestones. Adobe publicly shared its financial indicators and strove for transparency in its transition. Critical to the transformation, Narayen said, was creating a culture that enabled people to look at things transparently, acknowledge failures, and course-correct.

> First, we understood that there are employees who are excited, there are employees who are somewhat undecided, and there are employees who are resistant to change. We knew that we could not have a communication and change plan based merely on sending a daily email saying, "we are on a digital journey." We needed to guide people through the different phases of change. We do this by making them part of the vision and showcasing successful tangible examples of how digital has improved the lives of our customers. We tailored the communication to specific groups and ensured that the messages resonated with them.
> —SASKIA STEINACKER, GLOBAL HEAD OF DIGITAL TRANSFORMATION, BAYER GROUP[8]

To ensure engagement at all levels, Pernod Ricard started at the top, with senior management and board members. Within 12 months of launching its enterprise social network, Pernod Ricard had connected 84 percent of its worldwide employees with self-managing communities. This actively contributed to improving existing business practices and creating new ones. The communities were formed around business-relevant groups such as brand management or pricing. "Communities that are created on the network are free from geographical, functional or hierarchical boundaries," said chairman and CEO Alexandre Ricard. "Immediacy and discussion are now at the heart of relations between our employees, and have become essential in our relationship with consumers."[9]

To reach the next stage of its transformation, Pernod Ricard needed to cement new ways of working and encourage new behaviors. To do this, the company decided to enlist employees in co-designing the next phase of the digital transformation.

Pierre Pringuet, Pernod Ricard ex-CEO, explained: "With the first phase of our digital transformation, we have connected the organization and transformed the way we communicate, work and innovate. The second phase will help us to expand and accelerate this process. And its success is highly dependent on bringing our people with us on this journey."

By the end of 2019, an independent survey of Pernod Ricard employees found that 88 percent of its global workforce considered themselves engaged or highly engaged—well above the industry global average.[10]

• • •

Employee engagement is more a marathon than a sprint. It's easy to stay motivated in the early days with strong communication, visible engagement programs, town halls, baseball caps, and the like. But as time goes by, change fatigue sets in, and people often default to the old ways of doing things. Sustaining momentum is hard because it involves experimenting and then anchoring work practices until they become institutionalized. The way to win this marathon is to continually engage employees in the cocreation of the various phases of digital transformation.

Creating organizational momentum for digital transformation is about engaging employees at scale. It requires connecting the organization, giving employees and communities a voice to increase adoption, and institutionalizing new successful work practices.

Hacker's Toolbox

Launch and lead an engagement program. It will build momentum to turn your digital vision into reality. Identify a set of business-relevant communities of interest that will benefit most from best-practice exchanges and collaborative problem solving. For instance, a community of brand managers having to decide on the best merchandizing approach to promote a new product globally or a finance community tasked to harmonize global transfer pricing between internal entities.

Take inventory. Identify the various collaborative and productivity tools that have been deployed within the organization, e.g., enterprise social networks, cocreation tools, videoconferencing platforms, etc. Streamline and harmonize around a few compatible best-of-breed tools that can be used to connect employees across the organization. Be explicit about what tools to use for what purpose to give employees a voice and a practical purpose. Ensure employees have sufficient skills, training, and mentoring to engage and boost adoption (in coordination with HR).

Encourage, facilitate, and communicate best-practice sharing among communities. This can be done, for instance, with internal recognition or gamification or award programs. Once the business benefits are clear, adapt processes, rewards, and organization design to institutionalize successful new ways of working. Ensure your HR department uses digital tools to conduct regular employee engagement temperature checks so you can gauge progress.

Cocreate solutions. As engagement and collaboration increase, task communities with cocreating solutions to your most important business problems—for instance, as Pernod Ricard did in engaging employees in co-designing the next phase of its digital transformation. Ensure the problem-solving tasks are sufficiently detailed and practical to generate implementable solutions and are targeted at the right communities.

Self-Reflection Questions

Are your communications on digital transformation effectively conveying how it will make employees' jobs easier, better, or more fulfilling?

Are you focusing enough on user adoption versus the deployment of digital tools?

Are senior leaders "walking the talk"?

Are there opportunities for everyone in the company to take part in the conversation around digital initiatives?

Are you sensing change fatigue in the organization?

RELATED CHAPTERS

Creating a Clear and Powerful Transformation Objective (Chapter 1)

Building Urgency When Your Business Is Doing Well (Chapter 2)

Accelerating Digital Using Agile Methods (Chapter 10)

Working Across Silos (Chapter 25)

CHAPTER

5

TAKING AN INVENTORY OF EXISTING DIGITAL INITIATIVES

To orchestrate a winning digital transformation, one of the first steps is to determine where the organization stands today. Toward that end, digital leaders should conduct an inventory of the organization's existing digital initiatives in order to minimize duplications, understand dependencies, and ensure strategic alignment. This is often easier said than done, as information about these initiatives may be scattered among many owners and parts of the organization. In addition, some initiative owners may resist such a review, perceiving it as an exercise in centralization. To overcome such fears, successful digital initiative reviews require top-down support, clear communication of the digital transformation objectives, and a focus on the need for coordination, rather than control, of the digital team.

WHY IT MATTERS

Digital transformation leaders often confront a fragmented landscape of digital initiatives with varying levels of ownership and responsibility. This is especially common in companies with a decentralized organizational structure, where the locus of power resides in business lines/functions/regions/brands that enjoy a high level of autonomy.[1] One company with which we worked assumed it had a couple of dozen digital initiatives scattered throughout the firm. After a thorough audit, however, the company identified more than 160 distinct initiatives! Such situations are not unusual. In our experience, the "Let a thousand flowers bloom" strategy leads to precisely that: a thousand disconnected flowers. Uncoordinated approaches often result in a lack of consistency, duplication, difficulty in scaling, and, in general, wasted digital investments that negatively affect the firms' performance. For digital teams/units, the trick is to consolidate digital investments without appearing like "digital Caesars" who are hell-bent on wresting control from the operating units.

> As I walked around, I discovered more and more
> little units focused on digital and innovation.
> —FRED HERREN, FORMER CDO OF SGS[2]

BEST PRACTICES AND KEY INSIGHTS

Taking inventory of digital initiatives is a necessary, but frequently unwelcome, start to any digital transformation. Digital leaders face skepticism over their new decision rights, and existing initiatives owners must overcome their fear of a loss of control. As one executive observed, "It creates an impression that we are policing."

In our experience, many leaders overcome this negative perception by casting themselves as enablers, empowerment agents, and accelerators of their business partners' initiatives. Key to this exercise is establishing a high level of trust and sharing of information between the central digital teams and the operating units. Building trust with key stakeholders goes a long way toward ensuring information flows and obtaining alignment. On an individual level, Frances Frei and Anne Morriss describe the concept of a "trust triangle," which comprises three core drivers: authenticity, logic, and empathy.[3] In particular, most leaders struggle with displaying empathy. One way to display empathy is to put the needs of others first. In other words, by positioning themselves as helpful counterparts, digital transformation leaders will find that information flows more voluntarily. Of course, it also helps if the digital teams have an investment budget and/or rare capabilities, so that the operating units will immediately recognize the benefits that the central team can offer. Our research reveals three approaches that have worked for digital leaders: enabling, empowering, and accelerating.

Enabling

Some digital transformation leaders strive to be enablers by actively removing barriers to digital adoption. In that context, digital teams serve as a project
management office, working on an on-demand basis. This approach allows
leaders to build internal credibility and gather information about digital capability needs within the organization. As Guido Jouret, former CDO of ABB,
noted: "I show up, and say, 'I have teams who understand this IT side. If you
work with us, I'll provide my architects, my product managers, and put you in
touch with companies that have cool enabling technologies as well as software
development skills in these new technologies.'"[4]

Another enablement tactic used by many digital leaders is to appoint digital leads within business units and geographical regions. This creates a network of digital ambassadors who facilitate coordination and information
flows between the central team and the operating units. These digital leads
have both customer-facing and internal-facing roles, and are usually viewed as
an extended digital team. When Bertrand Bodson assumed the newly created
CDO role at pharmaceutical giant Novartis in 2018, one of his strategic priorities was establishing a portfolio of lighthouse projects—promising in-house
digital initiatives that would become the torchbearers of Novartis's digital
agenda. Creating a portfolio of lighthouse projects was a key step in Bodson's
strategy to make Novartis a leader in digital and data. The idea was to build
these programs with the business, gain the support of the executive committee, and rapidly demonstrate the potential of data and digital. Working closely
with Novartis's various businesses to uncover key needs, he persuaded 300 top
leaders ("digital champions") to make personal commitments on resource and
talent allocation.[5]

Empowering

A strict top-down approach rarely works in highly decentralized organizations, so it's best to empower the operating units. However, empowerment is
only effective when the entire organization is committed to the digital vision
and the senior leaders are strategically aligned. This requires strong leadership up front. Fred Herren, former CDO of SGS, the world's largest provider of
inspection, testing, and certification services, focused on building trust and a
culture of information sharing. He noted:

I want to provide the carrot, rather than a stick, so the organization comes to us. I congratulate them on the initiative, encourage them to make some money with it and to keep me posted. If the next day, another colleague comes to me with a similar initiative, I help to share the information between them. I've managed to get a lot of information coming my way because I'm not telling them to stop [their activities]. I walk around and ask people what's new and I always react positively. I don't think we should control everything.[6]

Accelerating

In order to rally the operating teams, senior leaders should emphasize that accelerating their digital transformation is a common goal. This tactic is often used when there's a need for tighter coordination of disparate initiatives or when there's strong competitive pressure to speed up the digitization of the business. COVID-19, for example, served as a digital accelerator for many organizations.[7] With acceleration as a rallying cry, mindsets can instantly shift from a self-interested to a more collective and collaborative way of working. At one oil and gas company, the leaders with whom we spoke described a fundamental shift in engagement between the central digital team and the business units once they made "acceleration" the central theme of their transformation.

"We run 'acceleration sessions' every month where an informal network of business unit representatives and the central digital team get together with the sole purpose of discussing how we can accelerate digital initiatives," one of the leaders told us. "We do exercises to clearly delineate our roles between digital corporate and the business units. The business units have their own space where they have ownership of the business case, delivery, and execution of their own digital initiatives. The role of the central digital team is to bring strategic alignment across the business units."

• • •

Taking an inventory of digital initiatives is an important early step in any digital transformation. Although centralizing information helps to minimize redundancies and create potential synergies, digital transformation leaders must also convince the rest of the organization that they aren't trying to take control of the initiatives themselves. Instead, they should adopt a collaborative approach based on shared goals. Success depends on establishing trust early so that the digital ambitions can be aligned to the various activities within the corporation. Once trust has been established, and leaders have an overview of digital initiatives across the organization, they'll be able to reprioritize the portfolio and the investments according to their transformation objectives.

Hacker's Toolbox

Map your business architecture. Identifying which individuals and which teams do what is an important step in understanding what is out there. Imagine using a giant pen to draw a circle around all the people, data, and infrastructure your organization has. This lets you see which resources are available in your organization's nodes and connections that can be brought to bear when changes are needed. Ask leaders representing those nodes and connections to appoint digital leads. These digital leads can help facilitate information flows, provide crucial insights about frontline needs, and act as a change agent on the ground.

Be visible and present. Taking inventory of digital initiatives is a key opportunity to demonstrate how you will collaborate with the rest of the organization. It is not a task to be delegated to others. Instead, we recommend creating opportunities to be visible by facilitating workshops, actively reaching out for information, and always being available for any questions that may arise.

Establish ad hoc working groups. Many digital transformation leaders establish working groups around new technologies (e.g., blockchain or AI), inviting anybody with knowledge and interest to join. These ad hoc working groups provide a window into the interests and experiments taking place throughout the organization.

Self-Reflection Questions

What prevents sharing information about digital initiatives?

How do you establish trust between the digital team and the operating units?

How can you enhance collaborations with initiative owners?

How can you show that you're not seeking to control all digital initiatives?

What information do you need to collect about digital initiatives?

Is there sufficient trust between the digital team and the operating units to reorient the portfolio of initiatives toward the key transformation priorities?

RELATED CHAPTERS

Aligning the Top Team to Drive Transformation Success (Chapter 3)

Funding Your Digital Transformation Program (Chapter 6)

Building a Balanced Portfolio of Digital Initiatives (Chapter 20)

Working Across Silos (Chapter 25)

Setting Up a Pipeline of Digital Initiatives (Chapter 26)

FUNDING YOUR DIGITAL TRANSFORMATION PROGRAM

Discussing industry disruption, digital vision, or road map priorities usually generates a great deal of excitement among executive teams. However, this excitement is rarely matched during discussions of how to fund digital transformation. In many cases, this is when all heads turn toward the CIO and the IT budget. But that's hardly the only, or the best, answer. Experience shows that however ambitious and clever, a digital program will be stillborn if it's not funded properly. But how can this be done? Available funds are constrained, budgeting cycles are out of kilter with digital ambitions, and the CFO is asking for a precise ROI. Yet the top team is convinced that, to thrive, the company needs to undertake the transformation now.

Funding a digital program is both art and science. It requires a clear understanding of the types of investment, the various funding models available, and a balanced portfolio of initiatives that will consider short- and longer-term returns.

WHY IT MATTERS

Digital transformation investment spending has exploded in recent years. Analyst firm IDC estimated that by 2023 it will represent more than 50 percent of all information and communication technology (ICT) investments, up from 36 percent in 2019.[1] But at the organization level, digital transformation differs from standard IT investments. Digital transformation is a journey, not a fixed project. And traditional metrics such as ROI do not capture the wider impact of digital investments. Funding is not limited to just the enabling technologies—the digital part—but also the human and organizational change—the transformation part.[2] The benefit of digital transformation is firmly on the adoption side, and this has a cost. Adoption costs, such as digital skills building, organizational change, communication, and training, have to be factored in early. Direct and indirect human capital costs must also be considered.

Some digital investments are trickier to justify than others, especially when executives are presented with no clear or realistic business case or ROI calculation. For instance, a process performance improvement is often easy to baseline, but an initiative aimed at boosting customer engagement with a brand might be harder, even though such an investment might be the most critical contributor to transformation success. In addition, CFOs are often hardwired to divert organizational funding to projects that can be clearly measured. This is when the digital strategy must come to the fore, so that the focus on the overall objective doesn't get lost. Value creation and growth targets for the overall digital effort must be clearly set in a way that covers both the initial capital expense (capex) and the running operating expense (opex). During funding negotiations, it is also critical not to lose sight of "North Star" ambitions.

The key to establishing funding clarity occurs during the early design phase of the transformation program. Some investments will be about building long-term capabilities, while others will be about exploratory or shorter-term experimentation. As much as possible, the program should be built around a series of agile sprints, not big-bang marathons. But realistically, some efforts will depend on scalable technology platform investments, and those might require a more traditional funding approach. Achieving a balance between short- and long-term outcomes in your transformation design should be matched by a balanced portfolio of funding models and sources.

BEST PRACTICES AND KEY INSIGHTS

The first step in funding a transformation is to shift the conversation from technology-related costs toward business value creation and enablement, such as customer or employee experience, competitive gains, or industry disruption. Digital leaders must also ensure that the financial requirements of the transformation are properly assessed. Partner closely with the financial community and/or dedicate financial resources to the transformation journey. But that won't be enough. Digital leaders will also need to categorize their transformation efforts, diversify their funding sources, and build a balanced funding portfolio.

Digital Investment Categories

Maintenance investments, such as website security or compliance projects, will have a clear line of sight to operational benefits. As such, they should conform to traditional methods of funding (ROI, budget cycles, etc.). Maintenance investments are usually funded by existing functional budgets. A global consumer packaged goods (CPG) company, for instance, needed to reintegrate hundreds of disparate websites onto a common hosting platform in order to harmonize the experience. The project was funded, managed, and delivered by the IT function within its standard planning procedure.

Foundational investments, such as core systems and platforms, are table stakes for the strategic success of your transformation. They are costly, and the benefits are often distributed across business units. They are usually funded centrally or by IT. But in all cases, they require a leadership judgment call. Detailed business cases are hard to compute, and without strong C-suite leadership, they won't happen. Early on, for example, Burberry realized that none of its digital transformation ambitions could be achieved within a common global enterprise resource planning (ERP) backbone. The CEO at the time, Angela Ahrendts, made the ERP delivery a priority for Burberry's CIO, and the project was delivered on time and on budget. The new, harmonized ERP allowed Burberry's digital services to be built on a strong common foundation.[3]

Exploratory investments, such as digitizing products or developing a suite of new services, are innovation driven. Although exploratory investments are more uncertain, they lend themselves to iterative and short-cycle developments, such as pilots, proof of concepts, minimum viable products, or incubators. These investments need to be big enough to succeed but small enough to manage the risk profile. Too much ROI discipline up front, and you might kill a good idea. Too late, and you may have a big sunk cost on your hands. Adopting a venture-capitalist mindset for innovation investment is best practice.[4] Mondelez, the global food manufacturer, invested in building "SnackFutures," an incubator design to test new disruptive snacking ideas in conjunction with partners and startups. Mondelez established a scaling process to further fund the ideas that looked more promising.[5]

> You have to put a cap on the amount of money you will invest in a digital transformation initiative and establish a time frame. That way, you are capping the risk. After a certain time frame, I showcase what I have achieved based on what I described previously, and then ask for the next tranche of funding. It has to happen incrementally. However, it is important to be agile and have a minimum viable product in the form of a quick win. Without that, it can be a bottomless pit where you continue saying "no, no, don't ask me about the ROI." Nobody will buy that.
>
> —MRUTYUNJAY MAHAPATRA, FORMER CDO, STATE BANK OF INDIA[6]

Funding Models

Westerman et al. describe how to diversify sources of funding for digital transformation.[7] These include:

Creation of funding capacity. There are ways to create funds from the existing budget envelopes. Many companies conduct initiative reviews at the start of their transformations, which are aimed at reprioritizing programs toward digital initiatives. If a portfolio review of digital projects uncovers areas of significant overlap, then duplicate projects could be combined or rationalized, and the resulting funds could be allocated to new digital projects. Other companies use the yearly cost-saving targets generated from the industrialization of their IT back office, and apply some (or all) of the savings toward digital investments. For example, one global FMCG company had a 3 percent target reduction annually as it industrialized its IT platforms. Senior leaders decided to allocate 1 percent of the savings to the bottom line and 2 percent to fund digital programs.

Central investments. These are enterprisewide investments that require coordination across entities. Foundational digital investments lend themselves to a central model. But they are also often used to fund innovation ventures such as incubators or innovation labs. Central investments are sometimes complemented with a charge-back model, where the investment is allocated across the business units that will profit most from the digital development over time. UK financial services company Lloyds Banking Group, for example, centrally decided to fund a complete replatforming of its IT systems. The decision was critical. It was a necessary investment to ensure the success of the digital transformation initiatives that would be built on top of the new platform.[8] In order to accelerate its digital transformation, ABB created "Matching Funds," which would double the digital investment made at the business unit level with money from the central digital fund.[9]

Local investments. When projects will directly benefit a business unit or a specific part of the business, local investment works well—e.g., when an e-commerce application mainly benefits one brand. Local investments are best, as they show real commitment from business units and increase the chances of adoption success. Whenever possible, they should be encouraged.

Partner-supported investments. These come in various flavors. Technology partners and startups can sometimes contribute to the investment in exchange for market access or a good use-case reference. You can ask partners for performance-based investments or a win fee should the pilot be scaled. Burberry, for instance, created a strong set of close partnerships with technology vendor Salesforce.

Table 6.1 summarizes the funding options.

Table 6.1 Funding Options

	Existing Capacity	Central Investment	Local/ Functional	Partner Supported
Maintenance	✓		✓	
Foundational		✓		✓
Exploratory		✓	✓	✓

Portfolio Funding Approach

Successful digital transformation depends on the kind of momentum that cuts across functional and departmental budgets. Most organizations have developed a central digital team or a subgroup of the management team to oversee the coordination and progress of the transformation. Looking at investment proposals on a stand-alone basis will not get you there. It is best practice for top management to consider funding from a portfolio across all investment categories. Some initiatives will have individual ROIs of their own, but others may have a strong ROI at only the portfolio level. Some ventures will be longer endeavors, such as a multichannel integration. Others may have shorter paybacks, such as the digital reengineering of a functional process. Balancing your portfolio will not only help to produce results in the short term; it will also derisk the transformation over time as projects get completed and new ones are started. Of course, the shape of the portfolio will depend on the scale of the digital ambitions, as well as the risk appetite of the corporation.

Hacker's Toolbox

Ensure financial support. Aim to have a strong finance executive on your digital team to measure, monitor, and report on the different categories of digital initiatives. Preferably, select a finance executive from, or with good links to, the internal finance function. Establish funding and reporting rules with your finance function and how digital investments will be managed, e.g., frequency of reporting.

Define your baseline investment. Conduct a thorough review of your current digital initiatives. Considering your digital transformation ambitions and their timing, reprioritize investments by delaying or canceling nonessential initiatives to create investment capacity for the digital program. Classify your digital investments by category—e.g., maintenance, exploratory—and gain agreement for funding models for each, e.g., central, business units. Allocate scaled funding levels (linked to delivery milestones) for each category/initiative.

Engage your ecosystem of external partners. Engage partners, such as technology vendors and consultants, by sharing your digital transformation ambitions and road map. Signal to your key partners that you are prepared to embark with them on your transformation journey long term, in exchange for resource, investment, or outcome commitments. Work with procurement to ensure contracting with selected digital partners is treated outside the normal process.

Conduct, at a minimum, a quarterly review of your digital investments. Involve senior management and representatives from the funding sources, e.g., business units. Review the investment as a portfolio, not as a collection of projects, in order to keep the integrity of the overall transformation program and reallocate investments as appropriate.

Self-Reflection Questions

Have you quantified the digital investments that underpin your transformation by investment types and timelines of benefits?

Are you prepared to stop existing projects and initiatives and reallocate the funding of your digital efforts?

Have you looked at savings from industrializing your IT as a source for digital funding?

Do you have the right governance structure and the finance function support to coordinate digital investments across silos?

Are you confident that you have a balanced portfolio of digital investments that will satisfy the need for short-term returns without compromising your longer-term goals?

What risks are you prepared to take to make the transformation a success?

RELATED CHAPTERS

Taking an Inventory of Existing Digital Initiatives (Chapter 5)

How to Get Your Board Onboard (Chapter 7)

Choosing the Right Digital Governance Model (Chapter 8)

Investing in Startups (Chapter 14)

Competing Against or Working with Digital Platforms (Chapter 19)

Building a Balanced Portfolio of Digital Initiatives (Chapter 20)

Setting Up a Pipeline of Digital Initiatives (Chapter 26)

Measuring the Performance of Digital Initiatives (Chapter 28)

Part Two

Hacking the Internal Organization

Setting Up the Right Organizational Dynamics

You have to have that organizational
principle behind the song.
—Tom Verlaine

We now turn from Part One, which was about building the foundation for digital transformation, to Parts Two to Five, which focus on what's above the ground. The main and upper floors are the visible parts of a building, where people spend most of their time. These floors need to be structurally sound and functional, as well as aesthetically pleasing. The same is true of digital transformation.

Establishing the right internal dynamics for transformation is critical for execution. The organization itself needs to be aligned and ready to be digitized. For a building to last, it needs to combine behind-the-scenes elements that must work, such as plumbing, electricity, and structural integrity, with functional and aesthetic elements, such as interior decoration, art, and technology. In digital transformation, the visible elements (tools, applications, and technologies) must work. But an equal (or greater) amount of effort should be expended behind the scenes, aligning with IT, defining a clear governance, and cleaning and securing your data.

In Part One, we spoke about the importance of aligning the top management team. Without alignment around a clear understanding of what digital transformation means for the organization—why you're doing it—it is unlikely to succeed. It's equally important to get your supervisory board onboard. Board members tend to be farther away from the business than the management team, and thus they may feel less pressure to transform.

In general, boards are also less digitally savvy than executives, and may not appreciate the resources, energy, and organizational change required for successful digital transformation. It's important to manage the board because its impact, as either an accelerator or a brake on transformation, can be significant.

In addition, many transformation failures can be traced to poor or weak governance. Governance needs to be tackled early, and carefully, as it will impact many of the downstream transformation activities. Good governance means clearly articulated roles, responsibilities, and decision rights for key stakeholders. It also requires an organizational decision about the level of integration (or separation) of your digital efforts, based on your ambitions and the culture of the organization. A one-size-fits-all approach to governance rarely works.

Early in any digital transformation, questions about the relationship between the digital team and the IT department will invariably surface. It's a tricky alliance that almost always contains overlapping and mutually dependent responsibilities. Without a well-functioning working relationship, these two groups will inevitably compete with each other for resources and management attention. We have even seen cases in which one side actively sabotaged the other. Hence, it's critical to maintain a positive relationship and strong alignment between IT and digital.

Data is an important source of common ground for IT and digital. Digital tools and technologies are rarely self-contained. They sit on top of infrastructure and draw on internal and external data. If the infrastructure is poor or the data is messy, your digital initiatives will fail to deliver.

Finally, there is agility. Agile methods and digital projects often go hand in hand, but their relationship is complex. Digital projects don't need to be implemented via agile methods, and agile tools can be applied to nondigital projects. Within a digital transformation program, it's critical to extract the best from agile methods to achieve a smooth execution.

Although many digital tools and technologies (AI, augmented reality, and distributed ledgers) are cool and sexy, the process of embedding them within an organization can be quite prosaic and mundane. Yet the efforts made behind the scenes to align the organizational context—around governance, data, and processes—can pay huge dividends down the line.

HOW TO GET YOUR BOARD ONBOARD

Balancing risk management, value creation, and long-term sustainability are the key roles of the board of directors (BoD).[1] To provide effective guidance on these topics, the BoD must consider the impact of digital technologies and business models, but to do this, the board members need to have an appropriate level of digital savvy. They also need to set up processes and governance structures to ensure that relevant insights about digital transformation are being considered. Finally, they need to establish a close and transparent relationship with executive management teams on digital topics.

WHY IT MATTERS

According to research, 63 percent of executives believe a partnership with the board is critical to the success of digital transformation efforts, and yet only 27 percent report that the BoD serves as an advocate for current strategies.[2]

Enlisting a digital-savvy board as a sparring partner is critical for:

1. Guiding and validating digital strategies and properly assessing digital opportunities and threats to the organization's business model

2. Providing oversight of digital transformation programs and ensuring that the digital road map, major projects, and investments are on track

3. Protecting the organization from cyber risks and ensuring data privacy, compliance, and ethics

A digitally savvy board also has a positive impact on financial performance. Recent research indicates that organizations with digitally savvy boards outperform others in areas such as revenue growth, profit margins, return on assets, and market capitalization growth.[3] Unfortunately, the same research shows that only 24 percent of organizations in the United States with revenues above $1 billion have boards that are digitally savvy.

BEST PRACTICES AND KEY INSIGHTS

Many organizations have recruited digitally savvy board members from born-digital firms such as Google, Amazon, or Uber. Others have appointed successful digital entrepreneurs. However, recruiting people with these backgrounds does not guarantee a digitally savvy board. Although such people will almost certainly inject an outside perspective and fresh thinking, they often lack any experience transforming a traditional organization. Therefore, it's best to complement these digital experts with *transformation* experts—people experienced in managing a digital transformation within a traditional firm.

Education Through "Digital Learning Expeditions"

Many management teams organize "digital safaris," physical visits to organizations that are either digital natives (such as Amazon, Tencent, or Google) or noncompeting companies with a successful track record of digital transformation (such as Starbucks or Schneider Electric). Because these safaris can be very effective learning journeys, we recommend bringing board members along. Stepping outside to see "what is possible and what 'better' could look like" enables board members to understand the strategic impact of digital on their organizations.

Although the visits themselves are useful, they should also include enough time for debrief sessions between board members and executive management to encourage debate on the potential impact of digital disruption and transformation. The inevitable downtime during these meetings can also provide a forum for board members and executives to privately and honestly discuss how the organization can shape its digital transformation to adapt to changing market conditions. Absent of debriefing sessions, expeditions may amount to little more than executive tourism.

Transparency

Allowing a huge digital knowledge gap to develop between executive management and the BoD can be counterproductive, as can a lack of transparency. To prevent this, Netflix encourages a transparent relationship between managers and the board by having board members regularly attend management meetings (via digital communication tools). "It's a good opportunity for board members to see the team in action and to meet several layers of the team. . . . You end up with more knowledgeable boards, not people who just drop in for dinner and a meeting," said Reed Hastings, CEO of Netflix.[4]

Leveraging Existing Governance Mechanisms

In most organizations, existing governance committees provide a useful forum for the board to gather information, discuss and formulate digital strategies, and communicate with high-level executives who are charged with developing and implementing the strategies. Some examples of committees include:

Strategy committees. BoD strategy committees are an ideal place to debate digital strategy and the evolving competitive landscape. We recommend, therefore, that these committees allocate sufficient space on their agendas for a thorough, ongoing dialogue about strategy and digital transformation. Since squeezing digital topics onto an already crowded agenda can be difficult, one company found a solution in a "tight-loose" format, which blends informal interactions with episodic formal meetings. Some board members, for example, work in a tag team with functional and business leaders to observe how business is executed from the ground up and how the company's culture and operating style are evolving with its digital strategy.

Technology committees. Some boards have established digital or technology committees at the same level as the audit or strategy committee. These digital committees assume an advisory role and facilitate discussions on digital matters to help make informed decisions.

A recent survey[5] revealed that increased interactions between CIOs and the board can lead to a more balanced mix of conversations covering digital risk, digital innovation, and technology investments, so board members can better understand how digitization is changing business models.

While only 9 percent of S&P 500 companies had a digital or technology committee in 2016,[6] this number has been increasing, as have "digital committees" that pair board members and key digital executives. Many of these committees also engage external experts and are sometimes formalized as "digital advisory boards."

One consumer products company created an advisory "ecosystem" that helps the committee brainstorm ways for IoT-connected systems to reshape the consumer experience.[7] This type of brainstorming and contextual learning can offset gaps in knowledge, and can open up fresh avenues for discussion around the strategic use of digital technologies.

> There are so many radical major transformative steps that Netflix has done since I've been on the board: DVD distribution into streaming over the web, moving international, committing millions of dollars in content, committing money to making the production. It's fascinating as a board member. . . . The management team is so thoughtful and open to dissension in the decision-making process that it makes very challenging decisions relatively easier because of the rigor of the process.
>
> —BOARD DIRECTOR, NETFLIX INC.[8]

Creating New Innovative Models

Evolving from a digital transformation into a sustainable digital business may require some organizations to develop new models to improve board engagement and effectiveness on digital issues.

Shadow boards. The desire among organizations to better connect with younger companies, as well as younger employees, has inspired the creation of "shadow boards," groups of employees who work with the board in an advisory capacity on strategic initiatives.

When GroupM, a marketing services conglomerate, needed to implement a three-year digital and cultural transformation, the South Asian market CEO created a youth executive committee. From its inception in 2013, the committee has been tasked with developing GroupM's Vision 3.0, making digital the core of its future growth. The shadow board developed several initiatives focused on both digitalizing contracts and strengthening partnerships with media owners, data providers, auditors, and startups. It also created a communication channel between management and lower-level employees. This initiative helped leverage younger employees' insights and diversify the perspective of board members.[9]

Reverse mentoring. Some companies have adopted reverse mentoring to create "buddy systems" in which board members are paired with digitally savvy employees to explore, on an informal basis, specific areas that are critical to digital strategy or transformation.

Getting your board onboard is critical for digital transformation success. Engaging your board to become an effective sparring partner on your digital journey requires education, transparency, good governance, and open dialogue.

Hacker's Toolbox

Ensure you have a direct line of communication with your board. Ensure there is sufficient space on the agenda to engage in the right conversations. Make sure these conversations are balanced between risk mitigation, such as cybersecurity risks, and technology-enabled value-creation opportunities. Schedule risk and growth discussions at different times to deliberately keep the two conversations separate.

Balance the digital savviness of the BoD. Encourage, or lobby for, a mix of digital experts and experienced transformation experts who have overseen, or been part of, a digital transformation in a traditional organization. Research points to having three digitally savvy board members as being a good balance to properly support your digital transformation efforts.[10]

Be sure your board experiences the digital change. When board members see and experience the real thing, they gain hands-on insights and become more engaged in the process. For example, when a global retailer implemented a new "click-and-collect" service, the company encouraged its board members to participate in the trial of the new service and welcomed their feedback comments and suggestions.

Create regular reporting mechanisms. Put in place structured mechanisms, such as dashboards or balanced scorecards, to provide consistent messaging on progress, roadblocks, and successes in the operational implementation of your digital transformation.

Self-Reflection Questions

How digitally savvy is your board of directors?

Have you established mechanisms for constantly updating the board about your digital transformation?

Does your board understand, actively support, and fund your digital transformation?

What level of transparency do you (or should you) have with your board?

Is there sufficient time on the BoD agenda for in-depth discussions on the strategy and implementation of your digital transformation?

Are you actively leveraging existing committees (e.g., strategy or technology committees) or new coordination committees (e.g., a digital advisory board) to steer and implement your digital transformation?

Have you established proper reporting mechanisms (e.g., a scorecard) for your board to monitor the progress and returns of your digital transformation?

RELATED CHAPTERS

Creating a Clear and Powerful Transformation Objective (Chapter 1)

Building Urgency When Your Business Is Doing Well (Chapter 2)

Aligning the Top Team to Drive Transformation Success (Chapter 3)

Funding Your Digital Transformation Program (Chapter 6)

CHOOSING THE RIGHT DIGITAL GOVERNANCE MODEL

Getting digital governance right is key to digital transformation success, but it's hard. The choice of governance model depends on the transformative ambitions of your organization, and for the model to work effectively, you must also take into account the underlying culture.

There's an ongoing debate about whether to completely separate or tightly integrate a digital team with the rest of the organization. In practice, this is a false choice. In general, neither extreme leads to a positive outcome. Hybrid approaches work better. Creating a distinct digital team will provide momentum, but finding the right points of integration will facilitate the operationalization of the initiatives. As organizations become more digitally mature, the need for a dedicated team will decrease as digital efforts become more embedded in the organization's operating model.

WHY IT MATTERS

One of the first decisions an organization must make is which governance model to adopt to translate the digital vision into a results-oriented reality. According to our research, 84 percent of organizations have established a dedicated group to oversee and manage digital transformation efforts.[1] However, digital transformation ambitions come in many flavors—from digitally enhancing the existing operations, to revamping customer experiences and operations in new ways, to reinventing business models. Each ambition will dictate a different model of governance.

Complete separation of digital teams allows them to think outside the current model and operational constraints. It liberates the transformation effort from the shackles of traditional processes and reporting, and it can also accelerate the effort. But separation carries a big risk of isolation from the day-to-day business, often leading to "ivory tower" syndromes, which make operationalization and scaling of the initiatives difficult to implement.

It's important to note that a "dedicated team" doesn't necessarily mean a "separated team." Indeed, there is strong evidence that creating a segregated digital organization, as GE did with GE Digital, can result in too much separation between the digital team and the rest of the organization.

Complete integration of digital teams provides proximity to current operations, which can make the transfer from digital experimentation to operations much more seamless. However, integration carries a big risk of incrementalism and duplication at the expense of fresh thinking, organizational learning, and true digital innovation. The trick is to find the right balance—to provide enough separation to kick-start digital momentum and also enough integration to facilitate the transfer of successful initiatives to the entire operation.

Then there's the issue of culture. Some organizations are highly decentralized, with a high level of autonomy in the business units. In such cases, separating a digital team has to be managed very carefully to reflect the day-to-day working of the organization.

For instance, many organizations have created a network of digital champions, giving the business units decision rights or influence over digital priorities. Other organizations have more centralized cultures and ways of operating. In these cases, prioritizing central coordination and harmonization of digital efforts might make sense. For example, because P&G has a long-established culture of strong central services supporting its global brands, the company was able to successfully replicate this governance model to implement its digital transformation.[2]

Our research has shown that organizations are evenly divided about whether digital should be a centralized or a distributed responsibility.[3] But in all the successful cases we've seen, a balance of separation and integration has been achieved. In other words, a hybrid model makes sense.

Digital transformation forces large organizations to perform unnatural cross-silo acts of coordination and sharing. That's why governance matters. But organizations also evolve and learn over time.

As digital maturity increases, and digital tools, technologies, and ways of working become an essential, integrated part of an organization's operating model, the way digital teams are structured and governed should evolve. Over time, many organizations can eliminate separate digital governance altogether.

BEST PRACTICES AND KEY INSIGHTS

Choosing digital governance models will be dictated by your digital transformation ambitions and organizational culture. The choice will also be influenced by how much coordination your digital initiatives require across the various organizational silos and how many shared resources you must deploy to succeed. Our research shows that there are four main governance models you can choose from:

1. **Business as usual (with light digital coordination).** The digital effort is driven by existing business and management teams, with a digital committee to coordinate initiatives. This model gives a simple mandate with no organizational or structural changes and is funded within existing P/Ls. The risk is the propensity to get stuck in day-to-day legacy business with incremental/bite-size progress and a lack of resource sharing.

2. **Digital leadership roles.** The digital effort is coordinated by a dedicated executive, such as a chief digital officer, with varying levels of resources and budget allocation. This model is used to accelerate efforts by providing focus, coordination, and resource sharing. The risk is linked to the level of responsibility and authority given to the leadership role, as well as the need for tight coordination with operational units.

3. **Shared digital units.** The main benefit of this model is pulling the specialized and scarce digital resources (e.g., AI capabilities) into a central hub. This model provides for an integrated road map of digital initiatives, harmonized ways of working, and strong cross-unit coordination through, for instance, a network of digital ambassadors. The risk is one of isolation from the core business, duplication of efforts, and tension with existing units like IT and marketing. Shared units can range from digital groups housed within existing structures

(e.g., IT), to digital centers of excellence, to organizationally separate and autonomous units.

The Dutch bank Rabobank decided to create a dedicated "Digital Hub" by pooling a set of fragmented corporate resources. The hub maintained some independence from the rest of the organization, so it could foster and promote a degree of flexibility and innovation.

Centralizing the hub, rather than separating it, also gave it access to existing corporate resources. As Rabobank's Chief Digital and Transformation Officer, Bart Leurs noted:

> In the Netherlands, we have decided to really move forward on digital, so what we have created is a Digital Hub within the company that should push forward the transformation. The Hub will pick up digital challenges, develop solutions for them, and then hand these solutions back to my colleagues in the business. At the start of the Digital Hub, what we have done is really look at all the customer journeys that we currently see at the organization, specifically those that can be digitized. I think we had around 100 customer journeys that we were looking at.[4]

4. **Greenfield ventures.** This model works best when you have digital ambitions that represent a drastic departure from current operations, such as the development of a new business model. It increases speed to market and allows for novel economic models, processes, and technology stacks. Risks include competition with the existing business, which may lead to duplication and infighting, as well as resource and cultural incompatibility with the existing business, making the migration from old to new more challenging.

   To leverage a large, existing client base, the French telecom operator Orange decided to expand its business model into digital banking. On the back of a prior banking infrastructure acquisition, Orange built a near-stand-alone greenfield venture, Orange Bank. The new venture was launched in a year, and the model has now been expanded to several geographies.[5]

Most organizations will choose hybrid versions of these models. Organizationally, the key is to properly align reporting, authority, decision rights, and budgets. The options are displayed in Figure 8.1.

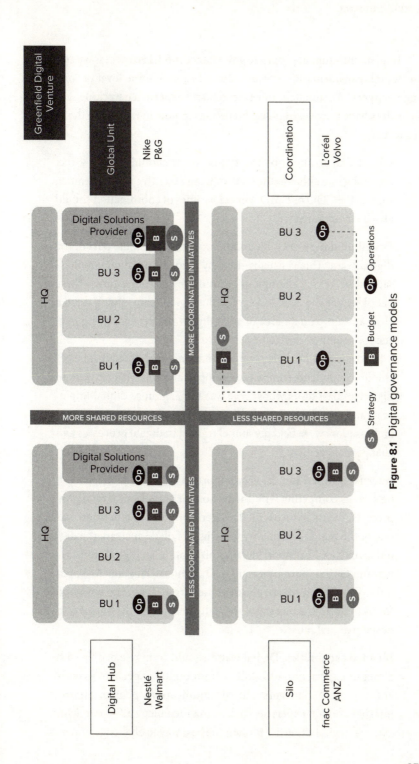

Figure 8.1 Digital governance models

Implementing an appropriate governance model is a necessary condition for digital transformation success. But it requires some level of "organizational surgery." Fortunately, our research and experience working with digital leaders have uncovered powerful lessons in how to maximize the chances of success:

Direct dial to the top. The digital team should have a direct reporting line either to the CEO or to an executive board member, such as the COO or CMO. Very close lines of coordination should also be maintained with IT.

Distributed networks. It's good practice to distribute part of the digital team. This is usually done by embedding "digital ambassadors" or "digital champions" within the lines of business. These people act as the eyes and ears of the digital team, giving them a clear and up-to-date idea of what digital projects are being pursued within the organization.

To support its digital transformation effort, Radiall, an electronic components company, developed and trained a network of digital ambassadors whose role was to harmonize digital implementations across all Radiall's facilities around the world. The ambassadors were field personnel trained in digital processes and change management.[6]

Internal competition. It's very important that the digital team not be seen as competing with the rest of the organization on digital projects, or indeed with IT. This perception of competition was one of the main reasons why GE Digital failed.[7] Instead, the digital team should support the organization in its digital transformation. Guido Jouret, former CDO of industrial giant ABB, put it this way: "My team are personal trainers. It doesn't do any good for us to do all the push-ups; we really need to get the business to develop digital muscle."[8]

Blended capabilities. Digital teams should comprise people with a mix of experience and skills—from digital experts to experienced project managers and communications people. Mixing internal domain expertise, such as maintenance and repair, with external digital expertise is often the best way to challenge underlying assumptions. Internal people will understand the culture and will deftly maneuver through the organization, increasing the odds of success. You will obviously need new skills and outsiders' perspectives, but balance is key. Too many outsiders will increase the chance of the digital team being isolated.

Charlotte Lindsey-Curtet, former director of digital transformation and data at the International Committee of the Red Cross, described it this way:

I have tried to bring people into my team from other departments. One of the strategic tech advisors worked in IT before, but was based in the field, so having knowledge of many years based on integrating things in the field is extremely useful. I think that trying to pick people from different parts of the organization has multiple benefits. They will leverage the trust they have from their own networks, their own integration, to actually look and say, "This is about working with people to enable how we move forward."[9]

Evolving models. The structure of the governance model and the type of support provided by the digital team will evolve over time. As digital competence and maturity grow within the organization, the need for separating the digital teams will decrease. Embed digital practices in your operating model as your organization matures.

Building a dedicated digital team was the preferred route of Energie Baden-Württemberg (EnBW), a regional energy and utilities company in Germany, when the company first launched its digital transformation. Sven Meier, director of digital transformation, explained how organizational structure, strength of existing business lines, and the integrated assets were taken into account for the decision: "We, as a digital transformation unit, are right in the middle of the organization. We are a vertically integrated company, and our digital transformation has to work with our assets. A spin-off digital structure would have been difficult to do."[10]

After two years of playing a central support role for the business units' initiatives, the EnBW digital transformation team began to observe redundancies across the organization. Therefore, community governance structures were created on a case-by-case basis to manage common initiatives (such as robotic processing) without central intervention.

Digital governance should not be left to chance. It is a key lever for digital transformation success. Full separation or full integration of digital teams rarely works. A hybrid approach that matches your ambitions and the culture of the company works best.

> Creating the digital unit, digitalONE, was momentous—it was an embodiment of a changing organization where silos are being broken down, teams and disciplines are merging, and a new common mindset emerges.
>
> —SABINE SCHEUNERT, VP DIGITAL & IT MARKETING/SALES, DAIMLER AG[11]

Hacker's Toolbox

Tackle your digital governance head-on; don't leave it to chance. Determine which digital governance models, most likely hybrid models, will best match your digital transformation objectives. For instance, to govern a cross-channel integration in retail will require heavy coordination between your customer front end, your back-office operations, and your IT team. Ensure your digital governance model is also compatible with the operating culture of your company, e.g., centralized versus decentralized, multigeographies, etc.

Be very clear and explicit about accountability. Formalize the remit of your digital team around assignment scopes, strategy, decision rights, operational accountability, and budgets.

Choose your digital leaders and roles carefully. Ensure a balance of both digital expertise, to deliver best-of-breed solutions, and good interpersonal skills, to navigate the organization and facilitate operational execution. A mix of external hires and internal experienced executives is often a good solution.

Ensure there is a process to adjust your governance model. Digital transformation demands change as your organization evolves. Over time, rotate leaders between the digital team and operations (and vice versa) to encourage harmonization and embed digital practices.

Consider relaxing your formal governance over time. As coordination and sharing of digital efforts become part of your culture, consider relaxing your formal governance structure by transferring more decision rights to business units while keeping a level of coordination to ensure consistency.

Self-Reflection Questions

Do you have an accurate sense of your portfolio of digital initiatives?

Is it clear who leads digital transformation in your organization?

Is your digital transformation progressing at the right pace?

Do you see competition between your digital team and the lines of business?

Do you sense that your organization is becoming more digitally mature—to the point where you could transfer more of your digital transformation to operations?

RELATED CHAPTERS

Aligning the Top Team to Drive Transformation Success (Chapter 3)

How to Make Digital and IT Work Together (Chapter 9)

Accelerating Digital Using Agile Methods (Chapter 10)

Building a Balanced Portfolio of Digital Initiatives (Chapter 20)

Making the CDO Role a Success (Chapter 23)

Working Across Silos (Chapter 25)

Measuring the Performance of Digital Initiatives (Chapter 28)

HOW TO MAKE DIGITAL AND IT WORK TOGETHER

O ver the last decade, traditional IT organizations and digital ventures have had a rocky relationship. Traditional (legacy) IT is often viewed as a major impediment to digital innovation, while digital is lauded as the engine of a better future. Truth is, the two must be closely coupled for a digital transformation to be successful. It takes the right mindset, a common vision of a better digital future, clear accountabilities, and proper governance mechanisms.

WHY IT MATTERS

Studies on digital transformations often cite archaic IT systems and applications as top obstacles,[1] and organizations find it easy to point the finger at IT as the "Department of No"—out of touch, old school, and bureaucratic. Although there may be some truth to this (in some organizations), the stereotype has encouraged various forms of separation between digital development and traditional IT.

Regardless of whether the IT department is on the cutting edge, digital transformation can't get very far without it.[2] Beyond isolated experiments or deployments of shiny new objects, digital implementation needs traditional IT support for enterprisewide scaling, especially when digital must interface with existing back-office systems or extract data that represents the core value of so many digital applications.[3]

With digital transformation, business and IT have become deeply intertwined. Unfortunately, duplicate responsibilities between digital initiatives and IT often lead to confusion, significant costs, and inefficiencies. We need a common front.

Whatever the digital governance model (CDO, digital unit, etc.), it is important to clearly define scope, accountability, and alignment between digital and IT leaders.[4] Without fail, a lack of alignment will lead to costly and painful integration down the road as digital efforts are scaled, which is a prerequisite for obtaining a healthy return on digital investments.

> Our entire leadership team is very engaged and animated around digital and tech and what it can mean for the company. It's part of the shared goals we have as a leadership team to continue to lead in terms of innovation and consumer facing technology.
>
> —ADAM BROTMAN, EX-CDO, STARBUCKS[5]

BEST PRACTICES AND KEY INSIGHTS

Digital transformation is about balancing the old and the new. This is also true for IT management. Efficient IT organizations are still crucial for keeping the current business ticking via complex back-office systems and operational backbone infrastructures, whether this is handled in-house or is outsourced. Companies still rely on these systems for the proper functioning of their traditional value chain, from procurement of goods and services to manufacturing, distribution, sales, and customer service operations.

But digital transformation has added new demands to the IT agenda, including rapid application development, innovative customer interactions, platform building, and the digitization of products and services. Effectively managing this dual agenda is paramount for digital transformation success, but it requires a mindset change for IT leaders because they must now align the demands of operational IT and innovative digital solutions. This dual agenda requires leaders to recognize and then manage a set of seven tensions (see Figure 9.1).

Managing these tensions requires a commitment from leadership. A main component in aligning IT and digital programs is to first agree on a structure that allows for a clear division of responsibility and accountability. It also involves clearly mapping out the current system landscape and the target architecture that will underpin digital developments.

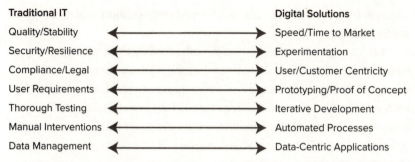

Traditional IT		Digital Solutions
Quality/Stability	←――――――――――→	Speed/Time to Market
Security/Resilience	←――――――――――→	Experimentation
Compliance/Legal	←――――――――――→	User/Customer Centricity
User Requirements	←――――――――――→	Prototyping/Proof of Concept
Thorough Testing	←――――――――――→	Iterative Development
Manual Interventions	←――――――――――→	Automated Processes
Data Management	←――――――――――→	Data-Centric Applications

Figure 9.1 Managing tensions between traditional IT and digital solutions

For example, the CDO-CIO team collaboration at CooperVision Inc., a manufacturer of contact lenses, used the approach of "decoupling front-end systems from back-end systems" to draw a clear division of responsibilities. CIO John Casella says that "decoupling" the customer's digital experience on its website (as much as practical) from core enterprise systems gave the digital team more control and responsiveness while minimizing extra work for IT. This led to clearer responsibilities and less conflict.[6]

Successfully aligning IT and digital ventures also depends on the governance model that has been adopted. In some cases, both IT and digital are within the same entity and reporting line, which allows a dual-mode IT model to be instituted. However, tight integration might come at the cost of incremental rather than radical innovation and slower time to market.[7] In other cases, a CDO or other executive(s) is charged with overseeing the digital unit. In that case, the digital unit acts as a bridge between IT and the business for the delivery of digital solutions.

Starbucks adopted this model very successfully with the appointment of CDO Adam Brotman as a sparring partner to CIO Curt Garner, both reporting to the CEO. Garner describes the alignment: "We have tiger teams or SWAT teams that are assigned to specific projects and goals. We've been able to knock a lot of time and cycles off the work by having the thought leaders for digital and technology and their teams all together and working towards the same objective. Everything from inception and brainstorming through to the service delivery is jointly owned, team-focused and very collaborative."[8]

Sometimes digital units are set up as independent entities from traditional IT. This has the advantage to provide focus and accountability for digital transformation, but it needs to be managed very tightly as there is a risk of isolation from the core business, which could generate sources of conflict with traditional IT.

Lastly, alignment can be strongly enhanced by establishing fluidity of resources between IT and digital—by creating a joint team with a dual focus on digital delivery and back-office integration or by dedicating key staff on each side to align objectives. CooperVision's CIO John Casella describes how he assigned a senior enterprise architect to the CDO team: "This manager understood the CDO priorities and marshalled IT resources for projects so they didn't have to work through the IT machinery."

Hacker's Toolbox

Get the setup right. Organizations may choose one of many different models to anchor their digital efforts, and this setup may change as the organizations continue their digital journey. Whatever model you decide to pursue, don't forget to plan alignment accordingly.

For example, if you implement a central digital group to push your digital agenda forward, make sure that the IT department is both informed and proactively involved. It's a good idea to use tools that create transparency and clearly show responsibilities and accountability, like the RACI (responsible, accountable, consulted, informed) mapping to clearly delineate the scope of work between IT and digital.

Create regular touchpoints. Successful digital leaders are well aware that successful alignment goes beyond lip commitments and requires real and tangible touchpoints. To make sure that alignment becomes part of the daily practice, put processes and roles in place that facilitate ongoing information sharing and increase trust between digital and IT teams.

Similar to business-IT liaison roles, digital-IT relationship managers can help to ensure ongoing adjustment and coordination. Information sharing can also be increased through physical proximity or regular shared events. To avoid internal rivalry, it helps to create a shared sense of ownership, for example through secondments and employee exchanges between digital teams and traditional IT departments.

Grow together. Alignment is not a static event or one-time task; it is a continuous process that evolves as the digital journey continues. Alongside increased digital revenues and responsibilities, power struggles and political conflicts may arise between digital and IT departments. While it may be impossible to avoid these struggles altogether, digital leaders can avoid breakdowns by continually reaching across the aisle and sharing both success and failures. IT and digital leaders should be responsible for regularly, and jointly, reporting on digital transformation progress and openly raising organizational, capability, or resource sticking points so they can be addressed.

Self-Reflection Questions

Are you seeing close cooperation and trust between your IT and digital leaders?

Are your IT leaders buying and actively supporting the digital strategy and the transformation required to implement it?

Is the scope of activity and accountabilities between IT and digital teams clear to you and the rest of the organization?

Are you receiving joint IT/digital progress reporting, or are you getting differing feedback from each side individually?

Are you confident that your digital transformation is being implemented at the right pace, or are you sensing that it needs structural or leadership changes?

RELATED CHAPTERS

Aligning the Top Team to Drive Transformation Success (Chapter 3)

Choosing the Right Digital Governance Model (Chapter 8)

Building and Managing Technology Infrastructure (Chapter 11)

Managing Partnerships and Ecosystems (Chapter 13)

Investing in Startups (Chapter 14)

Making the CDO Role a Success (Chapter 23)

ACCELERATING DIGITAL USING AGILE METHODS

An increasing number of organizations are employing agile tools and methods to accelerate their digital transformations.[1] Digital transformation requires speed and adaptability, and agile tools and methods support these efforts with their focus on short improvement cycles and experimentation. Despite widespread adoption, however, agile approaches to digital initiatives have met with varying degrees of success. This chapter explores the sources of this variance, and provides advice on how to set up and apply agile methods to digital transformation projects.

WHY IT MATTERS

Agile methods are not new. Although agile became associated with software development after 2001, its roots lie in manufacturing and quality movements in Japan.[2] What *is* new is how organizations are embracing agile methods as a means to drive their digital transformations.

Recent research reveals that more than two out of three successful digital transformations have leveraged agile management methods.[3] Agile methods and frameworks, such as Scrum or Extreme Programming,[4] represent an iterative development approach that embraces quick deployment, responsiveness to change, and an emphasis on customer needs. Agile practitioners also share a mindset that work should, in principle, be done in small, autonomous, and cross-functional teams.

While the benefits are clear, organizations experience many challenges when implementing agile, including resistance to change, difficulty in implementation, and unsuitable organizational structures.[5] Agile methods were originally designed for small and single-team projects. Although many organizations have successfully implemented agile in isolated areas, e.g., for a single team or business unit, most struggle to scale pilots to other parts of the organization.[6]

Moreover, while agile offers a useful framework for change management, it's not enough, on its own, to drive enterprisewide digital transformation. Research shows that even when organizations implement agile tools and processes "by the book," the benefits often fail to flow unless there's a mindset shift toward making organizational agility, not just project agility, the central focus of the change.[7]

> It's the leaders' responsibility to drive this change and
> it's continuous work; it's nothing you can delegate to a project
> or to a department—every leader has to do it.
> —FELIX HIERONYMI, VP AGILE TRANSFORMATION, BOSCH[8]

BEST PRACTICES AND KEY INSIGHTS

Digital transformation requires more than classic change management techniques. The change needs to be systemic to reflect the networked nature of organizations. It must also combine high levels of scale, interdependence, and dynamism.[9]

Although there are many implementation approaches, agile methods are particularly useful for driving collaboration across business units and functions, fostering continuous change, and promoting empowerment and autonomy in decision making. These are all important elements to ensure successful, and scaled, implementation of digital transformation. So what does it take to make agile effective?

Drive Collaboration Across Silos

When implementing a digital transformation, working across traditional silos is unavoidable. With a focus on organizing around cross-functional problem-solving teams, agile methods are well suited to fostering collaboration.

Organizations usually create teams that are small enough to collaborate closely but large enough to include the cross-functional skills necessary for project execution. Teams are given clear mandates and the autonomy to decide how to work. When done correctly, it pays off. Multidisciplinary collaborations have been found to produce higher revenues and profits because they can tackle higher-value problems more effectively.[10]

Take TDC, a leading Danish telecommunications company, which employed agile methods to accelerate its digital transformation. TDC had invested significant funds into digital for several years, but found that its initiatives took longer than anticipated and that consumer needs had shifted by the time the digital initiatives hit the market.[11]

In response, TDC launched cross-functional teams (consisting of product owners, commercial specialists, frontline experts, customer-experience designers, and developers) to design, test, and improve digital customer journeys. Initially launched as a small pilot, the initiative scaled into four "digital tribes" organized around their end consumers, B2B users, TV-based services, and systems infrastructure. These tribes were colocated, with each given end-to-end accountability to create engaging customer journeys in online sales and services.

In TDC's case, colocation and end-to-end accountability within each cross-functional team enabled the company to collaborate across traditional silos. And TDC realized significant benefits from this agile approach. Call volume, one of the largest cost drivers, decreased by more than 40 percent when customers were able to solve their problems online.

Drive Sustainable Change

Because digital disruption and transformation operate in perpetual and continuous cycles,[12] organizations need to develop new practices that support iterative changes and fast development cycles. Agile methods are often used to help align development with changing customer needs and trends. With their focus on iteration, agile methods can make development cycles more efficient.

Consider the case of Cisco, which faced difficulties in predicting long-term resource and work planning for its projects. The company decided to adopt agile methods for its product development process.

Long-term predictability can be difficult when using agile development, but one business unit at Cisco adopted a two-team structure, consisting of an "execution" team and a "planning" team. This enabled the business unit to constantly adapt to change while maintaining the ability to forecast and plan several quarters ahead.[13] Using agile methods, the planning team talked to early collaborative customers about new product features and translated these insights into engineering tasks for the execution team. While the development team worked on these projects, the planning team looked at specific tasks for the next two quarters and continued to seek out new customer needs. This parallel process ensured a continuous symbiosis between new development and business planning, which could be easily scaled.

Promote Shared Autonomy

The digital economy is highly dynamic. Keeping up with a rapidly changing business environment requires awareness and speed. Organizations need to develop a working culture based on fast feedback, quick decision making, and rapid adaptation. This isn't easy.

With agile development, teams are self-organized, autonomous, and empowered to make decisions. However, large organizations are complex systems, and there are many decisions that a single team can't make without impacting the wider organization.

To overcome this challenge, Swedish networking and telecommunications company Ericsson developed a community-based decision-making model, based on agile methods, which became the central decision-making body for large-scale projects. The community comprises 400 team members and product owners who are part of smaller "communities of practice," where specific topics are discussed among groups representing different parts of the business.[14]

The community usually meets once or twice a week, and meetings are led by a facilitator, with proposals for solutions prepared in advance. Decisions are made using "consent decision making," a technique in which people search for a tolerance range in which everyone can work. Ericsson reported several benefits to this approach, including higher employee motivation and better use of team members' knowledge.[15] Just as important, the approach helped the company make better decisions and commit to a common direction as it undertook new digital developments.

Promote Agile Values over Mechanics

Although some of the agile practices mentioned above can drive faster times to market and higher productivity, most agile experts agree that focusing on values and principles is equally effective.[16] When people understand agile values, they are more willing to embrace change. But it doesn't happen naturally.

When Volvo Cars introduced the Scaled Agile Framework in 2017, it also invested over 150,000 work hours in training the employees who were directly involved, along with 2,000 leaders.[17] As Anna Sandberg, head of Continuous Improvement & Change at Volvo's Product Creation, pointed out, "We wanted people to understand both the mechanics and the mind shift changes involved. We had leaders discuss and practice the new types of behaviors so they could better understand the results of those behaviors."

It's important to note that implementing independent agile programs is useful, but insufficient, for accelerating digital transformation. Organizations that successfully leverage agile methods for digital transformations focus not only on doing the mechanics but also on elevating mindsets to encourage autonomous teams, working through iterative and rapid processes, and promoting open communication across the organization.

> For us, the key was creating an environment which empowered teams to make their own mission- and values-guided decisions. Challenging the status quo where necessary, becoming self-disruptive, more entrepreneurial and innovation-led.
>
> —KEVIN COSTELLO, CEO HAYMARKET MEDIA GROUP[18]

Hacker's Toolbox

Choose your agile definition, methodology, and approach. The challenge of using agile is magnified by the many tools, labels, and methodologies that exist today.[19] The first practical step is to agree on what you're talking about, and more important, select an approach with a common methodology and language.

There are several frameworks for scaling agile that you might consider, including Scaled Agile Framework (SAFe), Large-Scale Scrum (LeSS), Disciplined Agile Delivery (DAD), and Scrum@Scale. These frameworks differ in team size, training and certification, methods and practices adopted, technical practices required, and organizational type.[20] Be sure to select the method that works best for your organization based on these differences.

Recruit agile evangelists in senior management. Research suggests that management support is critical for large-scale agile implementation.[21] Vistaprint, an online printing company, made sure its top executive team was trained using a course designed specifically for the company. A senior agile coach also participated in executive meetings for a year. As a result, several top executives became evangelists who encouraged other members of the executive team to adopt an agile mindset. A similar program was rolled out across the organizations for key leaders, who also became agile evangelists.[22]

Use coaches to accelerate learning by doing. It's difficult to explain how agile mindsets should be applied. Most organizations take a learn-by-doing approach via coaching. Coaches can watch for, and correct, problems as they arise. In particular, they can help draw attention away from tools and toward understanding principles and values. Both internal and external coaches can provide value. Internal coaches are often more accessible and know the specifics of the organization, whereas external coaches can provide an objective, outside-in view.

Self-Reflection Questions

What responses do you get from the people in your organization when they hear the word "agile"?

Have you experienced an agile program? Do you understand the organizational and mindset changes required?

Does your organization encourage and support a collaborative environment?

Can HR policies be changed to support and evaluate team effort instead of individuals?

RELATED CHAPTERS

Creating a Clear and Powerful Transformation Objective (Chapter 1)

How Best to Develop Digital Skills Within Your Organization (Chapter 24)

Working Across Silos (Chapter 25)

Scaling Digital Initiatives (Chapter 27)

BUILDING AND MANAGING TECHNOLOGY INFRASTRUCTURE

Because digital tools and technologies are all the rage, it's sometimes easy to overlook the underlying infrastructure that supports them. In the case of digital transformation, this infrastructure comprises two core elements: IT infrastructure that is stable and flexible and high-quality data assets that are secure.

Technologies such as databases, servers, network infrastructure, and enterprise software applications are not especially glamorous, but the success of any digital project hinges on them. Artificial intelligence, for example, is not a self-contained technology. In fact, unless it's plugged into a secure set of organizational systems, as well as accurate and compatible data sources, it's useless. A well-functioning technology infrastructure supports the whole digital transformation value chain—from data capture to storage, analysis, and dissemination of results—all in (or close to) real time.

WHY IT MATTERS

Abraham Lincoln once said, "Give me six hours to chop down a tree and I will spend the first four sharpening the axe."

The same logic applies to technology infrastructure. Without a proper infrastructure, management's resources and attention will be consumed with executing and maintaining core processes rather than figuring out how digital tools can generate new sources of value.

Technology infrastructure consists of a set of integrated and shared systems, processes, and data that together ensure operational efficiency and transparency.[1] When executives are asked about the main obstacles to proper digital execution, the limitations of existing IT systems are often cited as the number one roadblock.[2]

According to BCG, two out of three successful transformations were linked to business-led, modern fit-for-purpose technology and data platforms that supported the development and scaling of digital use cases.[3] Unfortunately, more than half of the companies in the study struggled with a lack of flexibility in their technology infrastructure.

GE invested billions in new technology, people, and processes to build an ambitious new division, GE Digital, to capitalize on the growth of digitization in the industrial world. However, the new division's marquee product—the Predix industrial internet platform—never lived up to its billing. Its main problem? It simply didn't work very well from a technology point of view.[4] Getting your technology infrastructure right is critical for digital transformation execution.

BEST PRACTICES AND KEY INSIGHTS

Paradoxically, recent advances have made it both easier and tougher to build a solid digital platform.[5] On the one hand, cloud, agile development methods, external code libraries, and easy-to-use development tools have enabled developers to build new digital solutions rapidly. On the other hand, these approaches can produce an uncoordinated mélange of tools and applications that collectively weaken, rather than strengthen, a digital transformation. Hence, the first step is to select a technology architecture that matches the organization's digital ambitions. But that won't be enough. Among the many challenges that a technology infrastructure must overcome, four have critical relevance. Two are linked to IT infrastructure (stability and flexibility), and two are related to data (quality and security).

Architecting Your Digital Infrastructure

The trouble with designing a technology architecture that will serve the organization's ambitions is that it must be built for efficiency *and* agility. For that reason, companies that have successfully executed a digital transformation have layered their technology infrastructure.

The first component is an efficient operational and transactional backbone. This is a traditional domain for industrialization, optimization, and efficiency, and it covers areas such as back-office systems and systems of records.

The second layer is an agile customer-engagement platform that covers areas from key transactions (such as payments) to the delivery of customized experiences and connections with ecosystem partners. This is a domain for user experience and quality service delivery.

The third component is a data and analytics platform that will use internal data and capture connectivity data to perform advanced analytics and/or build and test algorithms. This is a domain for insights and innovation.

Because of their differing objectives, each layer requires specialized management, capabilities, technology partners, and metrics. If this sounds complex, that's because it is. But choosing an architecture, up front, that matches the company's business ambitions will guide future technology investments and ensure the coherence of the technology/IT operation.

IT Infrastructure Stability

From an IT perspective, stability is closely linked to reliability, consistency, and usability. Reliability means that the infrastructure is consistently up and running, and is also immune to various shocks and adverse events. Consistency refers to the infrastructure's ability to provide a standard quality of service across operating environments, such as different operating systems or app ecosystems. Usability means that the infrastructure is easy to use. In sum, a stable IT infrastructure works most of the time, across a wide variety of use cases.

For example, most blockchain applications have relatively light infrastructure requirements: high processing speed and plenty of storage. Conversely, many AI solutions have high computing and network resource needs and require compatibility with data sources.

According to a study of CIOs, the enemy of IT infrastructure stability is complexity.[6] Typically, the more complex the infrastructure, the less stable it is. A positive development has been the growth of cloud solutions that tend to be more stable than on-premise systems since they are centrally managed and fit for purpose. For this reason, many organizations are investing heavily in cloud infrastructure to support their digital transformation programs. However, linking cloud solutions to legacy systems remains a significant challenge.

> The responsibilities of the CIO are shifting quickly. If I think about how the CIO has to look at things going forward and how we engage with the business, the CIO has to be a catalyst. We need to instigate innovations with our business architectures, our strategy, our operations, and our technologies. A CIO has to be a strategist. We have to partner closely with the business to align these strategies and maximize the value of the technology investments. If you step back and look across all industries, there is a core infrastructure renaissance underway.
> —TREVOR SCHULZE, CIO, MICRON TECHNOLOGY[7]

IT Infrastructure Flexibility

On the surface, IT infrastructure flexibility may seem inconsistent with stability, but the two go hand in hand. Infrastructure that is stable but not flexible is dangerous, as it is unable to adjust to changing conditions. Unfortunately, because many legacy systems (and some cloud solutions) are not very flexible, organizations struggle to keep up when the environments change.

Good infrastructure allows for the establishment of feedback loops, whereby successes and failures can be quickly flagged, analyzed, and acted upon. For instance, when Ticketmaster wanted to tackle the growing problem of "scalpers"—people who buy tickets ahead of genuine customers in order to resell those tickets at a premium—it turned to machine learning algorithms.[8] The company created a system that examined real-time ticket sales data, along with a holistic view of buyer activity, to block out resellers and reward legitimate customers with a smoother process. But as the company soon discovered, resellers adapted their strategies and tools in response to the new system. Ticketmaster's infrastructure was flexible enough to modify its pricing tool to include feedback loops, allowing its algorithms to keep up with the resellers' evolving techniques.

Sometimes it makes sense to differentiate between layers—e.g., between core back-office IT infrastructure and front-facing systems such as the websites and apps that work with customers and ecosystem partners. When it comes to integration with digital tools and technologies, this external-facing infrastructure is more than just a pretty front end.[9] It performs key transactions and connects back to the core platform to complete the work. The front-facing infrastructure needs to be more flexible than the back-office systems and should be designed accordingly.

Data Quality

Bad data is more than an annoyance. In 2013, the US Postal Service identified 6.8 billion pieces of mail (4.3 percent of the total) that was undeliverable due to bad data, costing the service more than $1.5 billion.[10] Fast-forward to 2020, when 20–30 percent of email addresses change each year,[11] and there are numerous data issues that can impact the effectiveness of a digital solution, including data incompatibility across different systems, duplicate data, lack of data currency, data inaccuracy, and data ambiguity. Indeed, one study published in the *Harvard Business Review* estimated that just 3 percent of companies' data met basic quality standards.[12]

It's often worthwhile to conduct a data quality audit.[13] These audits first establish a baseline of data quality standards, rules, and expectations, and then run checks across the organization to determine whether the data meets the required benchmarks. This audit should be followed by a data cleansing process.

Data Security

Cyberattacks are so common today that the importance of data security is hard to overstate. However, several practices can reduce the likelihood of being compromised.

First, most attacks exploit known vulnerabilities and can be addressed with relatively easy fixes. When a vulnerability in a piece of software is identified, a clock starts ticking; now it becomes a race between the software vendor (to develop a patch) and hackers (hoping to exploit the vulnerability). This race does not stop when a patch is released, as many software customers fail to quickly patch their systems. For example, Maersk was hit badly by the NotPetya virus in 2017, even though Microsoft had already released a patch that would have protected Maersk's systems from the virus, had Maersk installed it.

Second, routine maintenance and real-time monitoring can identify attacks and vulnerabilities and reduce the chances of future attacks. Standard practices should be followed, including the implementation of strong password policies, administrative privilege restrictions, and regular security audits. Random intrusion tests, including simulated phishing attacks, are also highly recommended. Because more than 90 percent of successful hacks and data breaches stem from phishing, the workforce should be educated on good and bad security policies, and best practices should be enforced for all users.

Finally, incentives should be aligned with security-friendly behavior. In the case of Maersk, the patch upgrade had been approved by senior management, but the IT administrators' bonuses were linked to uptime and other measures of current performance. Thus, the administrators had no incentive to implement the upgrade, as this would have slowed system performance.

Hacker's Toolbox

Fuse IT and business digital road maps. Technology infrastructure is often under the purview of the IT department, so close coordination with IT is important. Many first-wave digital transformations tried to go it alone (without IT) and failed.[14] Today, IT leaders drive digital transformation in some companies, while digital and IT leaders work closely in others. As business leaders become more tech savvy, and IT leaders and their teams become more business savvy, getting digital and IT to cooperate on infrastructure is a more realizable goal than ever before.

Don't avoid the tough fixes. Many organizations are using out-of-date, inferior, and unsecure systems, applications, and databases. Why? Because the prospect of changing them is so painful—e.g., if a system is critical to the company's operations, taking it offline might have unpredictable and expensive consequences. Unfortunately, legacy technologies are not like fine wines. They don't improve with age. In most cases, it's better to update the infrastructure as soon as possible.

Think about your digital platform architecture early. Empower your enterprise architects. You will need to have an appropriate target architecture in mind as you invest and transform your technology infrastructure. This synergy is critical for executing your business strategy.

Establish clear accountability for data management. Data, whether customer insights or operations and connectivity information, will most likely be at the heart of your digital transformation. Today, 57 percent of Fortune 1000 companies have appointed a chief data officer.[15] Even without a chief data officer, you will need clear data management accountability for governance, operations, innovation, analytics, and security of your data assets.

Educate the senior leaders. Don't tackle the complexity of building a proper technology infrastructure on your own. Share with senior leaders your architecture plans, the trade-offs being made, and the progress of your technology buildup.

Self-Reflection Questions

Is your technology infrastructure capable of supporting your objectives for digital transformation? What are the gaps, and how can they be bridged? What needs to be modernized? What needs to be replaced? What needs to be built from scratch or acquired?

Is your technology infrastructure both stable (reliable, usable, consistent) and flexible (adaptable, scalable) enough to meet the needs of your digital transformation road map?

Is your data quality high enough to support your digital activities?

Do you have sufficient data security protocols in place to prevent cyber incidents and mitigate the impact of potential attacks?

RELATED CHAPTERS

Part Three

Hacking the External Environment

Working with the Outside World

*It takes a lot of courage to show
your dreams to someone else.*
—Erma Bombeck

Creating the right internal conditions is a prerequisite for digital transformation success. But it's not sufficient in itself. No matter how tightly connected your employees or how big your R&D department, many answers to digital transformation execution will come from outside the organization. Digital transformation will make your organization more porous and open, and that's not a bad thing. But it does require a much deeper and richer understanding of the external environment, as well as an ability to absorb new insights.

In the digital age, the most successful organizations are not castles sitting atop mountains. They are office towers surrounded by busy streets and parks, plugged into the city infrastructure via transit hubs and shopping malls.

Successful organizations have developed a hyperawareness of external events. Why? Because the digital world is moving incredibly fast, often in unpredictable ways. An organization's ability to detect weak signals early (be they competitive, technological, environmental, or consumer led) is the best insurance policy against unpleasant surprises. Thus, hyperawareness has become a key organizational skill for digital business agility.

Earlier we saw that preparing the internal organization for digital transformation is not a solo sport. The same applies to the outside world. Building a strong ecosystem of partners should be at the core of your digital strategy. It will grant you access to competencies you haven't mastered and to technologies and solutions you don't possess internally. When well executed, it will also derisk and speed up your transformation efforts. But partnerships need to be proactively managed, and you will also have to dedicate resources and relinquish some managerial control to make them work.

Working with the outside world can also uncover valuable ideas and new sources of growth. Open innovation, or innovating with external partners, has accelerated over the last few years as organizations relentlessly search for new value-creation opportunities. Challenges abound, from selecting the right partners to managing intellectual property to bringing external innovation back in-house.

Working with startups can be an effective way to tap into emerging technologies and business models. For a long time, attention has focused on small, nimble startups disrupting large, established firms. But in our experience, the outcome of this "David and Goliath" opposition is more a story of cooperation than of competitive warfare. Nevertheless, effectively harnessing innovation synergies between corporates and new ventures necessitates that the right structures, incentives, and knowledge sharing are properly orchestrated.

Lastly, digital transformation isn't solely about innovation and competition. It also has important ramifications for ethics and sustainability practices that cannot be brushed aside. Privacy, security, diversity, and environmental considerations have come to the fore of the digital transformation agenda. Unfortunately, in many instances, these ethical and sustainability practices have been managed in a highly fragmented way inside organizations. This approach is no longer possible. Responsible and forward-thinking organizations have made these issues an integral part of their digital execution. And in the years ahead, it will become more pressing for others to follow suit.

Opening your organization to the outside world is no longer "nice to have." It will make your organization smarter by being more alert to competitive dynamics, consumer behaviors, technology evolution, innovation opportunities, and environmental responsibility.

BUILDING HYPERAWARENESS INTO YOUR ORGANIZATION

Disrupt or be disrupted? This oft-used mantra reveals the fundamental conundrum that businesses face as digital disruption becomes a major force across all industries. In rapidly changing environments, an organization's ability to detect and monitor weak signals of forthcoming industry and consumer shifts helps provide crucial information about external and internal factors—factors that impact an organization's opportunities and risks, competitive position, and, ultimately, its very survival. We describe this ability as hyperawareness.

Hyperaware companies are less likely to be taken by surprise. They're also harder to disrupt because they can sense their own vulnerabilities and adjust their business models and processes accordingly. Organizations can build two types of hyperawareness that are critical for success: behavioral awareness and situational awareness.

WHY IT MATTERS

Many executives struggle to imagine their digital future in an ever-shifting landscape.[1] But what most do understand is that failing to have an early warning system leaves them vulnerable to competitive surprises that could threaten their long-term survival. With iconic incumbents such as Dell Computer, Safeway, and DuPont replaced by Facebook, Under Armour, and Gartner, Inc., on the S&P 500 in just five years,[2] many executives believe that more than one-third of their industry's top 10 incumbents will be displaced by digital disruption.[3] That said, many executives must still learn to distinguish between genuine disruption and mere hype to avoid unhealthy collective thinking and bad decision making.[4]

BEST PRACTICES AND KEY INSIGHTS

Recognizing weak or early signals of a change can provide organizations with a head start in preparing for what's coming next.[5] Hyperawareness is the ability to sense what's happening throughout an organization's operations—among workers and customers and in the broader environment—and make informed decisions based on these insights. In particular, two types of hyperawareness are critical for success: behavioral awareness and situational awareness.[6]

Build Behavioral Awareness

Behavioral awareness is the ability to deeply understand what employees *and* customers value, as well as how they think and act. To exploit this capability, companies need a methodical but organizationally safe way to facilitate information flows from the edges to those with decision rights.

Through Employees

Collecting information through employees is important because they are closest to the customers and partners. They know what customers love and what they complain about. They also know when a strategy isn't working, and will respond enthusiastically to initiatives that really matter. A common mistake that leaders make is isolating themselves from the people who can tell them what's really going on, and underestimating the difficulty of creating a culture of candor, where employees can share constructive criticism. Organizations have to build various mechanisms to promote information flows from employees to decision makers.

Spanish fashion retailer Zara, for example, actively trains its store managers and sales associates to elicit feedback from customers about what they like, dislike, and would purchase if it were available. Employees are also expected to communicate their own ideas about what will or won't sell. These insights are captured in Zara stores worldwide and reviewed by product designers at corporate headquarters.[7]

Other organizations employ reverse mentoring, which pairs younger employees with senior executives to provide fresh insight into emerging trends. These mentoring programs aren't just casual conversations. They are carefully structured to assure confidentiality and commitment.[8]

Finally, some companies employ anonymous feedback mechanisms to not only encourage feedback, but also gauge which ideas or criticisms have broad support. Google Moderator, a service that uses crowdsourcing to rank user-submitted questions and ideas, was originally developed to allow individual Google employees to anonymously submit questions at meetings. Other employees voted on these questions, and those that received the most responses would rise to the top of the list in real time. The service was quickly adopted at Google's weekly "all-hands" meetings to help the moderator address the most pressing issues on employees' minds.

Through Customers

Collecting information about customers has evolved from observable "snapshots-in-time" formats (such as customer surveys and focus groups) toward the use of mobile-phone and sensor data to uncover hidden patterns. Chinese retailers, in particular, are demonstrating how to get it right. The decline of retail is now a familiar story in the Western world, with iconic companies such as Walmart and Marks and Spencer forced to close stores, but retail in China is experiencing a resurgence, thanks to the concept of "new retail."

Hema, Alibaba's tech-powered fresh-food supermarket, embodies the new retail, which integrates online, offline, logistics, and data across a single value chain. Alibaba relies heavily on analytics to understand its consumers—how they buy and what they prefer to buy—to drive its retail strategy. Consumers can search for product information in-store by scanning a product code, place an order for home delivery (30-minute delivery within a three-kilometer radius [not quite two miles]), make a payment, and even order fresh food (including live seafood) to be cooked and eaten in-store—all via a dedicated Hema app. Hema knows everything about its customers: their phone numbers, purchasing history, payment and financial activities, and home addresses—and tailors its offerings accordingly in real time. According to company reports, Hema stores' sales per unit area are three to five times higher than those of other supermarkets.[9]

Build Situational Awareness

Situational awareness is the ability to define changes in an organization's business and operating environment to understand which ones matter. For many organizations, social media listening has become a critical tool for capturing insights about their business environment. In 2013, General Motors created a global Social Media Center of Expertise with a staff of approximately 600, distributed across five regions. The staff monitors hundreds of GM-owned and third-party social sites and vehicle-owner forums, using a range of digital technologies, including collaboration and analytics.[10] GM uses the data gleaned from over 6,000 customer interactions per month to improve its relationship with customers.

Other organizations integrate periodic deep-dive activities to help make sense of their business environment. Intuit, a business and financial software company, dedicates substantial management time to examining external market shifts every three to four years. As Albert Ko, former chief transformation officer, explains, "We really ask ourselves and bring in outside-in thinking of what could disrupt us and what are the disruptive forces that could dramatically spill over."

Intuit's exercise is usually undertaken by the C-level, as well as 100 top leaders and beyond, with the executives devoting 20–50 percent of their time over several months to identifying emerging trends.[11] In 2012, the team identified social, mobile, cloud, and data as disruptive trends and then aligned the company's internal businesses to these trends. In 2017, the team repeated the exercise with external strategic thinkers, operational Intuit leaders, 500+ customer observations, and 225 interviews with external companies. As a result, investments were reallocated to address eight major trends. "We follow the mantra of reroofing while the sun is shining," said Ko. "We are constantly looking to improve our house, both in terms of how we operate and new growth opportunities."

Although organizations are under pressure to anticipate changes in their business environments, a significant amount of management's time is occupied with overseeing the operating environment (comprising physical assets such as oil rigs, manufacturing plants, vehicle fleets, buildings, and other facilities).[12] Increasingly, the internet of things is a key digital enabler of operational awareness. The ability to track the status of production assets can drive significant operational efficiencies.

Consider the case of Dundee Precious Metals, a Canadian mining company that connected its entire European gold mine (located near Chelopech, Bulgaria), including assets such as conveyer systems, lights, fans, the blasting system, and even the miners themselves. Miners, drivers, and supervisors can now communicate by voice from anywhere, aboveground or below, including areas of the mines where voice communications have been historically hindered by a lack of radio or cellular signals. The mine's entire network, along with collaboration tools, analytics, and mobile devices, enables the company to understand its operations in real time.[13]

> We want to see exactly what is going on, as it is happening, rather than waiting for the shift change.
> —MARK GELSOMINI, DUNDEE PRECIOUS METALS[14]

Keep in mind that digital is a double-edged sword. On one hand, it's the leading cause of industry and business disruption today. On the other, it's a powerful tool that can be leveraged to spot and exploit opportunities. Because hyperawareness capabilities enable organizations to quickly respond to the changing digital environment, they are vital to digital strategy formulation. As such, they should become an ongoing part of every organization's business processes.

Hacker's Toolbox

Search for leading indicators. In *Seeing Around Corners*, author Rita McGrath encourages us to look for leading indicators—information about events that have yet to happen.[15] Leading indicators are often qualitative, taking the form of hypotheses. For example, a global transportation company might anticipate a retail slowdown if it observes the size of its customer shipments decreasing. The objective is to feed these leading indicators into an early warning system to facilitate your organization's preparedness.

Identify digital signals in other industries. To detect signals of how digital technologies might affect your business, look beyond your industry and business. Keeping abreast of emerging digital technologies in one industry can send alerts to another. For example, while extended reality technologies might primarily serve as tools for gaming, the adoption of these technologies may be an important signal that other industries (such as medicine and education) should recognize.

Leverage your ecosystem. Often, organizations don't have the internal expertise to interpret weak signals on their own. Rather than working by themselves, many organizations find it beneficial to work with partners that have expertise and insights in areas they don't.[16] Partnering with startups is a good avenue for testing new technologies. Collaborating with other large companies in different industries is also an efficient way to explore long-shot ideas.

Determine what is not relevant. Becoming hyperaware also involves determining what matters and what doesn't. Disruption is rarely defined and almost never measured. Equally, the influence of hype around disruption is hard to gauge. To understand and predict genuine disruption, pay close attention to actual industry data such as aggregate revenue, profit, or market share changes/gains.

Self-Reflection Questions

Are you leveraging diverse viewpoints from employees and customers into your business decision making? Do you tend to home in on one scenario to the detriment of others?

How much direct contact do you have with thought leaders and entrepreneurs outside of your organization? How often do you expose yourself and your organization to areas where the future is unfolding today?

Has your ability (and that of your senior leadership) to make sense of what's going on in the marketplace diminished in a significant way?

Do you have a deep understanding of what customers want and need? Do you have systems in place to track changing customer expectations?

RELATED CHAPTERS

Building Urgency When Your Business Is Doing Well (Chapter 2)

Investing in Startups (Chapter 14)

Implementing Open Innovation Effectively (Chapter 15)

Working Across Silos (Chapter 25)

Staying on Top of New Technologies (Chapter 29)

MANAGING PARTNERSHIPS AND ECOSYSTEMS

Should an organization partner to deliver its digital transformation? On this question, business leaders are deeply divided. Some argue that because digital transformation is at the core of their strategies, few (if any) components of the implementation should be outsourced. Others highlight the benefits of enlisting outside organizations: increased speed, access to key capabilities, and the quality that a capable transformation partner can bring to the transformation. So what's the answer? Our research has found that leading digital organizations often adopt a hybrid approach. They carefully build on their internal capabilities, but also rely on trustworthy strategic partners.

WHY IT MATTERS

Digital transformation presents many challenges in terms of capabilities (i.e., "We can't do this because we don't know how") and capacity (i.e., "We can't do this because we don't have enough resources"). Heightened market pressure forces organizations to become more and more specialized to differentiate their products and services, exacerbating the need for collaborators in noncore areas.

Today, external partnerships are a key element for pushing the digital journey forward to reduce an organization's risk exposure.[1] But this is where it gets tricky. Many partnerships are time-boxed and transactional, such as some IT outsourcing projects.[2] Digital leaders will need a more strategic approach to find companions to partner with them, stay the course, and truly transform the organization. Finding the right partner or network of partners and building and maintaining trust, as well as continually aligning expectations, are cornerstones of a successful digital partnership strategy.

> Sometimes, you use a partnership because they're doing something you simply couldn't do yourself. You couldn't recruit that kind of skill into your kind of business. You couldn't access a particular talent pool or a particular group of customers. Sometimes, we also use partnerships just for pace. Even as the digital business sitting on the side, if you like, of a large organization, still we can't operate at the pace that some of our digital-native and start-up partners can. We try our best to use Agile, but the way they use Agile is simply better than we are ever going to be able to do.
>
> —ANDREW REAR, CEO, MUNICH RE DIGITAL PARTNERS[3]

BEST PRACTICES AND KEY INSIGHTS

To locate digital transformation partners, it helps to look beyond the usual business relationships. Most organizations benefit from acquiring different types of partners, including both high-level and truly strategic partners, as well as a network of tactical partners. However, organizations with a long history of managing supplier relationships can easily fall into the trap of using a traditional supplier approach. This works well in areas like IT outsourcing or industrial automation, which usually focus on clearly defined tasks and tend to be transactional in nature.[4] Here, huge outsourcing contracts, with clear provisions for service-level agreements and penalties, are the norm. However, such an approach often limits the creative freedom and innovative developments needed to execute a successful digital journey.[5] We recommend, therefore, that digital leaders look beyond their procurement departments to build an ecosystem of suppliers and trusted strategic partners that can exploit long-term opportunities, as well as delivering clearly measurable short-term benefits.[6] Table 13.1 breaks down the options.

Table 13.1 Digital/IT Suppliers Versus Strategic Transformation Partners

Digital/IT Suppliers	Versus	Strategic Transformation Partner
Office automatization Digital marketing inititatives Supply chain digitization	What?	Codeveloping a digital vision, road map, and execution plan
Regular procurement/ contracting supplier	How?	Partner relationship based on goal alignment and trust
Ecosystem of suppliers and contractors for various projects	Who?	A small number of key partners

Find the Right Partners to Use as a Catalyst for Your Transformation

Many business partnerships are inherently uncertain and risky,[7] making it all the more crucial to carefully vet potential candidates to ensure they can meet your goals and serve as catalysts for the transformation.[8] But often the list of potential partners is long and the choice is difficult. Organizations should not take this decision lightly because this initial step may well determine the success or failure of their digital plans. Take, for example, the partnership between a unit of the pharmaceutical giant Novartis Sandoz and Pear Therapeutics, which aimed to leverage a prescription smartphone app for substance abuse therapies. At first glance, it seemed to be a good match. The partnership combined the global power and expertise of Novartis with the technological edge of Pear Therapeutics in the fast-growing digital healthcare market. Yet for reasons involving "leadership change" and "focus on cost and capital allocation,"[9] the relationship soured, leaving both parties with little to show for their efforts. What was viewed as a key strategic partnership by Pear Therapeutics was, from Novartis's perspective, probably seen as a simple supplier relationship. This is why alignment and transparency are such key elements of successful partnering.

Although tactical partnerships are not novel to digital transformation, and many large organizations have considerable experience with them, a strategic partner is a different animal. To pick the right strategic partners, organizations should consider three key dimensions: complementarity, experience, and ambition.

Complementarity

How well do they complement existing capabilities and capacities? Digital partnerships need to be purpose driven so that all the partners complement the others' technological and innovative strengths.[10] By working together, the partners each reduce their own exposure to the substantial risk and uncertainty that comes with novel technologies, while also maintaining their ability to explore and experiment with various new developments.[11] Organizations can choose among a wide range of potential partners, depending on the purpose.

If an organization is seeking outside-in innovation, partnering with a startup may be a good solution. If a company lacks skilled tech experts and needs help leveraging a new technology, one of the digital giants (e.g., Google, Microsoft) might provide the right value. If the firm is looking for a partner that will bring both technology and expertise to the table, teaming with a digital consultancy could be the solution. Digital leaders should also consider multiple partnerships—or a network of partners—if it suits their needs. But beware: the more parties that are involved, the more effort that is required to successfully manage the partnership.

Experience

Do they have prior experience partnering for (digital) business transformation? Working as equal and strategic partners—rather than in client-vendor or supply relationships—can be challenging. It requires a careful balancing of multiple, potentially conflicting, interests. To make the partnership work, executives must be open to sharing competitive insights and information with their partners while simultaneously safeguarding their organization's best interests.

This is especially true of digital transformations, which affect all parts of an organization and its business model, and where an atmosphere of distrust can quickly transform a strategic partnership into a transactional relationship with little benefit for either party. Prior successful experience with partnership networks is usually a good indicator that a would-be partner will live up to its promises and expectations. An established track record allows digital leaders to evaluate candidates based on their past partnership performances.[12] Unfortunately, some consultancies take the opportunity to learn about digital transformation on the job, at the client's expense.

Ambition

Will they provide the desired speed, quality, etc.? There is nothing more frustrating than wasting time, energy, and other resources only to find out that partners are not on the same page. For many organizations, embarking on digital transformation requires radical changes to all aspects of their business model and identity. To be of value on this journey, a digital partner must understand the organization, its strategy, and its ambitions inside out. A technology partner that downgrades a priority halfway through the transformation can have a massive negative impact on digital success. With this in mind, look beyond financial criteria, and instead seek out a company that will be a good match for the organization's ambitions—e.g., speed and quality—so that the partner will serve as a transformation catalyst rather than a millstone around the neck.[13]

A good example of a positive approach to partnering is global fashion brand Burberry. Former CEO Angela Ahrendts had an early hunch that fashion retail was changing dramatically, so she actively engaged with different partners to open up her brand for new types of consumerism. Burberry pioneered this approach by building a digital supplier ecosystem and by entering into a key strategic partnership with Salesforce. Ahrendts worked closely with Marc Benioff, CEO of Salesforce, to establish a strategic partnership that would become the main driver for Burberry's transformation into a "social enterprise." On top of this strong foundation, Burberry built a network of tactical partners, working with Google, Apple, and Snapchat in the United States, as well as WeChat and Alibaba in Asian markets. Doing so turned Burberry from a "tired brand into a digital powerhouse."[14]

Build Trust and Alignment Around Common Goals and Expectations

When it comes to digital partnerships, especially on a strategic level, sharing information and data is a key element. This can be a difficult paradigm shift, particularly for traditional organizations that grew big by closely protecting their IP. Concerns about risk and security are dominant. To overcome this barrier, organizations should determine what data they are willing to share and what data will remain proprietary.[15] Even then, it will be necessary to build mutual trust. According to research, building interorganizational trust requires two main elements: evidence of prior trustworthy actions and continuous commitment to the partnership.[16]

As with every family, however, the true strength of the relationship is tested during tough times. Disagreements or conflicting interests are unavoidable parts of partnerships, and the key is not to avoid them but to confront them directly and transparently, so the relationship can grow and continue afterward. Digital partnerships need to be agile.[17] Partners need to continually evaluate if their return on investment still outweighs the costs of the partnership and to proactively communicate if goals or expectations are changing. Partnership management can be a difficult and tedious task, especially if multiple partners are involved.[18] Thus, it's important for a dedicated top executive to sponsor and drive the partnership agenda to ensure a successful partnering approach.

$$\bullet \quad \bullet \quad \bullet$$

Today, very few corporations have the power to pull off a successful digital transformation on their own. Trustworthy partners can help accelerate the digital journey by providing expert digital skills that are hard to find. Making the best out of partnerships is both an art and a science, so organizations should consider the three key criteria discussed in this chapter when seeking partners for digital transformation: complementarity, experience, and ambition.

Hacker's Toolbox

Look for complementors near and far. Look for digital partners that will complement your own capabilities instead of "brand names" with international reputations. Sometimes teaming with a smaller, local organization can create a much more valuable partnership than competing for the attention of global digital players. A good way to start is to leverage local business networks and talk to companies with similar challenges about their experiences and recommendations.

Don't compete with your partners. If a partnership harbors competition and mistrust, it won't last very long. When entering partnerships, strive for a balance of power and mutual trust among partners, highlighting the benefits that each party brings to the table. Transparency among key stakeholders is key to match expectations and build trust. Partnerships tend to develop dynamics of their own, spiraling into either vicious or virtuous circles. Be alert for early signs of abuse or distrust, and confront them openly to turn a potentially downward spiral into positive momentum.

Take a systematic approach to choosing your partners. Before entering into a partnership, answer the following questions:

- Why do you need this partner—capacity or capability?
- Do you know exactly what you want (tactical project), or do you want to codevelop the outcome with the partner (strategic project)?
- Do you match with the partner in terms of ambition?
- To what extent are you willing to share your data and IP with this partner?

Self-Reflection Questions

Are you still aligned with your partners in terms of goals and ambition?

What if you lost a partner? How would this change your digital transformation journey?

How can/do you measure partnership success?

Do you have dedicated roles in place to make sure you get the most out of your partnerships?

RELATED CHAPTERS

Investing in Startups (Chapter 14)

Implementing Open Innovation Effectively (Chapter 15)

Competing Against or Working with Digital Platforms (Chapter 19)

INVESTING IN STARTUPS

Many organizations are encouraged to invest in startups to learn about emerging trends, to help them become more innovative, and to share in the gains when the startups are sold or go public. The outcome of these partnerships, however, is often disappointing. Established companies fail to learn much from startups, and startups fail to improve their odds of success by working with established companies. To effectively harness synergies between established companies and new ventures, our research suggests that organizations should design appropriate structures and incentives to enhance their corporate investment mechanisms and facilitate knowledge and access between both parties.[1]

WHY IT MATTERS

Increasingly, companies are turning to networks of external partners to accelerate their efforts to innovate and compete. One key group of digital innovation partners is startups,[2] which are often perceived as innovating closer to the customer and working in entrepreneurial and agile ways. Indeed, many organizations have established startup incubators, accelerators, and/or corporate venture capital (CVC) units to benefit tactically and financially from startups' knowledge and capabilities.[3]

However, previous studies have identified long lists of shortcomings with such collaborations, and recent research reveals that collaborations between startups and established companies are tenuous: 45 percent of established companies and 55 percent of startups are either "dissatisfied" or "somewhat dissatisfied" with their partnership.[4]

Clearly, there is a large opportunity for both established companies and startups to gain from partnering, but getting it to work for the benefit of both is not easy.

BEST PRACTICES AND KEY INSIGHTS

We recommend three concrete steps to gain the most value from investing in startups.

Establish Structures Built on VC Practices

First, set up a separate structure to work with startups. Most corporations already have departments that evaluate new investment opportunities, such as merger and acquisition (M&A) teams, innovation units, and business plan competitions. It's tempting to integrate startups into these entities. But working with startups is substantially different from other corporate partnering or investment activities.

We recommend establishing a unit built on venture capital industry best practices. These include hiring VC professionals who understand how to successfully navigate the VC ecosystem. Hiring at least one experienced venture capitalist has been correlated with ongoing CVC unit success.[5] These professionals bring deep practice knowledge of structuring venture deals, as well as an established network to source promising deals.

Take the case of South Korean electronics manufacturer Samsung, which formed Samsung NEXT as a software and services innovation subsidiary. As a hardware manufacturer, Samsung was keen to quickly improve (and integrate) software and services. To achieve this, NEXT was staffed with venture capital, M&A, industry experts, and other professionals to immediately create and scale breakthrough software and services. Leveraging its $150 million venture capital investment fund, Samsung NEXT aimed to support early-stage startups with pre-seed to Series B investments.[6]

> Start-ups and corporates do often have different objectives;
> this is what both parties need to understand and internalize.
> —DR. ULRICH SCHNITY, CTO OF AXEL SPRINGER[7]

Once an established company chooses to invest in a startup, we recommend that it *not* request strategic rights as part of the funding arrangement. These rights may prevent startups from reaching fair market value when they are sold. In addition, call options, the right to match an acquisition offer, etc., can scare off potential acquirers, which risk losing the acquisition to the CVC-sponsoring organization. Asking for strategic rights may also steer the most promising startups away from CVC deals. Founders and existing investors may worry that the exit price will be compromised.

Incentivize Collaborations with Startups

Second, startups typically expect to gain nonfinancial benefits from the partnership, such as access to corporate knowledge and resources and exposure to potential customers. In reality, these benefits tend to be overstated, since there is little to no incentive for corporate employees to collaborate with the startups.

The solution? Top management should make cooperation a fundamental part of corporate culture by actively encouraging employees to collaborate with startups—and by doing so themselves. This helps to demonstrate commitment and relevance. Moreover, companies should adopt corporate incentive systems that will help match employees (with relevant skills and knowledge) with the startups. These incentive systems may include participation in compensation schemes paid to the investment team. Temporary secondments of corporate employees to startups, and vice versa, also help to increase understanding and collaboration. We also recommend establishing internal bridge roles or linked teams composed of employees acting as intermediaries between the startups and relevant corporate entities.

GV (formerly Google Ventures) and Germany's Metro Group are good examples of CVC units committed to creating value for their portfolio companies. GV has dedicated teams that make sure its portfolio companies interface with Google technology and talent. Metro Group grants portfolio companies preferential access to its international store network and its customer base of independent hospitality businesses.[8]

Facilitate Knowledge Sharing and Communication

Third, poor communication is often the chief cause of failed partnerships between startups and established companies. Thus clear and effective communication protocols should be established, so that the right people in the corporation gain necessary insights about new industry trends, opportunities, and threats. For example, by involving the CVC unit in corporate strategy discussions, innovation activities, and digitization committees, companies can foster the transfer of insights from startups to the relevant corporate stakeholders.

It is also important to create clear processes around IP ownership rights. If startups worry that the corporate partner will steal their best ideas or technology, they will not collaborate fully. At the same time, complex processes involving the sponsoring company's legal department might scare away startups. The best approach is to establish simple rules regarding IP rights—rules that are clear to all parties from the start.

It can also be helpful for startups to provide regular information updates, new technology seminars, and meet-and-greets to expose their ideas and insights to as many corporate employees as possible. Through regular and continual contact between corporate employees and startups, a culture of sharing and learning, beneficial to both sides, can be established. We suggest that corporations define clear processes and structures that allow CVC units to capture and share insights gathered from their work with startups.

Such processes can be fostered through close links between the customer-facing part of the established company and the startup. The Metro Group developed a process that catalogs both internal and customer pain points and then links them to startups in its CVC ecosystem that offer relevant solutions. The company also holds regular meetings to explore how these startups can work with the company and its customers to resolve problems.[9]

Another example of cooperation is the way Airbus set up the UP42 ecosystem with the help of BCG Digital Ventures in 2018. Designed to help develop the growing geospatial solutions market, the platform offers access to earth observation and terrestrial data, provides data processing algorithms, and gives developers the infrastructure they need to run their code. UP42 benefits greatly from the "unfair advantage" that Airbus grants it—specifically, access to high-quality satellite images and tremendous domain experience built over decades. It complements these key assets with external data and analytics to provide a comprehensive environment for geospatial solutions.[10]

• • •

In theory, partnering with startups provides a win-win for both sides. Startups gain access to capital, valuable corporate resources, industry know-how, advice, and, perhaps most important, contacts and sales leads. For corporations, benefits include the possibility of above-average financial returns connected with any venture capital investment, along with strategic benefits such as access to new technologies or insights that may otherwise be unavailable. However, none of these benefits are likely to accrue unless the established company and the startup actively invest time, energy, and resources into the partnership.

Hacker's Toolbox

Clarify which type of CVC you are setting up. If you are setting up a CVC to work with digital startups, then make a very clear decision up front whether you are creating a financially driven CVC, a strategically driven CVC, or some combination of both. Your structure, processes, and targets will be quite different depending on your answer. Try to avoid what Scott Orn and Bill Growney describe in a *TechCrunch* article as tourist CVCs,[11] or ones that reflect a desire to be part of the CVC game without a clear set of objectives in mind. CVCs driven primarily by financial considerations act very much like traditional VCs—their main objective is to return capital back to the parent. Strategic CVCs care a lot more about finding new sources of business value and getting access to complementary resources and technologies. In either case, it is a good idea to hire VC insiders, who understand the nuances of this very idiosyncratic area of finance, then give them a great deal of autonomy to run it in the most appropriate manner.

Provide incentives for employees to work with startups. Incentivize key people in the organization to share in the success of the startup. People are busy, and without a clear reason to work with startups, most people will not do so, or do so superficially. These incentives may go as far as to include a share in the exit price of the startup, similar to the incentives given to the CVC team.

Don't be greedy. Insisting on being able to match any acquisition offer, insisting on having a first right of refusal, or insisting on sharing sensitive information can scare off startups with the best growth potential. For this reason, compared with traditional VCs, CVCs often end up working with second-tier companies.[12] If you insist on including these terms in contracts with startups, make sure that the potential outcomes are appealing enough—that is, that you offer other compensating benefits such as access to key knowledge or technologies—to attract the best companies.

Self-Reflection Questions

Gaining value from startups won't happen by itself, even if you invest in them. Are you doing enough to ensure that learning travels both ways?

Are people in your organization incentivized to work with startups? Is there anything in it for them?

What are the benefits and the long-term competitive advantage of a potential collaboration?

RELATED CHAPTERS

Managing Partnerships and Ecosystems (Chapter 13)

Implementing Open Innovation Effectively (Chapter 15)

Staying on Top of New Technologies (Chapter 29)

IMPLEMENTING OPEN INNOVATION EFFECTIVELY

Open innovation, or innovating with external partners, has been around for a long time.[1] Despite its widespread popularity, the results of open innovation programs are a mixed bag, as companies often struggle to make it work.[2] Challenges abound, from protecting intellectual property, to selecting the right external partners, to investing the required time and money to bring innovation back in-house. Yet research shows that open innovation practices have been accelerating over the past few years.[3] Why? Digital technologies have made it significantly easier for organizations to tap external innovation sources and acquire the capabilities to compete in a rapidly changing world. However, balancing internal innovation with externally focused open innovation requires organizational and mindset shifts. Research shows that the organizations that are aware of these challenges, and that proactively formalize their open innovation practices, are more likely to reap its rewards.[4]

WHY IT MATTERS

Innovation projects today overwhelmingly rely on digital technologies, but many organizations lack the capabilities to develop them in-house.[5] So to accelerate innovation, many organizations are opening up their innovation processes by sourcing external as well as internal ideas and pathways to market. Indeed, 78 percent of large companies in North America and Europe have adopted open innovation practices.[6] These organizations are increasing their financial support and allocating more full-time resources toward open innovation. But it's not plain sailing.

Open innovation requires clearly identifying which digital competencies will be strategic to an organization's future, as well as requiring an understanding of where such competencies can be accessed externally. Moreover, it's necessary to rebuild an innovation architecture to manage both internal and external resources and to ensure the transfer and scaling of successful ventures. Open innovation helps companies acquire capabilities in the short run, and building capabilities internally sustains competitive advantage in the long run, but how do digital leaders achieve the right balance?

BEST PRACTICES AND KEY INSIGHTS

According to research studies, organizations that purposefully design openness into their innovation efforts are best positioned to capture its advantages.[7] Many organizations find it relatively easy to launch open innovation activities such as innovation labs, hackathons, or corporate accelerators,[8] often by using intermediaries. But it's much harder to leverage external knowledge and embed capabilities into an organization's internal processes, beyond very limited structures or one-time events. So what does it take to really open up innovation?

Successful organizations design and implement open innovation by shifting their mindset toward external sources. They build or rebuild their innovation architectures from the ground up to incorporate both internal and external sources.

Creating an Open Innovation Mindset

Developing a mindset of open innovation can be a difficult shift for traditional organizations. It represents a marked departure from the "not invented here" syndrome that has plagued companies for decades. It's more evolution than revolution, and it takes time.

Global industrial leader Siemens has a highly decentralized operating structure built around four main sectors: energy, healthcare, industry, and infrastructure. When the company launched open innovation programs in 2008, many people were skeptical and/or confused. As Tomas Lackner, head of Open Innovation & Scouting, noted: "Siemens as a company already had lots of connections to the external world, with more than 2,000 collaborations with roughly 1,000 universities! Obviously, the number of collaborations was not the point we wanted to address. Rather, we wanted to connect experts, both inside and outside of Siemens, and who didn't know of each other before and who perhaps had already developed ideas and technologies that matched with our needs."[9]

To encourage open collaboration and innovation in the Siemens culture, Lackner first initiated companywide "innovation jams" using online discussions that allowed people to rapidly share and discuss specific innovation topics. Lackner was also instrumental in developing TechnoWeb in 2009, an internal social media tool that helped network more than 35,000 experts within approximately 1,200 technology-oriented communities at Siemens.[10] Having encouraged internal collaboration around innovation, Siemens was able to step outside its firewalls.

Lackner and his team also developed a series of idea-generation contests with external participants and universities to scope out joint research projects. In 2016, Siemens launched "next47," an investment arm and startup accelerator to further open itself up to disruptive ideas. Through these successive external ventures, Siemens's innovation community was able to evolve its open innovation mindset and embrace the benefits of external collaboration over the past decade.

A study of open innovation at NASA provides further insight. The study revealed that while an open innovation model led to scientific breakthroughs at record speeds, the most resistant scientists and engineers saw open-source methods as a challenge to their identities as innovative problem solvers. In contrast, those scientists who embraced open-source methods shifted their identities from "hero problem solvers" to "solution seekers."[11]

Managers should encourage and reward solution-seeking behavior by recognizing those who find solutions in creative ways.

Identifying and Accessing Critical Capabilities

When companies have the digital capabilities to innovate, there is no need to go external. In fact, it can be counterproductive, exposing the company's innovations to the outside world and making IP harder to protect. In addition, it's fair to assume that some external partners will be working with the firm's competitors. But with the ever-increasing demand for advanced digital skills such as IoT or machine learning, most companies will have no choice but to seek external input. (See Figure 15.1.)

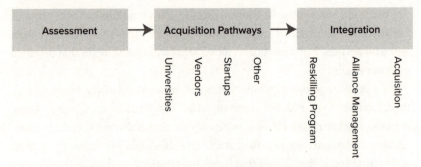

Figure 15.1 Identifying and accessing digital capabilities

It's critical to acquire a detailed understanding of which digital capabilities will help you to successfully transform and differentiate. Accessing data science expertise might be critical for the long-term health of a retailer, for instance, but it might not be for a real estate management company that needs to understand only sales and rental trends.

> For the long run, you have to be clear on what capabilities will be strategic, enable differentiation and potential innovation—invest in building these capabilities in-house now. Outsourcing these strategic skills will limit achieving differentiation, and mostly provide parity with competitors that are leveraging similar outsourced partners.
>
> —FARHAN SIDDIQI, CDO, AHOLD DELHAIZE[12]

The next critical step is choosing the best external routes to these capabilities, be they universities, startups, technology vendors, or others. With this mapping in hand, companies can develop a coherent portfolio for their open innovation program. Next comes the task of how to integrate these capabilities. This can be achieved through the reskilling of employees, alliance management, or outright acquisitions.

Monsanto, now part of Bayer, had a strategic need to develop data science capabilities. In addition to external partnering, the company launched a reskilling program that eventually grew its data science community to 500 members, with many biologists and process chemists turning into data scientists.[13]

Philips Consumer Lighting embarked on its open innovation journey in 2010, and has continually refined its integration of external technologies through a clear alliance management process. Philips's alliance management comprises a small team of professionals who negotiate contracts, obtain agreements on key performance indicators, and develop tools to evaluate the partners' perspectives on partnership evolution. The group is also responsible for managing regular meetings and project workshops to support effective knowledge transfer.[14]

Outright acquisition of companies to capture capabilities (aka "acquihire") can also be effective when speed is of the essence. In 2019, restaurant chain McDonald's acquired a number of startups to speed access to key capabilities in dynamic personalization, automation, and voice-based technologies.[15]

Embedding a New Innovation Architecture

Pursuing open innovation in an uncoordinated way rarely works. In fact, studies have shown that taking a hands-off approach generates poor results.[16] The pursuit must be orchestrated through a clear and coherent innovation architecture, starting at the top. First, a clear logic is required for how and where open innovation ventures contribute to either growth strategy or business model evolution. Second, it's good practice to have a senior executive oversee the innovation investments and efforts across the business to ensure focus and knowledge flows and to avoid duplication. Third, it's important to be clear about the time horizon and the expected return for each open innovation project.

James Swanson, former CIO of Monsanto, quickly realized that he needed a clear innovation architecture to drive Monsanto's transformation from a seed producer to a solutions provider from 2014 to 2018. At the time, Monsanto committed to investing in digital technologies, so it could gather and study all the data underlying decision making on farms. But thanks to a scarcity of in-house digital skills, Monsanto had to turn to external sources for certain capabilities in big data and analytics infrastructure, AI, and cybersecurity. To tap more external innovation sources, Monsanto built a data science center of excellence, using a centralized data platform driven by API and microservices, to run hundreds of AI models to improve supply chain and commercial activities.[17]

"You have to look at your assets and where you need a partner," said Swanson. "For us, data and our scientific understanding of the data are tremendous assets. We've realized that internal capabilities are critical, as well as our networks and the modernization of our infrastructure."

There is no one-size-fits-all approach to building an innovation architecture, but clear goals help determine the type of external sourcing required, as well as how best to connect it to the organization. For example, some open innovation will be long term and science/technology led, such as a research partnership with a university. Others will focus on discovery and incubation, such as startup accelerators and incubators. Others might be investment led, such as venture incubation or acquisitions.

Managing innovation architecture is a complex endeavor. It's a balancing act between managing internal and external sources and figuring out how to best transfer and scale successes within your operational organization. It often requires dedicated innovation teams, some organizational surgery to ensure proper transfer (such as a testing sandbox for startups), and an understanding and proactive support from your internal functions, like HR and legal.

Hacker's Toolbox

Build the team. Ensure that key individuals, scouts, and gatekeepers are in place to build open innovation capabilities. Scouts identify advances in science and technology, and gatekeepers support the transfer and dissemination of external knowledge and technologies into the organization. Not only do these roles help build an organization's external network with different partners, but they also make open innovation visible within the entire organization.

Establish outcome metrics to measure the success of open innovation initiatives. The two leading outcome metrics often used by organizations are the amount invested into open innovation projects and the number of technological opportunities introduced to the organization.[18] While the relevance of these metrics could be debated, the point is that successful organizations approach open innovation in an organized way through the application of metrics.

Ensure top management support. Be sure senior executives are overseeing the open innovation activities to ensure coherence with the firm's growth strategy or business model ambitions. Several studies point to the role of top management support in open innovation success. Senior management is especially crucial for ensuring organizational commitment and support. While these executives may not be expected to have the skills of a practitioner, they should appreciate the skills and needs of the people they are asking to run open innovation.

Self-Reflection Questions

Who is accountable for innovation within your firm?

Do you have a good grasp of which digital capabilities you need to develop over time?

Can you develop those missing capabilities in-house fast enough, or do you need to access them through external sources?

If you need to access these capabilities externally, are you clear on the best sourcing strategy—e.g., partnerships, universities, startups, etc.?

Do you have the right internal innovation processes and leadership to bridge your internal and external innovation sources?

Are you clear about how open innovation ventures will contribute to business results and over what time horizon?

RELATED CHAPTERS

Building Hyperawareness into Your Organization (Chapter 12)

Managing Partnerships and Ecosystems (Chapter 13)

Investing in Startups (Chapter 14)

Building a Balanced Portfolio of Digital Initiatives (Chapter 20)

How Best to Develop Digital Skills Within Your Organization (Chapter 24)

MANAGING DIGITAL TRANSFORMATION RESPONSIBLY AND SUSTAINABLY

The ethics and sustainability of digital transformation are likely to become more pressing in the coming years. To date, the focus has largely been on the negative impact of poor ethical and sustainability practices, such as cyberattacks, privacy breaches, and excessive environmental damage. However, well-managed practices can lead to benefits, such as improved customer loyalty, higher revenues, and lower costs. Today, digital ethics and sustainability efforts are highly fragmented across organizations. To address this, forward-thinking organizations are setting up corporate digital responsibility (CDR) offices to oversee and coordinate ethical and sustainable digital practices.

WHY IT MATTERS

Over the past few years, two of the most significant global business trends have been *sustainability* and *digitization*. Sustainability revolves around humanity's relationship with the natural world, while digitization focuses on the virtual world. Without obvious common roots, these trends have developed more or less independently. However, the worlds are about to merge. Digital ethics and sustainability will become a major factor in digital transformation.

In some places, they already have. The risks to organizations from poor or unethical digital practices are escalating and can no longer be ignored. Imagine the damage caused by a misogynistic or racist AI chatbot (e.g.,

Microsoft's Tay[1]), the impact of a security or privacy breach (e.g., Equifax[2]), or the environmental harm caused by poorly disposed of computer equipment.

For digital transformation leaders, the pressure to quantify and reduce the social and environmental impact of digital systems and technologies is sure to mount. For the moment, most companies address digital ethics and sustainability in a fragmented way—if they address them at all. Although the risks are clear, there's also a significant opportunity to differentiate based on digital sustainability practices. In short, there are many rewards to consider, as well as risks.

BEST PRACTICES AND KEY INSIGHTS

COVID-19 provided an interesting test case for digital ethics. For example, mobile phone apps that track the location and movement of people were deployed across the world. These apps were designed to provide a societal benefit by reducing the spread of the virus. However, questions have arisen about the impact of the apps on people's privacy. The extent to which the data was aggregated and anonymized varied greatly by country. Organizations, such as Apple, Google, Facebook, and many telecommunications companies, had to make difficult choices about how to balance ethical responsibilities to their customers, governments, and employees.

COVID-19 is merely one example of how digital ethics and sustainability practices are assuming a greater role in digital transformation. The pandemic highlighted the fragmented nature of current practices, as well as the dangers of too little coordination.

To address these problems, some companies are bringing together the various sustainability practices relevant to digital transformation under the umbrella term "corporate digital responsibility."[3] Although CDR is a subset of corporate social responsibility (CSR), a well-established entity in many organizations, CSR functions often lack the digital knowledge and skills needed to effectively manage CDR.

CDR is defined as *a set of practices and behaviors that help an organization use data and digital technologies in socially, economically, technologically, and environmentally responsible ways.* Thus, four CDR categories are relevant to digital transformation: social CDR, economic CDR, technological CDR, and environmental CDR. Each of these four categories contains components that could create significant opportunities for competitive differentiation (see Figure 16.1). If they aren't appropriately addressed, however, the opportunities could also become threats.

Social CDR
- Ensuring data privacy protection for employees, customers, and other stakeholders
- Promoting digital diversity and inclusion
- Pursuing socially ethical practices

Economic CDR
- Replacing jobs done by humans in a responsible way
- Ensuring that outsourcing of work to the gig economy is done in a responsible way
- Respecting data ownership rights, i.e., by reducing piracy

Technological CDR
- Ensuring ethical AI decision-making algorithms
- Not producing or using digital technologies that could harm employees, customers, or other stakeholders
- Implementing responsible cybersecurity practices

Environmental CDR
- Following responsible recycling practices for digital technologies
- Following responsible disposal of digital technologies, including extending technology life span
- Following responsible power consumption practices

Figure 16.1 The four categories of corporate digital responsibility

Social CDR revolves around an organization's relationship to people and society. Included in this area is data privacy protection for customers, employees, and other stakeholders. Social CDR also incorporates aspects of digital diversity and inclusion, such as bridging the increasing divide between digital haves and have-nots across geographies, industries, social classes, and age.[4]

> We have a responsibility to protect your data, and if we can't then we don't deserve to serve you.
> —MARK ZUCKERBERG, FACEBOOK CEO[5]

Economic CDR relates to responsibly managing the economic impact of digital technologies. Much has been said about the replacement of human jobs by robots and other digital technologies, and this is certainly a relevant part of economic CDR. Yet CDR also encompasses the creation of new jobs that are enriching, purposeful, and interesting. (Emerging evidence suggests that the so-called gig economy creates jobs that are often uninteresting, repetitive, and underpaid.)[6] There are also questions regarding fair monetary compensation for the data's original owners.

Technological CDR is linked to the responsible creation of technologies themselves. For example, biased or inaccurate AI decision-making algorithms can lead to unfair or discriminatory practices, as has been noted among many recommendation engines.[7] Other technologies can also have harmful effects on society. Facebook, among others, banned so-called deep-fake videos that realistically apply false or misleading statements to real people.[8]

Environmental CDR concerns the link between digital technologies and the physical environment. There are many issues here, including the responsible recycling or disposal of old computer equipment. The extension of obsolescence cycles by one year, for example, can have an enormous impact on the environment. There are also calls to reduce the amount of power used to support data centers or bitcoin mining.

Many organizational processes, practices, and projects can address the digital aspects of social, economic, technological, and environmental responsibility. Unfortunately, they are rarely coordinated or optimized. Some, like cybersecurity, tend to be the responsibility of IT departments, while others, like workforce automation, may fall under the purview of operations. Other elements may sit with HR, legal, engineering, R&D, or particular lines of business. It's time for all the elements to be collectively coordinated to ensure better risk mitigation and rewards capture.

The responsibility for this consolidated approach could rest with a CDR office. The purpose of this office is not to create additional governance, establish new bureaucracy, or add a bottleneck for progress. Its purpose is to bring visibility to relevant initiatives and also to promote ethical and sustainable business practices by coordinating and overseeing the role of digital technologies. For example, Italy's insurance giant Unipol has established a group to monitor and implement its board-approved "Personal data protection and valoriza-tion policy" that combines multiple aspects of digital responsibility and ethics.[9]

Indeed, organizations need to take a hard look at how their digital tech-nologies and practices are impacting employees, customers, and society at large. Failure to do so may lead to employee resistance, as we have seen recently in companies such as Google and Amazon,[10] or to falling revenues and profits as civil society pushes harder for more responsible practices. Lack of action could also prompt more stringent regulations, such as the European Union's GDPR legislation, which includes severe penalties for noncompliant behavior or inaction.

But CDR is not just about risk mitigation. There's a substantial upside as well. Organizations that are able to manage data, technology, and digital practices in a sustainable way can benefit from more loyal customers, happier employees, higher-quality recruitment, and better margins.

As the sustainability and digitization trends gain momentum, digital eth-ics will become increasingly relevant for digital transformation, both to mit-igate risks and to find new sources of advantage. Unless organizations take a synergistic and coordinated approach to corporate digital responsibility, they will find themselves in trouble with customers, employees, and regulators.

Hacker's Toolbox

Figure out your current digital ethics and sustainability landscape. Launch an organization-wide review of digital ethics and sustainability practices, using Figure 16.1 as a guide. Establishing a portfolio view will help to set the groundwork to ensure that digital ethics and sustainability practices are consistent, mutually reinforcing, and nonoverlapping. Gaps should also become more apparent.

Add governance. Establish a CDR group to coordinate the development and delivery of digital ethics and sustainability practices. This group doesn't need to own or control the practices, nor does it need to ensure compliance. Its responsibility is to provide advice, coordination, and visibility of different practices across the organization. At a minimum, the CDR group should include a representative from IT (for cybersecurity), legal (for privacy and related personal data protection practices), sustainability (for environmental impacts), and HR (for digital diversity and inclusion). For some organizations, a commercial representative should also be present if data monetization is a consideration.

Include digital ethics in digital project planning. Ensure that digital ethics and sustainability are considered and included in the planning process for digital projects. For example, a digital project charter could include the consideration of digital risks and benefits.[11] In addition, a digital ethics checklist could be included or embedded in all digital projects. An example of such a checklist has been created by data science collective Driven Data.[12]

Self-Reflection Questions

Are you taking a fragmented approach to dealing with the sustainability aspects of digital transformation?

Are you quantifying the benefits of good digital ethics and sustainability practices, as well as the costs of poor ones?

RELATED CHAPTERS

Taking an Inventory of Existing Digital Initiatives (Chapter 5)

Implementing Open Innovation Effectively (Chapter 15)

The Characteristics of Agile Digital Leadership (Chapter 21)

How to Leverage Digital for Organizational Resilience (Chapter 30)

Part Four
Hacking the Business Model Transition

Creating Value in New Ways

*Without leaps of imagination or dreaming,
we lose the excitement of possibilities.
Dreaming, after all, is a form of planning.*
—Gloria Steinem

Most of the buzz around digital transformation comes from stories of business model disruption—e.g., how Uber disrupted taxis or how Amazon disrupted retail. In reality, few companies can become digital giants with sky-high valuations. But any organization can become a disruptor. Exploring the opportunities and risks of digitally driven business model transitions is critical for achieving growth and/or navigating your organization toward the next competitive S curve.

Successful new business models create value for customers in new ways. This is difficult to achieve in the best of times, but even more so when it's done through the creative use of digital tools and technologies. One common shift is from products to services and solutions—e.g., transitioning from selling a physical good (such as a router) to selling a subscription (such as a networking service). Moving from products to services is a common strategy for gaining recurring revenue and avoiding the so-called commodity trap that often accompanies a maturing product business. But these transitions are tricky. They require not only changes to the product/service offering, but also changes to many organizational functions, such as engineering, product development, sales, and marketing. Furthermore, managing profit margins for digital services isn't easy.

When shifting from products to services and solutions, one of the main challenges is convincing customers to pay for digital services. Although customers often appreciate the value of digital services attached to physical objects, such as a monitoring service for industrial equipment, they aren't always willing to pay for them. Even if they love a service, they may have trouble quantifying its true value. In addition, they're often uncomfortable with an external party gaining access to their internal data, like the operating efficiency of their equipment.

Shifting from product to solution is the most common, but not the most complex, form of business model transition. Platform strategy has that distinction. Over the past 20 years, platform companies have seen a remarkable rise in size and power. As of early 2021, the largest companies in the world were platform companies. They have built powerful network effects that make them extremely difficult to compete against. Nevertheless, in some cases, it is possible to build competing platforms, particularly in niche areas. And if you can't beat them, you can join them. An important digital strategy component is exploring ways to tip platform dynamics in your favor, whether you're building your own platform or working with someone else's.

All digital transformation programs contain a mix of digital projects with different objectives, time horizons, and risk levels. Some will focus on radical change and brand-new business models; others will be less ambitious. Creating a balanced portfolio of digital initiatives—one that factors in relative risks and rewards over time—is critical. Focus too much on the short term, and you may miss large disruptive trends or sources of value. Focus too much on long-term disruption, and you may miss opportunities to create value by digitizing your current business. Digital transformation is not a single thing, but a well-managed portfolio of relevant digital initiatives.

MOVING FROM PRODUCT-CENTRICITY TO SERVICES AND SOLUTIONS

Digital transformation is blurring the traditional divide between products and services for B2B and B2C companies. We live in a world in which an abundance of data, from customer transactions and usage to connected machinery and objects, is opening up myriad opportunities to create additional value for customers. Digital transformation is forcing traditional product-centric organizations to move to service-based selling in the quest for recurring and higher-margin offerings. This isn't easy. Moving from products to services and solutions is a business transformation journey that must be planned and managed.

WHY IT MATTERS

Shrinking product life cycles, product commoditization, and new digital business models are driving lower margins and pushing more companies to seek new recurring-service revenues. Some industry surveys estimate that 65 percent of global manufacturers are already using a service-based selling model as opposed to a product-based one.[1]

Digital transformation has accelerated this shift and is blurring the lines between product and service. Why? Because it has reduced the tangibility of offerings by digitizing some features of both products and services. In addition, the availability of vast amounts of data from transactions and sensors is generating many opportunities to complement product offerings with usage and optimization insights that can substantially improve customers' operations. IoT applications are further accelerating this trend by shifting the emphasis from physical goods (capex) to service-based models (opex).

Digital economics are also challenging the notion of asset ownership as a competitive model. In many sectors, such as aviation or mobility services, the management of assets has been outsourced to third parties with innovative outcome-based and/or usage-based business models. This is turning the product-centric model upside down.

Adding a strong service layer provides significant upside and has become an integral part of digital transformation strategies. But shifting from products to services, and expanding the service portfolio to include an outcome-based model, is far from an easy endeavor. It's a true transformation effort, and even the best and brightest may stumble. It might make sense for the company's customers, and for its financials, but does the firm have the organizational capability to deliver?

BEST PRACTICES AND KEY INSIGHTS

Strategically, some companies see shifting from products to services/solutions as a way to grow revenue and margins. Others see shifting more defensively, as a way to keep existing customers loyal and increase barriers to entry. Whatever the ambition, success will depend on how the service strategy is implemented. The process starts with a good strategy, but it must end with clear customer benefits and an invoice.

Successfully scaling services capabilities and overcoming a traditional product-centric mindset takes time. There is no silver bullet, and it cannot be done in one go. It's difficult and risky to transition from simple service add-ons to a core product (such as maintenance and repairs) to outcome-based solutions (such as "hours in flight"–based models in jet engines). Therefore, successful companies have adopted a phased approach when shifting to services by adapting the required organizational capabilities at each stage. (See Figure 17.1.)

Service delivery is critical to success, and new capabilities need to be developed in many core processes: customer relationship, service supply chain, service operations, partner management, and engineering—all supported by strong digital enablement. Oftentimes, at least at the outset, companies have to build (or ring-fence) capabilities into separate business lines, with their own accountability, to properly scale their services and solutions portfolio.

Product Augmentation	Solution Portfolio	New Business Model
Provide services for product offering augmentation (servicing the installed base)	Develop data-driven value-added services portfolio with clear customer benefits	Offer new service-based business models that radically change usage or operational performance
e.g., maintenance contract, reporting, spare parts . . .	e.g., predictive maintenance, usage-based . . .	e.g., outcome-based, subscription . . .

Increasing Organization Capability

e.g., pricing, commercialization . . .	e.g., solution design, solution selling, service delivery . . .	e.g., value proposition, economic modeling . . .

Figure 17.1 Transformation journey: from products to services

Shifting to services will also require a mindset change. Over time, the culture will need to evolve from a cost-plus mentality to value-based selling. As former Cisco CEO John Chambers famously said: "You win customers by selling them what they need, not what you want them to buy. If you truly focus on your customers' success, you can build a relationship for life."[2]

> The role of a CDO in an industrial company is about taking a traditional company with a traditional portfolio that primarily sells hard assets—such as jet aircraft engines or wind turbines—and trying to help that company transition to a set of digital services that can be operated at greater efficiencies. This is crucial because we all know that the future is going to be the data coming off these hard assets.
>
> —BILL RUH, FORMER CEO, GE DIGITAL[3]

In addition, moving to more complex outcome-based solutions fundamentally changes the go-to-market approach. Commercialization involves more complex buying groups, with involvement from both asset owners and operators, resulting in much longer sales cycles and more complex contract negotiations. But when it's implemented successfully, the move to more complex outcome-based solutions can make a big difference to your digital transformation.

Michelin's haulage business was facing commoditization, thanks to competition from low-cost competitors and environmental pressures. Despite the superior quality of its tire products, it was becoming harder to extract value. A big part of Michelin's digital transformation, therefore, was to connect services to its products. Because tires have embedded sensors, giving the company valuable data on usage, distances, and maintenance needs, Michelin decided to develop a service portfolio. This allowed it to move from a transactional relationship with customers to one in which the company would "charge by the kilometer" with a usage-based managed-service model. The new "Michelin Fleet Solutions" offers transportation companies comprehensive tire management solutions for their vehicle fleets with a three- to five-year contract period.

The service suite was designed to bring tangible benefits to Michelin's haulage customers: better cost control, more fuel efficiency, seamless fleet maintenance, and much more environmentally friendly service. Michelin's business model change was not smooth sailing at first, but it allowed the company to learn valuable lessons and establish new service-based revenue streams. It's also helping the company to cement long-lasting customer relationships and brand loyalty.

Many B2C companies have adopted similar strategies in their digital transformations, but with marked differences. Services and solutions in B2C markets often take the form of added functionalities and information through app-based solutions. Services are designed to enrich the customer experience, build engagement, increase loyalty, and gather valuable customer data on transactions and behaviors to upsell and cross-sell. Monetization is often downstream, and based on increased customer engagement.

The Nike+ runner app and Starbucks's mobile app are examples of successful service-based digital strategies. Other B2C companies have chosen hybrid approaches using complementary products and services. Apple, for instance, has substantially increased its reach by leveraging its core products (iPhone, iPad) with its complementary iTunes digital service platform.

• • •

In all probability, your digital transformation will, over time, demand that you shift part of your business from products to services and solutions. This shift opens up opportunities to create massive value for your business and your customers. But it also requires substantial changes to a firm's capabilities. It's a complex endeavor with many pitfalls. It demands a progressive approach to structure, market, and sell services. It also requires careful customer-centric experimentation to get the mix right. It's a true business transformation and must be planned and managed as such.

Hacker's Toolbox

Start with an inventory of the services that you currently offer, even for free. Then task a data team with determining which data sets—e.g., from customers and connected products/machines—could be monetized, which could provide added customer benefits, and how.

Analyze your customers'/users' pain points in detail. Use techniques such as job to be done, customer journeys, day in the life of, etc., to identify how you can improve customers' experiences or operational performance to add value to their business. Translate these needs into a portfolio of new service-based offers and prioritize them according to their ease of implementation versus economic return.

Walk before you run. Develop a phased strategy. First, extend your current product offerings; then add more complex services, and finally move to new monetization methods or business models (e.g., outcome-based). Continually ask the "Why would customers pay for this?" question. Run joint workshops with existing customers or engage lead users to experiment and test responses and iterate. Work out the capability development needed (organization and skills) at each stage of your phased strategy—e.g., solution-selling skills—and align your hiring and workforce development programs.

Avoid high customization of services. This will drive up costs and will not deliver on margin performance. Make sure you industrialize/automate your back office and standardize the service-delivery process.

Self-Reflection Questions

Are your core-product margins being commoditized under competitive pressures?

Do you have a detailed understanding of your customers' pain points (in terms of usage and processes) that your business could alleviate through new digital services and solutions?

Can you substantially increase customer engagement and loyalty by providing new data and information that your customers value?

Do you have the digital capability required in terms of service innovation, commercialization, and service delivery?

Do you understand the mindset shift required for your organization to successfully market new digital services, or do you need a new organizational construct to make it happen?

Have you considered radical changes to your existing business model by challenging current industry norms and practices?

RELATED CHAPTERS

Creating a Clear and Powerful Transformation Objective (Chapter 1)

Taking an Inventory of Existing Digital Initiatives (Chapter 5)

Building and Managing Technology Infrastructure (Chapter 11)

Convincing Customers to Pay for Digital Services (Chapter 18)

How Best to Develop Digital Skills Within Your Organization (Chapter 24)

Scaling Digital Initiatives (Chapter 27)

CONVINCING CUSTOMERS TO PAY FOR DIGITAL SERVICES

A common component of digital transformation journeys involves either a move from products to services and solutions or the addition of a service layer on top of a product. Here, we cover a particularly challenging part of this second component—convincing customers to actually pay for digital services. In many industries, the unfortunate reality is that these services are given away free or at very low cost.

Monetizing digital services requires multiple steps, some internal and others external. First, you need to spend a significant amount of time considering the benefits of the service to customers. You can build it, but don't expect them to come!

In addition, in most B2B environments, customers come in different guises—"approvers" (such as company bosses), "negotiators" (such as purchasing managers), "payers" (such as budget owners), and "users" (such as operators). For each type of customer, the value of the service should be specifically and clearly communicated.

Second, relevant stakeholders in the value chain—such as salespeople, agents, and dealers—must be properly incentivized to sell the service. And third, the service needs to be priced appropriately so that it will sell.

WHY IT MATTERS

People are accustomed to paying for physical products, but often balk at paying for intangible products or services, especially when these are information-based and digitally delivered. For example, we will happily buy a stamp to send a physical letter, but very few of us will pay to send an email, or even to use email software. As a consequence, many digital services are supported by other revenue streams (such as advertising), bundled into products (such as online photo storage for cameras), or simply offered for free (like internet access in hotels).

Thanks to this, many customers now assume that "digital goods should be free." In fact, this is not the case. Digital services are often quite expensive to produce and maintain, including costs for ongoing development, software licensing, data acquisition, hosting, and connectivity. Thus, convincing customers to pay for digital services can make a big difference to overall profitability.

BEST PRACTICES AND KEY INSIGHTS

Augmenting products with digital services is very common as organizations shift from one-off product sales to recurring sources of revenue. This trend is particularly common in the industrial world, where connected products, equipment, and machines have become rich sources of real-time data. This data generates insights and benefits that can be monetized in various ways. For example, predictive and preventative maintenance can improve efficiency and reduce running costs, and usage data can help reduce defects and improve product quality, which are a significant source of costs in the industrial world.

Despite these benefits, many clients are skeptical about adding connectivity to their products or equipment. Among other concerns, they worry about ownership and responsible usage of the data that is generated. Even if they accept the value that can be created from operational data, they are often unwilling to pay for it. A common refrain in the B2B world is "By all means, connect my machines, but I want exclusive access to my data, and I don't want to pay for it."

Caterpillar is an interesting case in point. The company sells large pieces of machinery for the construction, mining, and transportation industries. The benefits of connectivity were clear for Caterpillar and its customers. For customers, it could lead to reduced downtime, increased productivity, fuel efficiency, and better asset management (a surprising number of machines get lost). For Caterpillar, it could lead to more and better understanding of equipment usage and customer behavior, insights for product development, and increased revenue from spare parts. In short, connecting machines was a win-win proposition for both Caterpillar and its customers.

By the start of 2015, Caterpillar had all the basic pieces in place—a clear mandate to drive digitization from the top and a dedicated team to develop and deploy digital services (named "CAT Connect"). The team put together a set of services designed to benefit Caterpillar, its dealers, and its customers.

But after five years of effort, less than 10 percent of the company's connected equipment included digital services for which customers were paying, forcing Caterpillar to foot the remaining costs. By 2019, the team conceded defeat, and most attempts to sell digital services were dropped. The focus of CAT Connect was repositioned to drive Caterpillar's sales of spare parts.

What went wrong?

Clearly Communicate the Value of the Service to Each Type of Customer

Caterpillar made a common mistake—one that, at first, doesn't seem like a mistake at all. It assumed that customers would be interested in a service that adds significant value to their businesses. But the benefits were never articulated clearly enough in terms that mattered to the customer. Since very few customers were proactively asking for such a digital offering, they didn't see the need to pay for it. Moreover, many customers were skeptical of the new service. They wanted to know what Caterpillar was doing with their data. Some worried that their data would be shared with their competitors, many of whom were also Caterpillar customers.

Caterpillar also failed to distinguish among different types of customers. Equipment operators, site managers, purchasing managers, and business owners all had different perspectives on the value of the service. For example, purchasing managers were focused on minimizing costs and were not too concerned with post-sales usage. More often than not, their position was "Give it to us for free." Meanwhile, operators worried that their performance was being monitored by their bosses. And although site managers often had the most to gain from the digital services, they rarely participated directly in the purchasing process.

The challenge of convincing B2B customers to pay for digital services requires you to consider all potential stakeholders in the buying network and then develop arguments that resonate for each one regarding the value of the service.

Convincing customers to pay is also an issue in the B2C world. Digital giants like Google, Facebook, and TikTok sidestep this challenge by generating revenue from advertising while maintaining the core service for free. But this is not a sustainable model for most organizations. The revenue-generating capacity of advertising is simply not sufficient to cover the costs of offering the service. A common approach employed in the online world is the freemium business model, where the basic service is offered for free while advanced features are available at a cost.

Freemium models are typically based on two approaches: feature limits and usage limits. For example, the free version of Spotify allows users to stream most music (albums, playlists, or curated radio stations) on shuffle play, but ads are played between songs and users are limited in their ability to skip to the specific songs they like (feature limits). In many cases, feature and usage limits are combined. Evernote does not allow offline usage and offers no customer support (feature limits). It also restricts file size and uploads (usage limits). The key to creating a successful freemium model is to give consumers a big enough "taste" of the experience to appreciate its value, but not so much that they have no incentive to upgrade.

Dropbox's freemium model has been relatively successful. It offers two gigabytes of storage for free with very few feature limits. Users who reach the storage limit often convert to paying customers because the hassle of moving all their files is greater than simply paying the subscription fee.

Make Sure Your Organization Is Set Up to Sell Services

It sounds obvious, but selling services is very different from selling products. As we have seen earlier, most product-centric organizations are optimized around certain sales processes and cycles. For example, products are often sold as discrete bundles—sell it, book it, and then move on to the next one. Services, by contrast, are often sold, paid for, and consumed over longer periods of time.

In 2015, when Cisco decided to shift its revenue from 10 percent services to 40 percent, this caused major changes in the organization. Not only did products need to be redesigned to include services (and entirely new services developed), but the culture of "box shifting" needed to be changed, incentives for salespeople needed to be updated, and the marketing and sales organizations had to be redesigned.

> We're trying to move from selling equipment to selling services. We are merging the technologies of tomorrow with the buildings of today to put the "smart" into smart buildings. We are changing our business profoundly towards a platform business. This means combining products and services over the lifetime of a building.
>
> —TOMIO PIHKALA, EXECUTIVE VICE PRESIDENT, KONE CORPORATION[1]

In the case of Caterpillar, the CAT Connect team was largely separated from the engineering teams that designed the equipment, the operations teams that manufactured and shipped the equipment, and the sales and services teams that interacted with customers. This isn't necessarily a bad thing. Often, digital units are smothered by the traditional organization. But in this case, the CAT Connect digital-as-a-business focus was never fully embraced by the rest of the organization. Consequently, the digital team had a hard time integrating the service offering into products, and its digital services play was neither well understood nor adopted by other parts of the company.

Ensure All Relevant Stakeholders Are Incentivized to Sell the Service

Digital services often fail to generate revenue and profit, not only because customers are unwilling to pay for them, but because salespeople are unwilling to sell them. This was the case with Caterpillar. Understandably, since the regular sales team was not significantly incentivized to sell CAT Connect, it didn't do so. When selling a construction machine worth $300,000, adding a $20-per-month service contract hardly seemed worth the sales rep's time. As a result, the sales team often brought in the digital team only as an add-on, when the sales team was in danger of losing a client.

In addition to internal salespeople, other players often need to be incentivized. Like many B2B players, Caterpillar rarely interacts directly with end customers. The company conducts the majority of its sales through a network of dealers and distributors across the world. Some of them regarded CAT

Connect as a threat because it created a direct connection between Caterpillar and the end customers. They worried that Caterpillar would sell spare parts directly to customers rather than through them. The dealers needed to be trained on the benefits of CAT Connect and incentivized to offer the service.

Be Smart About Pricing

Because a service is intangible, and the incremental costs of delivering it are typically small, there is a temptation to underprice it. This is a mistake. A service should not be priced based on the cost of producing and delivering it, but on the value it delivers to the client. This value may be based on improved effectiveness, better productivity, saved time, or other benefits. As stated above, if the benefits and the value are clearly articulated and perceived by stakeholders, there is a much better chance of pricing services appropriately.

Some common methods can enhance customers' willingness to pay for services attached to products. For example, the cost can be bundled into an existing maintenance contract or subscription service to avoid a separate sales and invoicing process. Outcome-based pricing, which links the cost of a service to some basket of preagreed benefits, can increase willingness to pay, as a reduction in benefits is typically easier to justify than an increase in costs.

• • •

Digital services are notoriously hard to sell, especially if they are add-ons to physical products. However, they can often create significant value for customers. Benefits of the services need to be clearly communicated, based on their value, to each relevant stakeholder. To be successful, organizational processes and incentives often need to be adjusted to ensure that the services are being properly marketed and sold.

Hacker's Toolbox

Figure out which services you can charge for. Get a handle on what digital services you are offering, and how much you are charging for them, including services that you are currently offering for free. Organizations are often unaware of the portfolio of digital services on offer and are surprised to find that many more exist than they expected. In their article "Bill It, Kill It, or Keep It Free?,"[2] Wolfgang Ulaga and Stefan Michel argue that the first step in the transition from "free to fee" is to organize services into those that customer are willing to pay for and those that they expect to be offered for free. Start by focusing on the ones you feel they will be willing to pay for.

Get the pitch right. Make sure that the benefits of the digital services you want to charge for are very clearly articulated. This should be provided in language that your customers understand. For example, "Reduce machine downtime by 30 percent" or "Decrease time to market by an average of two weeks." Tailor your value messaging to different types of customers.

For example, purchasing managers might value immediate cost savings, operators might value effectiveness gains, and managers might value productivity improvements over time. It seems obvious, but unless they clearly see the value, customers will not pay. Avoid unnecessary complexity or too many service variants—there is normally no need for more than three service tiers. Simplicity is key to understanding.

Get your salespeople onboard. Make sure your salespeople both understand how digital services work and are trained and incentivized to sell them. Many organizations today are shifting from selling products to selling services and solutions. However, salespeople who are good at selling one are not necessarily good at selling the other.

Cisco embarked on a major retraining program to prepare its salespeople to sell the company's service and solution portfolio, but it initially neglected to adjust the sales incentive structure. Initial results were disappointing. After an internal review, it changed the incentive structure to ensure that salespeople were rewarded as much to sell services as products.

Be very clear on how customer data is used. Many organizations, particularly in B2B settings, are concerned about their data falling into the wrong hands. They may like a digital service, and be willing to pay for it, but they do not want their internal data to be owned (or even handled) by a third party.

You can approach this issue by providing assurances of appropriate data handling. For example, the data can be made accessible at any time to the customer, it can be anonymized, and it can be stored secured in a compliant location. A case in point—after a few instances of "Zoombombing" in early 2020, Zoom added layers of security to its communication service.[3] It also provided assurances of data residency to comply with different regulations, such as GDPR in Europe.

Self-Reflection Questions

Could you explain the value of your new service to a typical customer in 30 seconds?

Have you made sure that your salespeople are trained and incentivized to sell this service?

Have you priced the service realistically and competitively?

Have you clearly articulated to customers how their data will be used?

RELATED CHAPTERS

Building and Managing Technology Infrastructure (Chapter 11)

Managing Partnerships and Ecosystems (Chapter 13)

Moving from Product-Centricity to Services and Solutions (Chapter 17)

COMPETING AGAINST OR WORKING WITH DIGITAL PLATFORMS

During the last decade, one of the most important disruptions in digital competition has been the emergence of dominant market positions by multisided platform players. Some, like Airbnb in hospitality or Uber in transportation, have focused on specific industries. Others, like Google or Amazon, have disrupted (or have the potential to disrupt) multiple industries. Fewer and fewer industries are untouched by platform players. So for any company mapping its digital strategy and transformation, platform economics are now impossible to ignore.

Does this mean that all organizations should aim to become digital platforms? Probably not. Successful platform strategies respond to specific economic and market conditions, and they are hard (and expensive) to get right. However, if building a digital platform is beyond the reach of an organization, there are still strategic moves that can help the firm participate in, collaborate with, or leverage existing digital platforms and ecosystems.

WHY IT MATTERS

Today, 7 of the 10 most valuable organizations in the world (by market capitalization) are platform companies. At the beginning of 2020, Apple, Microsoft, Alphabet, Amazon, Facebook, Alibaba, and Tencent represented more than $6.3 trillion in market value.[1]

The attraction of platform strategies is the ability to scale extremely fast using network effects. In essence, the value of the platform is tied to the number of users, because platform participants benefit from the presence of others.

For traditional organizations, this matters: platform owners can leverage their large user base to expand their offering, as Uber did with Uber Eats. Or they can enter entirely new markets with a different economic model, as Google Maps did with navigation. With platforms, the competitive advantage shifts from the supply side (assets and barriers to entry) to the demand side (scale and interactions among participants).

When crafting digital transformation strategies, thinking of the business through the lens of platform strategy is more critical than the outcome itself. Why? First, a platform strategy is the most ambitious and disruptive move that an established organization can make. Platforms create markets. But in order to work, they also require that the organization coordinate the behaviors of multiple parties with (sometimes) differing agendas. Second, as much as platform thinking can pinpoint potential new sources of value for an organization, it can also uncover strategic vulnerabilities. However, the vulnerabilities may be overcome by building platforms or participating in third-party platforms.

BEST PRACTICES AND KEY INSIGHTS

The most common type of platform is two-sided, creating interactions between two participants. On one side is the producer who creates or owns the value—e.g., the property owners on Airbnb. On the other side is the consumer of value—e.g., the renters looking for holiday properties on Airbnb.

A first critical step in a platform strategy is to thoroughly understand the expectations and behaviors of both sides and the nature of the interaction that will draw buyers and sellers together. The second step consists of working out how to scale these interactions, often described as the "chicken-and-egg" problem. One side of the platform will matter most for scaling. In the case of Airbnb, it is pointless trying to attract people looking for holiday homes until there's a sufficient inventory of rental properties. So one side of the platform will need to be proactively activated or subsidized through, for instance, differentiated content or financial incentives. This is the route to scaling fast, but it needs to be well managed because, in the case of financial incentives, it can become very costly.

PayPal cofounder Peter Thiel described how the early explosive growth of the service was both exhilarating and scary: "New customers got $10 for signing up, and existing ones got $10 for referrals. Growth was exponential, and

PayPal wound up paying $20 for each new customer. It felt like things were working and not working at the same time; 7 to 10% daily growth and 100 million users was good. No revenues and an exponentially growing cost structure were not. Things felt a little unstable."[2] Incentives work, but they need to be phased out at some point.

> A platform is when the economic value of everybody
> that uses it exceeds the value of the company that creates it.
> Then it's a platform.
>
> —BILL GATES[3]

The third step is to design an economic model capable of generating revenues, and profit, over time. When both sides of the platform are independent of each other, or when the platform has achieved sufficient scale, the model becomes attractive because the company can charge both sides for services. For example, Airbnb charges renters a service fee of approximately 14 percent, depending on the listing, but it also charges hosts a fee of 3 percent for every completed booking. In addition, Airbnb collects commissions from ancillary offerings (ecosystem complements) such as cleaning services, organized tours, chauffeured cars, chefs, etc.[4]

Finally, to work effectively over time, a platform needs rules of engagement for all participants. Platform owners must decide on the level of openness for elements of their platform (APIs, source code, IP rights, etc.), and this requires trade-offs. The more closed the platform, the more it can be tightly integrated, and the more an organization can control pricing. The more open the platform, the faster the company can innovate externally by, for example, leveraging third-party developers to build complementary apps to enrich the platform. However, this can lead to fragmentation, and may also relinquish too much control to ecosystem partners.

Therefore, governance and curation of the platform are important. They will protect the quality and the integrity of platform interactions and will regulate the ecosystem. To achieve the right balance, organizations must cultivate good use of the platform without abuse. To this end, digital leaders must determine who will participate, how to create and divide value, and how to fairly resolve conflicts. The essential components of a well-governed platform are quality, transparency, and fairness. Apple exercises "bouncer's rights" on its platform to exclude low-quality apps, pornography, and hate speech and to minimize the risk of viruses.

Network effects and scale play out differently across markets and/or industry sectors. For digital leaders, the trick is identifying the value that's being created and captured across the network.

Choose Your Platform Battle: The 4Bs

What kind of platform strategy should a company choose? (See Figure 19.1.) The answer depends on how the firm plans to adapt to platform competition (by either proactively or defensively participating) and whether its focus will be internal or external.[5]

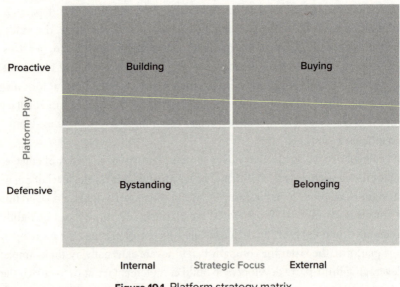

Figure 19.1 Platform strategy matrix

Building

Although platforms share common economic characteristics, they come in different shapes and sizes. The media often lauds the success of large platforms like Uber or Airbnb, but those are hard to build. Many have tried, but few have succeeded at such a scale. On the other hand, many smaller (or more targeted) digital platforms have carved out strong competitive positions in B2C and B2B markets. To establish sufficient scale and a stable economic model, platforms need strong leadership, vision, and staying power.

Founded in 2005, Etsy is a marketplace that aggregates sellers of hand-made and vintage products, ranging from paintings to jewelry to bespoke furniture. Most sellers are independent artists who contribute to Etsy's positioning as the go-to place for artisanal craftsmanship. The platform's success is also linked to high repeat-purchase rates and a community in which sellers and buyers are encouraged to socially share their preferences and buying habits. Today, Etsy is the biggest global platform for craft goods. It now operates in over 150 countries and, following an IPO, had a market cap in 2020 of more than $17 billion.[6]

Despite its lower visibility, the industrial world also offers strategic opportunities for platform plays. In 2018, the 112-year-old German steel and metal distributor Klöckner & Co. launched XOM, a proprietary online platform, to distribute its products. Moreover, the company invited its competitors to join. This move positioned Klöckner's platform as an independent digital marketplace for anyone buying or selling steel, metal, and other industrial products. To ensure fair and transparent access for competitors, XOM is run independently from the core business, and it even competes with Klöckner's own business.[7]

Buying

When disruption is pounding on the corporate gates, acquisitions can be a viable, though frequently expensive, path to success. Beyond competitive pressures, the logic for platform acquisitions includes additional capabilities, existing client bases, and established technology infrastructures.

In its battle with Amazon, Walmart scaled its marketplace position through its $3.3 billion acquisition of Jet.com in 2016. In 2018, Walmart employed a similar approach to capture a share of one of the world's most attractive retail markets, buying a majority stake in Flipkart (India's biggest online retailer) for $16 billion.[8]

Those global platform moves were expensive, but not every play needs to be on that scale. Founded in 1744, Sotheby's is one of the world's largest brokers of art, real estate, and collectibles. In 2018, Sotheby's bought five-year-old Viyet, an online retail platform for antique furniture and decorative objects, to broaden its business beyond auctions and reach younger, more digitally savvy customers.[9]

Platform strategy can sometimes reveal new sources of growth in adjacent or complementary markets. When luxury powerhouse Richemont, owner of brands such as Cartier, Montblanc, and IWC, undertook a quest for growth in the stagnant market for high-end watches, it identified an adjacent area that was growing and profitable—preowned watches. A variety of online marketplaces had sprung up to facilitate the purchase and sale of used watches. The sophistication of these marketplaces surprised many in the industry, who'd assumed that people would not spend thousands of dollars on a watch they could not see or touch. Yet billions of dollars of used watches were being traded online every year. Richemont had to decide whether to build its own online platform, work with an existing platform, or buy one. It chose the third option with the purchase of Watchfinder, a UK-based marketplace for preowned watches, in 2018.[10] Although integration of Watchfinder with the much larger and more conservative Richemont group was not seamless, both sides learned a great deal. By 2020, Watchfinder had become one of the fastest-growing watch marketplaces, and it even opened offline stores.[11]

Belonging

For many smaller or niche players, building a platform with scale and network effects is not a realistic option. Joining or participating in an established platform may be the only viable path. This can be a worthwhile strategy when the company's products or services are important complements to the platform's offering, or when brand power is strong enough to enhance an existing platform's appeal. Of course, joining an existing platform means that organizations must adhere to an existing set of rules and an established governance. It can also create dependencies and increase the bargaining power of the platform. Moreover, organizations must be careful to retain control of their data. But in certain cases, this can be a much faster and cheaper entry route for a platform strategy.

Global luxury brands from Kenzo to Burberry to Versace joined Luxury Pavilion, a subset of Alibaba's Tmall.com, as an entry channel into the lucrative Chinese luxury market, which entailed lower risk and costs than trying to build their own platform ecosystems.[12] Luxury Pavilion allows these brands to target young affluent buyers: 80 percent of customers on the platform are under 35.[13]

It's not always possible to address both sides of a two-sided market. In these cases, a company should focus on capturing value from just one side. @Leisure, a European vacation-rental marketplace, was facing severe competition from global travel platforms such as Booking.com, Airbnb, and Expedia. Rather than grappling for both travelers and vacation-home owners, it concentrated most of its resources and attention on the supply of quality properties. It was a risky strategy. The company ceded control over the platform's demand side (travelers), but by focusing on high-quality services for homeowners, it could build a portfolio of attractive vacation properties. Sometimes it's better to focus almost exclusively on one side of a platform rather than splitting focus (and resources) between both sides.

Bystanding

Some organizations will have neither a clear opportunity nor the investment capacity to participate in platform plays. Platform strategy is not for everyone. Choosing to be a bystander is a strategic choice in itself. Nevertheless, organizations should still consider and analyze how platform economics could influence their performance and whether existing or new platform players could disrupt their core businesses. Some organizations take the regulatory route to defend against platforms, but often this merely delays the inevitable, rather than preventing it. Building alternative digital pathways to transact directly with customers is a good way to keep control and avoid the economic price charged by platform owners.

As another defensive strategy, some organizations have formed coalitions with other players. Founded in 2017, ADAMOS is a manufacturer-neutral IoT software platform for Germany's mechanical engineering sector. It is a consortium of 12 companies that cooperate closely to develop apps and digital applications on a common platform.[14]

• • •

Launching a successful multisided platform ecosystem requires specific economic conditions, heavy investment, and a strong dose of luck to reach profitable scale. Not every company should try to become the platform leader in its industry. But companies that cannot create their own multisided platforms can still use platform economics to partially transform their business models or find an economically viable role in the platforms operated by others. Whether or not a company participates in platforms, platform thinking is a useful strategic process—one that enables organizations to uncover new sources of value and enhance their digital transformation strategy.[15]

Hacker's Toolbox

Make platform economics an integral part of your digital strategy. Examine opportunities to significantly reduce transaction frictions and balance the interests of participants on all sides.

Run scenarios. Assess where strategic platform plays could be viable from a business and operating model perspective.

Decide how to ignite your platform. Define what is the best side to start with, how to ignite participant growth, and how to solve the chicken-and-egg problem in an economically viable way.

Define the platform curation principles. Establish a set of rules for operating the ecosystem effectively and fairly.

Define where and how to win. Analyze the strategic options for implementing your platform play from a viability and cost perspective: participate in an existing platform or buy an existing platform player in your core or adjacent market. If no platform plays are viable, define an alternative defense strategy to reconfigure and transform your operations—e.g., partnerships, etc.

Self-Reflection Questions

Do you and your senior team truly understand the economics of platform competition in your industry—now and in the future?

Are you confident that you've explored every potential opportunity and threat from platform competition while formulating your digital transformation strategy?

Do you have a clear path forward and dedicated resources to implement a platform strategy?

As external events change, do you have a process for regularly reviewing the nature of platform competition in your industry?

RELATED CHAPTERS

Creating a Clear and Powerful Transformation Objective (Chapter 1)

How to Get Your Board Onboard (Chapter 7)

Building Hyperawareness into Your Organization (Chapter 12)

Managing Partnerships and Ecosystems (Chapter 13)

Building a Balanced Portfolio of Digital Initiatives (Chapter 20)

CHAPTER

20

BUILDING A BALANCED PORTFOLIO OF DIGITAL INITIATIVES

Senior leaders often struggle to craft a digital transformation that balances strategic risk with speed of execution. Should short-term improvements be prioritized over larger strategic shifts? How can we demonstrate ROI from our digital investments? How fast will our industry be disrupted? What level of risk are we willing to tolerate on innovative new business models? These are tough questions to answer simultaneously.

Part of the problem is that digital road maps are designed as if each digital initiative had the same impact, time horizon, or risk level. But, of course, that's not the real world. Digital leaders consciously manage their digital transformations as a strategic portfolio over time, balancing the need for short-term improvements with longer-term strategic and business model evolution. And they must do so within a risk profile that both leaders and key stakeholders are comfortable with. Portfolio management is the link between digital strategy and execution.

WHY IT MATTERS

Getting a clear picture of how digitization will affect your industry, organization, and competitive position is a complex exercise. It's about managing both offense and defense—about understanding the opportunities that digital technology brings but also the potential vulnerabilities that the business faces. Offense is about understanding how digital transformation can help the organization create more value. Can we enhance our customer experience through digitization? Can we obtain a step change in performance by connecting our operations and our products? Can we disrupt our industry, or an adjacent industry, using our digital competencies?

Conversely, defense is about understanding where the organization might have vulnerabilities and identifying the major sources of risk. How is digitization going to impact our value chain or our current business model? How are products, services, pricing, or distribution likely to evolve? Are there digital initiatives that should be canceled or technologies that should be retired? Are there areas where new entrants or adjacent competitors are likely to disrupt our existing revenue streams? Do we have the right competencies to respond? And what is the likely time horizon for this change to happen?

These are questions that a digital strategy should be able to answer. But it's only the start. Once the digital landscape has been properly mapped, leaders must shape their digital transformation program accordingly. Balance is key. Too much focus on reconfiguring existing operations or short-term gains might expose the organization to increasing risks of digital disruption. Too much focus on reinvention might lead to constant exploration with little business impact, as well as neglect of the currently profitable business lines. So what's the answer?

BEST PRACTICES AND KEY INSIGHTS

Successful digital transformation portfolios have a clear focus on the *what* and the *how*.[1] The what is about balancing the scope of your strategic digital initiatives. It's about unlocking sources of value in current operations and uncovering new value creation opportunities by evolving the offering and business model. The how is about executing the digital transformation at the right tempo—understanding the speed at which each component of the digital strategy must be implemented. It's also about assessing the ability to execute using the capabilities the organization currently possesses versus the need to access external resources.

The What of a Digital Transformation

As strategy is translated into a transformation program, it's important to frame digital initiatives according to their impact on current operations. Two dimensions are critical. The first is the breadth of the reconfiguration needed within the current value chain or delivery system. These days, pretty much every core process and every function can be reconfigured more efficiently using digital technologies. For instance, most core processes of an HR or finance department can be automated, and data can be used to increase the personalization of a customer offering. The second dimension is the level of reinvention needed. Digital leaders need to gauge the level of reinvention required in their core offering and business model. This will require vision and creative skills, and more often than not, it will also require opening up the organization to innovative partners that can help the organization through the reinvention.

Reinventing the business model can be a "bet the ranch" strategic move, such as moving to a platform-based business model. General Electric, with its move to the "industrial internet," is an example of such a radical step.[2] At the same time, such a move doesn't necessarily have to "make" or "break." Many enhancements to a service offering or business model can be executed without creating massive risks to current operations, while still generating significant business returns.[3] Figure 20.1 shows how to map digital initiatives across these two dimensions.

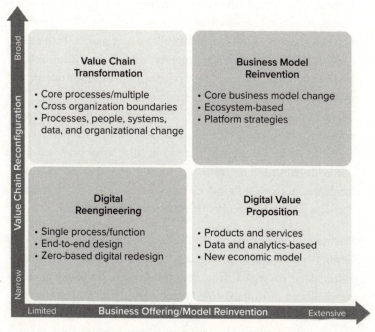

Figure 20.1 Mapping the digital initiatives:
the *what* of your digital transformation portfolio

Digital reengineering. Some initiatives will have a narrow scope within the value chain, e.g., a single function or process. Although reengineering has gotten some bad press, the opportunities that digital technology creates to reconfigure and modernize existing operations should not be overlooked. Zero-basing and reconfiguring existing processes will provide reasonably short time frames to ROI, so they are essential portfolio components for demonstrating early successes.

Value chain transformation. These initiatives often cut across traditional boundaries of the firm, e.g., functions or geographies. They are, therefore, more difficult to execute because they require a higher level of coordination and change management support. Retailers attempting to design seamless customer experiences across their channels is a good example of value chain transformation. These initiatives are complex and will invariably impact existing processes, systems, data, people, and organizational structures.

Digital value proposition. Reinventing offerings or business models need not be disruptive. It can be about combining products and services in new and innovative ways or making better use of available data. For instance, property and casualty insurer Tokio Marine augmented its traditional offering by providing a one-time insurance offer in partnership with mobile operator Docomo. It offers insurance for narrowly defined periods (e.g., a day, an afternoon, etc.) for lifetime events such as borrowing a friend's car or going skiing for a weekend.[4] Such innovative value propositions can be developed in a reasonable time frame and do not require fundamental changes to the existing value chain. They are usually derisked by using experimentation and proof of concept.

Business model reinvention. Reinventing business models is, by far, the most challenging of digital transitions. The drivers are either major strategic threats or a significant opportunity to create value and disrupt existing industry practices. Such transformations invariably involve an external ecosystem of partners, a substantial reskilling and skill acquisition exercise, and, more often than not, some surgery to the existing organizational structure. GE's Predix platform play is a good example of such a radical move.[5]

Not all digital initiatives are created equal. To successfully execute a digital strategy, it is essential to get a good handle on the different types of initiatives and to ensure that the portfolio is sufficiently balanced so that risk and return can be adequately managed.

Is there a generic best practice on how to balance a portfolio? Unfortunately, no. The shape of the portfolio will very much depend on the competitive situation. In the initiation stage, a high dose of digital reengineering might be appropriate (50–60 percent) to demonstrate quick wins and justify further investment. Another 30–40 percent might be dedicated to reconfiguring and digitizing core processes, while 10–20 percent might be targeted at new value propositions or business model exploration. Organizations deep in executions will have substantial value chain transformation initiatives (70–80 percent) as they reinvent their existing customer experiences and connect their operations. Exploring and experimenting with new value propositions/business models will require the remainder of the digital investment.

> At Jawwy, we are building a digital mobile operator model with the organizational DNA and agility of an internet player. Our strategy is not about price. It is about designing and launching a best-in-class customer experience that is fully digital end-to-end.
> —SUBHRA DAS, CEO, JAWWY (AN STC SUBSIDIARY)[6]

For organizations that are already being heavily disrupted and in defensive mode, digitizing the existing business might be akin to rearranging the deck chairs on the *Titanic*. They may have a 20–30 percent investment dedicated to replatforming core systems or integrating data. But in highly disrupted environments, the risk profile for the business will be higher—as will the overall shape of the digital portfolio, with the bulk (70–80 percent) focused on moving to the next S curve.

The How of a Digital Transformation

Determining which digital initiatives are needed to face the brave new digital future is important. But finding the right tempo and means to execute the transformation is even more critical. Why? Because balancing speed, risk, competence building, and financial capacity is a complex but essential ingredient for execution. Leaders will be confronted with competencies they do not have, technologies they have not mastered and/or do not own, unfamiliar ways of working, untested new business models, and even cultural barriers that will have to be overcome. A tall order.

Executives need to focus the how of execution on two critical dimensions: time to implementation and make/buy/partner decisions for accessing key capabilities. Speed of execution will be driven by external factors: the rate of technological upheaval and/or the intensity of competition. But it will also be strongly influenced by internal factors: the company's current digital competency versus the competency it needs, familiarity with the core technologies, and any changes that must be made to the existing organizational model. Accessing key capabilities is critical to execution. Figure 20.2 shows how to map execution routes across these two dimensions.

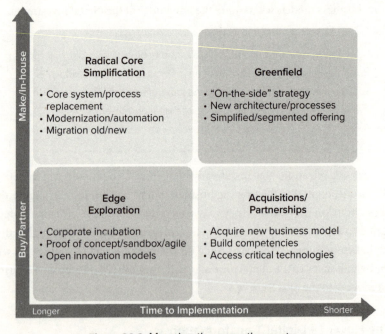

Figure 20.2 Mapping the execution route:
the *how* of your digital transformation portfolio

Edge exploration. When technologies are unproved and the benefits unclear, the exploration route is appropriate. Building incubation or innovation sandboxes will allow the company to test potentially transformative applications in a controlled environment. This will mean opening up the organization to external parties such as startups, incubators, technology vendors, or universities. Edge exploration is a good way to mitigate risk while leveraging potential sources of value. But it is not a fast path to success. Identifying promising applications takes time in large organizations, and scaling up a successful pilot is a complex organizational endeavor.

Radical core simplification. Sometimes what needs to change is clear, but it requires a major overhaul of core processes and underpinning systems. These major business simplifications occur, for example, when the cost base has become unacceptably high or when a technology platform has been overtaken by nimbler, faster, and easier-to-maintain alternatives. When Lloyds Banking Group, for example, launched a four-year automation and replatforming of its core banking processes, it managed to reduce the number of unique business processes from 700 to just 23.[7]

In this respect, digital portfolio management can be as much about what to cut as what to add, and there are times when it is necessary to remove a system or cancel a digital project. Doing so can cause resentment and lead to passive or active resistance. Therefore, the political sensitivities around rationalizing digital initiatives need to be carefully managed, and may sometime require senior leadership intervention.

To succeed, such simplifications require the utmost leadership attention, strong internal program management, and financial commitment to stay the course. Migrating to simplified core platforms, such as a new data management system or an automated process, is not a short-term endeavor.

Acquisitions/partnerships. When the competitive pressures are so great that organic development would take too long and put the company at risk, acquisitions or external partnerships become viable execution options. There are many reasons to go external.

The competence gap might be too big, the necessary skills might be rare and expensive, the technology platform might be a competitive differentiator, or it might be simpler and cheaper to buy a new business model rather than build one. Spanish-based bank BBVA, for example, acquired Simple (a US bank with no physical branches) in 2014 to develop its digital-only business model.[8]

Of course, partnerships carry interface management costs. Digital acquisitions are also as risky—and can be as expensive— as any other acquisition. But very often, they can provide a shorter route to execution than organic development.

Greenfield. When simplifying the core business proves too difficult or lengthy, when acquisitions are too expensive, or when a new digital culture is essential to succeed quickly, an organization can pursue a greenfield option. This is about building a new and simplified operation "on the side" of the core business, sometimes with a different brand.

The greenfield option is attractive because the organization can start with a blank canvas, creating a unit that is digital from day one, with a much-simplified offering, operations, and new digital talents. It's like building a startup within a large company.

For example, tire company Michelin created a new entity called "Michelin Solutions" to manage new digital business models around proactive fleet management for its B2B customers.[9] However, greenfield operations require strong top-down leadership to ensure the business can take off successfully. Corporate antibodies from the parent company often spring into action to defeat the new model, particularly if cannibalization of existing business lines becomes inevitable.

Of course, none of these execution routes are mutually exclusive. Leaders can hedge their risk by pursuing multiple portfolio options. What's important is to think through the execution routes as the digital strategy is developed and to constantly iterate as opportunities arise or the competitive climate changes.

Consider the case of Heineken, an independent global brewer with a presence in over 180 countries.

To digitize its routes to market, Heineken embarked on radical core simplification initiatives. It developed a centralized transformation road map, and it launched pilots in selected markets to empower local teams and identify key customer needs. The initial pilots were scaled to additional markets only *after* a local "minimum viable product" solution had been validated. In parallel, Heineken built centralized capabilities to roll out its digital solutions globally. This approach helped it to launch its B2B e-commerce platforms with hotels and restaurants.

But Heineken took a very different approach for Beerwulf, its direct-to-consumer e-commerce platform for craft beers. Hans Böhm, managing director of Beerwulf, realized that "designing a new direct-to-consumer business model would require a fundamentally different approach, much more focused on taking consumer feedback to refine our proposition, and being willing to test and learn—and fail—as we learned what worked. We couldn't run it in a business as usual, big corporate kind of way."[10]

Therefore, Heineken elected to greenfield Beerwulf as a separate "startup" outside the regular business structure. This approach freed Beerwulf from constraints on reporting and resource allocation that would have slowed the venture down if it had been treated as just another "digital project" inside the regular business. As a result, the fledging venture was also able to set up a separate, but compatible, IT architecture. This was key to achieving the flexibility and speed required.

Think Portfolio

Too many digital transformation road maps are static, failing to balance strategic and competitive risks with the speed required for successful implementation. To ensure a proper linkage between strategy and execution, a digital portfolio needs to be reviewed regularly (quarterly) with the senior team and business unit leaders. These reviews should focus not only on digital resources that are missing or capabilities that need to be developed, but also on technologies that need to be rationalized or retired if they are duplicated, redundant, or out of date.

To succeed in digital transformation, it is crucial to turn ambitions and strategy into a balanced portfolio of initiatives, with short- and longer-term outcomes. Digital leaders must also use the full panoply of execution routes to cope with the pressures and magnitude of the digital transition—within a risk profile that leaders and key stakeholders are comfortable with.

Hacker's Toolbox

Take a portfolio approach to your initiative road map.
Assess technical/market risk, timing horizons, capability requirements, and the complexity of your transformation. Ensure that digitizing the existing operations and finding new sources of growth match your strategic ambitions.

Map out the best execution routes to deliver your portfolio. You will most likely have a mix of execution routes that match the timing and complexity of execution.

Align at the top. Ensure that the top team, and probably your board, is comfortable and aligned with both the what of your transformation and the how of your plan to execute the digital strategy. Highlight financial investments and the expected rate of return.

Use the portfolio approach in communication. It will provide a good overview of your digital strategy to the relevant stakeholders, including timing and organizational complexity.

Conduct regular reviews of your portfolio. Review both the what and the how with your top team and gauge against the competitive situation and timing for implementation. At a minimum, you should review your portfolio quarterly.

Self-Reflection Questions

Do you think dynamically about your balanced digital transformation portfolio? Is portfolio mapping part of your overall digital strategy? If not, course-correct.

Do you have a process to conduct quarterly reviews of your portfolio of initiatives against ambition, competition, and risk profile?

Do you regularly assess your portfolio of execution routes to ensure you can meet the timing required by the competitive environment?

Have you involved all stakeholders—from digital leaders, to corporate strategy, to HR, to finance—to align everyone around what executing the digital portfolio means for the business?

RELATED CHAPTERS

Aligning the Top Team to Drive Transformation Success (Chapter 3)

Taking an Inventory of Existing Digital Initiatives (Chapter 5)

Managing Partnerships and Ecosystems (Chapter 13)

Measuring the Performance of Digital Initiatives (Chapter 28)

Part Five
Hacking Digital Transformation Leadership

Leading People and Organizations

Do not follow where the path may lead.
Go instead where there is no path and leave a trail.
—Muriel Strode

In previous chapters, we've seen the wide array of activities that you have to get right to successfully execute your organization's digital transformation. It's a daunting task, and none of these activities will happen through a simple mandate. Digital transformation has to be led. In this part, we switch our focus to the individual level and explore the people side of digital.

By design, digital transformation creates organizational and managerial tensions: experimentation versus perfection, autonomy versus control, data versus intuition, speed versus accuracy, and many others. They have to be managed, and it's very contextual. Sometimes traditional leadership traits (such as tight operational control) are critical to execution. But in other circumstances, traditional leadership traits can be counterproductive—e.g., trusting your intuition when the data from a digital experiment points the other way. There are no natural-born digital leaders. True digital leadership is about balancing tensions and seamlessly shifting between styles as the situation dictates.

Leadership credibility is hard to gain and easy to lose. With digital transformation, the credibility mountain is even harder to climb. Many organizations have created new roles for digital leaders that are cross-functional, multicompetency, and global. Often, these new digital roles come with vague job descriptions, limited direct reports, and huge scopes of responsibility. Chief digital officer roles, for instance, have become very popular in the last few years. But unless the objectives and authority levels are clear, a CDO's tenure will be short-lived.

So how can digital leaders stay the course? Sustaining leadership credibility requires a careful balance between deep digital competencies and the interpersonal skills required to navigate through the organization, culturally and politically. Sometimes you can't have both in the same person, so team building is key.

Digital leadership is also about raising the skills of the entire organization. At some point during the transformation, the skill gap will come to the fore. Employees are rarely a homogeneous population. Some will have the skills and foresight to buy into the digital program very quickly; others will need convincing and training; still others will be scared and skeptical of the learning curve ahead of them. Leadership is the ability to plan for, and cater to, all these populations to move your digital transformation forward. Longer term, it's about building a culture of lifelong learning.

Lastly, one of the most common obstacles to digital success is the organization's culture and structure. Reorganization is rarely the way out. Digital initiatives will cut across traditional silos, whether they are by business line, function, or geography. Collaboration and agile ways of working are keys to execution. Strong leadership is needed to foster collaboration across silos through incentivization and the flexible deployment of resources to digital priorities.

None of these acts of leadership are one-time shots, or easy. But actively leading people and organizations through the tensions created by digital transformation will significantly increase the chances of success.

THE CHARACTERISTICS OF AGILE DIGITAL LEADERSHIP

Despite what you may read, digital leaders are not all "new age" management gurus who reject traditional leadership orthodoxy. The evidence suggests that the most effective digital transformation leaders are those able to balance the tensions between traditional and emerging approaches to leadership. We refer to these tensions as *the expert* versus *the learner, the constant* versus *the adaptor, the tactician* versus *the visionary, the teller* versus *the listener, the power holder* versus *the power sharer, the intuitionist* versus *the analyst,* and *the perfectionist* versus *the accelerator.*[1]

We found that digital leaders who manage to balance these tensions must excel in three distinct capabilities. First, they need to build a level of self-awareness to understand their natural tendencies among the different tensions. For example, they may realize that that they are not very good listeners. Second, they need to develop a set of practices and behaviors that help them to compensate for these weaknesses. For instance, to force themselves to stop talking and to listen instead. Third, they need to build contextual awareness to know when to use one side of the tension or the other. For example, to know when to listen and when to speak.

WHY IT MATTERS

In recent years, many management articles and pundits have claimed that old-style command-and-control leadership is "out" and a new way of leading is "in."[2] In other words, instead of telling people what to do, leaders should ask them questions; instead of sticking exactly to plans, they should adjust goals as new information emerges; instead of working from one's gut, a leader should rely on data to make decisions, etc. This advice is particularly directed at digital leaders.[3]

Let's call the old-fashioned leadership model "traditional" and the new one "emergent." Here's the challenge: in the current environment, characterized by digital disruption, most executives need to be good at both styles of leadership. That is, any leader who relies solely on positional authority will run into trouble. Business, technology, and workforce expectations are changing much too quickly for that approach to be sustainable. At the same time, any leader who fully eschews striving for perfection, who never tells and only listens, and who shares but never holds power, will also struggle to be effective.

The key to leading a successful digital transformation is effectively balancing the tensions.

BEST PRACTICES AND KEY INSIGHTS

First of all, there is no single best approach to leading digital transformation. Digital leaders need to understand the tensions that are created between the traditional and emergent approaches to leadership. Then, they need to develop coping mechanisms to deal with them.

Tension 1: The Expert Versus the Learner

Traditionally, leaders built their careers by developing deep expertise in some area of the business. The assumption was that this knowledge would bring superior insight to organizational challenges. In the emergent approach, leaders accept that their specialized expertise is limited (in some cases obsolete) and are open to learning from others. This is especially true of digital knowledge, as people who are tasked with leading digital transformations cannot possibly be expected to know about all the relevant digital trends and technologies. Instead, they need to tap into a network of knowledge experts who can provide them with the necessary insights.

> In the long run, the learn-it-all always wins over the know-it-all.
> —SATYA NADELLA, CEO MICROSOFT[4]

Tim Westergren, cofounder of streaming radio platform Pandora, was able to blend the two. He was an expert in the traditional music industry before he founded Pandora. However, because Westergren was in new territory when the company adopted a freemium business model, he had to rely heavily on insights and knowledge from employees and partners. He came to understand that a key to his success was combining his deep knowledge of the industry with an openness to learning from others about new trends and technologies.[5]

Tension 2: The Constant Versus the Adaptor

The traditional approach to leadership values decision-making conviction and consistency. Good leaders "stick to their guns." By contrast, the emergent approach recognizes that in fast-changing environments, decisions must often be reversed or adapted, and that changing course in response to new information is a strength, not a weakness.

Early in his career, Jim Whitehurst, CEO of open-source software company Red Hat, decided to release a product that wasn't completely open source, which was against company policy. Not surprisingly, the product failed. When he openly admitted his error, employees and colleagues quickly moved past the mistake and continued to see him as trustworthy.[6]

Tension 3: The Tactician Versus the Visionary

The traditional approach calls for operational clarity and well-defined plans. The emergent approach suggests that leaders must have a clear vision for where they want to go, without necessarily needing a concrete road map for how to get there. If this tension isn't managed wisely, leaders run the risk of providing no "North Star" for their team members. On the other hand, if they are not grounded in reality, they may serve up lofty, unrealistic, or intangible goals.

Vas Narasimhan, CEO of Novartis AG, believes that predictive analytics and artificial intelligence will revolutionize the healthcare industry. Therefore, he invested significantly in AI and challenged different parts of the organization to find their own way to deploy the technology.[7] Most teams welcomed the initiative, but Narasimhan noticed that they often struggled to link AI to their daily work. Thus, he also paid close attention to the day-to-day processes that would enable these "bigger, bolder moves" to achieve results for the pharmaceutical giant.

Tension 4: The Teller Versus the Listener

The traditional approach to leadership calls for leaders to tell others what to do and how to do it. The emergent approach values listening carefully to others before deciding. If this tension is not managed wisely, leaders run the risk of missing important information that resides in the team. Conversely, if leaders refrain from providing their viewpoint, they miss the chance to apply their own digital transformation knowledge.

Angela Ahrendts, former CEO of Burberry, was not a digital expert. But she entered her role with a clear point of view on the industry: that the fashion brand needed to become relevant to a generation of millennial shoppers in order to thrive.[8] And these millennial shoppers were all online. But when it came to specific operational decisions, she sourced ideas and opinions from a wide range of people and partners. This led to a successful digital transformation of the brand and a near doubling of Burberry's operating profits during her tenure.

Tension 5: The Power Holder Versus the Power Sharer

The traditional approach suggests that leaders must lead from the top, make decisions, and take actions independently. In contrast, the emergent approach values empowering others to achieve goals. If this tension is not managed well, leaders run the risk of alienating and marginalizing promising talent. Alternatively, they may undermine their own authority by sharing power too broadly.

Marco Bizzarri, CEO of Gucci, wields his executive power by managing the financial part of the business while giving Gucci's creative director, Alessandro Michele, space to focus solely on what he does best—the design. Bizzarri knew when to empower, creating a shadow board of millennial employees to advise the fashion giant's executive team.[9]

Tension 6: The Intuitionist Versus the Analyst

Per the traditional approach, leaders nurture their "expert gut" to make intuitive decisions. Using the emergent approach, however, leaders base decisions largely on data. If this tension is not properly managed, leaders run the risk of making decisions based on outdated and biased heuristics. On the other hand, if they ignore their inner compass, they risk overlooking valuable insights gleaned from their extensive experience.

Barbara Coppola, chief digital officer of IKEA, advocates for data-driven decision making and data standardization globally, while giving regions the latitude to innovate to suit their immediate markets.[10] Because data and certain metrics are standardized across regions, these can be benchmarked easily against all other regions, as well as globally. The benchmarking standardization tactic provides an overall picture, and from this picture, intuitive hunches about which regional innovations could be experimentally expanded or leveraged globally can be obtained.

Tension 7: The Perfectionist Versus the Accelerator

The traditional approach asserts that leaders should take the time to deliver a perfectly finished product. The emergent approach calls for leaders to acknowledge that doing something quickly, and failing fast, is often more important than doing it perfectly. Due to a fear of imperfection, leaders run the risk of delaying the launch of key initiatives or directives. Conversely, moving initiatives forward without ample consideration and testing can lead to embarrassing results.

Charlotte Lindsey-Curtet, former director of digital transformation and data at the International Red Cross, strives to maintain an impeccable, privacy-by-design approach to protecting the identity of refugees. However, she also explores ways to connect refugee families via new technologies, such as biometrics, because speed is a critical factor in family reunification.[11]

Coping Mechanisms to Become a More Effective Digital Leader

In many situations linked to digital transformation, an emergent approach to leadership is preferable to a traditional approach—data is valued over intuition, listening is preferred over telling, power sharing is valued over power holding, and so on. However, this is not always the case.

At times, the emergent approach can be unproductive, slow, or inappropriate. For example, trusting the data was difficult during the COVID-19 pandemic as (1) there was little history on which to build reliable insight, (2) much of the available data was confusing or contradictory, and (3) the situation changed frequently. Thus, intuition gained increasing importance during the crisis. By the same token, when the impact of the pandemic hit many companies, vision became less important than tactical considerations linked to short-term survival.

Thus, digital leaders need to move between the traditional and emergent approaches as the context requires. Three capabilities are required to make these shifts:

> **Self-awareness.** Understanding one's natural tendencies is an important first step. Where is your comfort zone? What's your default position? All leaders have natural tendencies toward one style of leadership or the other, and this may differ depending on the tension. It's rare for leaders to always be fully traditional or emergent. There are a number of ways that leaders can discover their leadership styles. They can use diagnostic tests, conduct interviews with peers, and work with coaches. In the digital world, they can gain insight about themselves from real-time feedback apps or from online forums in which community members post comments and provide assessments.

> **Learn, adapt, practice.** Once leaders know their natural tendencies, they can work to develop a portfolio of microbehaviors to address the tensions that they don't manage well. For example, they can work on their listening skills or learn to work faster, even at the expense of perfection. This process can be enhanced by formal coaching. Each leader should find ways to build capabilities that are at odds with their natural styles across all seven tensions.

> **Contextual awareness.** Becoming a more effective digital leader means not only expanding one's current leadership approach to incorporate new behaviors, but also knowing when to put more focus on one side of a tension or the other. This requires both contextual awareness and emotional intelligence—sourced directly from the leader or from the leader's social environment. Through programs such as reverse mentoring, leaders can rely on the diversity embedded within their workforces to give them advice on when it's appropriate to favor one approach over the other.

• • •

Agility is not about being one type of leader or another—empowering, humble, or traditional. Successful digital leaders must seamlessly shift between different leadership styles as needs arise. Being able to shift requires balancing the tensions between the traditional and emergent approaches. Self-awareness, an adaptive and flexible leadership approach, and contextual awareness are all required to succeed as a digital leader.

Hacker's Toolbox

Figure out your own leadership baseline. It is difficult to be self-aware about one's own leadership tendencies, especially when it comes to digital disruption. Take a leadership assessment to become aware of your natural leadership style. We recommend the Hogan Agile Leader assessment,[12] but many options are available. All of them can provide deep insights into leadership behaviors. Once you are aware of your natural leadership tendencies, it becomes easier to adapt them to changing situations.

Get help—you don't have to do it alone. Work with a qualified leadership coach to improve self-awareness and develop a set of coping mechanisms to manage the tensions between traditional and emergent leadership practices. Set specific targets and goals. For example, if your tendency is to be a teller rather than a listener, set a goal for what proportion of your time you will spend listening. Or if your natural inclination is to follow your gut, force yourself to become familiar with analytics tools so that you can easily access the data yourself, rather than having to ask someone each time you need clarification. Work with the coach to assess your progress against the targets. As an alternative to a coach (or in addition to one), you can work with a trusted colleague who has a very different leadership style—e.g., someone who is a very good listener, works quickly, or listens carefully to data. Learn from that colleague's practices.

Test and learn. Playing against your natural leadership style is difficult. Rather than trying to accomplish it all at once, define a small set of projects on which to apply and test new leadership practices. Use these projects to test your abilities to work across the tensions. Refine your approaches based on the results. If possible, seek assistance from a colleague or coach.

Self-Reflection Questions

What are your natural tendencies across the seven tensions? To which side do you default most often, especially when under stress?

How can you improve your leadership capabilities across the nondefault sides of each tension?

Are you giving yourself enough time to consider the context before taking a leadership action?

Are you making sure that your leadership peers and subordinates are also aware of their leadership tendencies?

RELATED CHAPTERS

Aligning the Top Team to Drive Transformation Success (Chapter 3)

How Digital Leaders Can Establish and Maintain Credibility (Chapter 22)

Making the CDO Role a Success (Chapter 23)

HOW DIGITAL LEADERS CAN ESTABLISH AND MAINTAIN CREDIBILITY

With increased awareness of digital transformation, organizations have appointed a number of leaders to new digital roles. For any leader, credibility is difficult to build and easy to lose—and digital leaders have an even higher mountain to climb. Digital roles are cross-functional and multi-competence by design. Internal candidates understand the underlying culture and how things are done, but for external hires, this is an extra hurdle. Of course, digital competencies are important for the job, but so are the interpersonal skills needed to navigate the organization and build credibility. Therefore, clarifying the scope and responsibilities of the role up front is critical. A number of concrete actions can be taken by digital leaders to smooth the path of digital transformation execution.

WHY IT MATTERS

Over the last decade, we've seen a steady increase in digital transformation directors, chief digital officers, chief data officers, and other digital roles. By 2019, for example, 21 percent of global companies had a CDO position.[1] For some executives, the new digital roles have provided an amazing platform to learn new skills and produce an impact on their companies' strategic direction. For others, the roles have been a curse, forcing them to fight cross-silo battles, convince business line owners of the value of digital initiatives, and constantly justify their own existence. And in many cases, the "shelf life" of digital roles has been short. Our research shows that, on average, the tenure of a chief digital officer is 2½ years.[2]

Why?

Implementation of digital initiatives requires end-to-end coordination and collaboration, which is not a well-developed muscle in large organizations. Moreover, digital transformation is often seen as the latest management fad, or as something linked to complex technologies that only IT departments understand, or as a distraction from running the "real" business. Hence, in many organizations, digital efforts amplify the traditional resistance to change.

To compound the difficulty, our research shows that 70 percent of digital transformation leaders are hired from outside the companies.[3] The temptation to source externally is strong. Injecting new blood from a born-digital company, or from someone who's already been through a digital transformation in a large corporation, can more easily kick-start a transformation program. But because corporate "antibodies" are what they are, the risk of "tissue rejection" is real.

> For a successful digital transformation, stamina is just as important as speed because as you go along, hurdles invariably emerge.
> —RAHUL WELDE, EVP DIGITAL TRANSFORMATION, UNILEVER[4]

Credibility depends on whether people believe that a leader has the knowledge and skills to do the job (perceived competence), and whether they have faith in a leader's values and dependability (trustworthiness).[5] The same is true of longevity. Therefore, stamina is also important.

BEST PRACTICES AND KEY INSIGHTS

Every digital leader would like to discover the magic bullet for success. Unfortunately, there isn't one. A big part of success is asking the right questions up front. It's also about taking concrete actions, and setting up corporate mechanisms, that have a proven track record.

Asking the Right Questions Up Front

Two questions, in particular, should be asked up front.

How Ambiguous Is the Role?

For some leaders, the role can be very clear and the assignment well defined— e.g., improving data integration or boosting online marketing. The more the role leverages the leader's technical skills, the clearer the scope. But more often than not, digital leaders are given roles with high-ambiguity objectives, such as formulating a digital strategy or executing an enterprisewide digital transformation. These will require a good balance of competence and credibility.

In such cases, digital leaders should insist on taking the time for a discovery and design phase. This will allow them to get a grip on the inventory of existing initiatives and to understand the company's digital ambitions, priorities, and implementation time scales. Lastly, they will need to mobilize the various business stakeholders and align them on a digital road map.

As a digital leader, don't allow ambiguity to fester. Define the scope of the role, and make sure you have a good grasp of "what good looks like." As Mrutyunjay Mahapatra, ex-CDO of the State Bank of India, explained: "The first [thing to get right] is senior leadership buy-in. Digital transformation projects are not IT projects and require business buy-in. Top leadership needs to be invested right at the outset of the program."[6]

What Organizational Levers Does the Leader Possess?

When the objectives are nebulous, the means to achieve them are usually ill-defined. Beyond a clear line of reporting for decision making, digital leaders must learn how the transformation will be resourced and funded and what decision rights they will have. In addition, building a coalition of executive support is a good practice. It will help build the internal credibility required to avoid being marginalized.

Concrete Actions That Enhance Credibility and Success

Certain behaviors can affect how people assess their leaders' competence and trustworthiness and, in turn, their credibility. Behaviors that project competence include emphasizing future outcomes, taking action, and communicating effectively. Behaviors that project trustworthiness include acting consistently, communicating openly with others, and offering support to employees and stakeholders.[7] Successful digital transformation leaders employ an array of approaches to enhance their chances of success.

Make Some Noise

Leaders should enlist the support of communication teams to transmit and market the strategy and objectives of the digital transformation. If need be, they should brand the transformation program. Other noisemaking initiatives might include organizing regular town hall meetings or virtual conferences to engage all parts of the organization. In every case, leaders should communicate widely, transparently, and often about progress and achievements.

Send Strong Signals

A leader should make visible moves that depart from the organization's traditional ways of working. This will intrigue people, demonstrating that the leader has the authority and drive to do things differently. Ibrahim Gokcen, former CDO of Maersk, the global shipping company, discovered that people at Maersk didn't give trust by default:

> You have to make some visible iconic moves. Not big bang stuff, but small moves which have a large impact. I built a small room. Some people called it an innovation room; others called it the visitor room. I called it a design center. People were like, "What is this? A room?" I decided to put some uncommon furniture in to show how the physical space impacts how we work. It was to show the spirit of design thinking and user experience. I spent money to build that room with video and touch screens. It showed people that something new is happening. Something is changing.[8]

By creating a real and physical change, Gokcen was able to send a strong signal that he had top management support to change things.

Find Quick Wins

Even when the digital ambitions are high and the road map complex, quick wins matter. Ideally, digital leaders will have an initiative that they can conclude relatively fast, or an existing end-to-end initiative that they can accelerate. If this isn't possible, a succession of smaller quick wins can also have a huge impact on the credibility of the digital program.

Gerd Schenkel, former director of Telstra Digital, introduced a series of quick wins aimed at servicing Telstra's customers through social channels and at introducing CrowdSupport—a forum in which customers help other customers. Having a portfolio of quick and visible wins, alongside activities requiring meaningful investments, helped Schenkel manage expectations, both internally and externally: "You can only afford a small number of large things, and if one goes off, then financially the agenda is derailed. So if you don't have any quick wins, you haven't moved forward."[9]

Build a Coalition of Believers

Internal politics and resistance to change are traditional hurdles for any transformation effort. Very often, "the way we do things around here" is not overtly stated, but embedded in unwritten rules and invisible structures. To achieve tangible success, digital leaders need the support of influential business line leaders. This coalition needn't be formal, but it must be nurtured. For those appointed to a digital role from within the company, creating a coalition of support is an easier task. They will know the key movers and shakers. However, it will still require effort to ensure that the digital program has business- and personal-agenda interests for unit leaders. Diego De Coen, former CDO of tobacco giant JTI, put it this way: "You cannot tell a general manager, who is a very powerful person, to do things in a certain way. As long as they are successful, they do things in their own way, with their own investment."[10]

If the leader has been appointed from an external organization, the learning curve is steeper. That being said, we've seen examples of newly appointed leaders successfully partnering with influential company insiders to engage business leaders and remove organizational obstacles.

• • •

Digital competencies are a necessary condition for digital leaders, but so are interpersonal skills. Clarify the digital program's expectations and your role within it. Make a number of visible moves early; then use a coalition of supporters in the business to help you navigate the organization, build credibility, and stay the course.

Hacker's Toolbox

Search out iconic moves. Look for possible iconic moves in things that are widely known and regularly encountered and yet small enough to create cheap and quick effects. Keep in mind that it's not so much about making digital progress as it is about demonstrating the ability to create change.

Build a stakeholder map. Build a detailed stakeholder map of the business leaders with whom you should partner. Nurture this network by ensuring that they have access to critical knowledge, and if possible, allocate some of your leadership responsibilities across your network.

Communicate your strategic intent. Similar to setting your organization's digital transformation objective, it is important to ensure that people working with you understand your strategic intent. Strategic intent refers to the aligning of direction and pace of motion, instead of defining a vision or a strategy.[11] While it communicates what you hope to achieve, it also provides freedom for others working with you to provide input and collaborate on how to reach the objective together. It provides an opportunity to build trust.

Make the entire team look good. When selecting quick wins, focus on accomplishments that make the entire team look good. The team must make real and direct contributions to business success. Work with at least one respected member of the new team to brainstorm collective quick wins. A focus on collective quick wins also helps establish your credibility as a leader.

Self-Reflection Questions

Is your role as a digital leader clear to you and to the rest of the organization's stakeholders?

Do you have the organizational resources and levers to achieve your objectives?

What behaviors and actions can help project competence and trustworthiness for you and your team?

What visible signals and quick wins can you undertake to build your reputation?

Do you have an aligned view of "what good looks like" for your digital transformation?

RELATED CHAPTERS

Building Urgency When Your Business Is Doing Well (Chapter 2)

Taking an Inventory of Existing Digital Initiatives (Chapter 5)

Funding Your Digital Transformation Program (Chapter 6)

Choosing the Right Digital Governance Model (Chapter 8)

The Characteristics of Agile Digital Leadership (Chapter 21)

MAKING THE CDO ROLE A SUCCESS

The role of chief digital officer is widely popular, but research shows that CDOs rarely last long. Many CDOs are set up to fail. To avoid costly mistakes, firms should carefully design the CDO role around the following aspects: organizational anchoring, funding, jurisdiction, and decision rights.

WHY IT MATTERS

Research has shown that many CDOs are saddled with vague job descriptions and success measures when they start their tenure.[1] Average tenure is just about 2½ years, compared with 5 years or more for CEOs.[2] Their mission is described as being "in charge of the digital transformation," but they often lack both concrete authority and clear objectives.[3] Such uncertainty and ambiguity can lead to battles for jurisdiction with other established executive roles, like CIOs and CMOs, that negatively affect the performance of the entire firm.[4] On top of this, newly hired CDOs often face the problem of having to transform the whole firm at once, without having a plan that details how or where to start.[5]

BEST PRACTICES AND KEY INSIGHTS

Setting up the CDO role for success is not an easy task.[6] Countless organizations hire a CDO because they feel the need to put a name in charge of digital, but in reality they are often unprepared and don't know exactly what this person should do. Without a clear idea of expectations, responsibilities, and authority, CDOs are set up to fail. This is frustrating for both the CDO *and* the organization, and may incur substantial costs. Through our research and experience, we have identified four aspects that must be carefully considered when introducing the CDO role: organizational anchoring at the top level, independent funding, clear jurisdiction, and end-to-end decision rights.

Organizational Anchoring

Anchoring the CDO role within the organizational hierarchy, along with the role's reporting relationship, directly influences (1) the digital agenda and (2) the chance of success. For a truly companywide digital transformation, the CDO should be anchored in the top management team, ideally reporting directly to the CEO.

As the VP in charge of digital transformation at a leading global oil and gas company explained, direct access to the CEO is a crucial element in acquiring the backing and freedom to act that's necessary to get the digital journey off the ground—without that, a CDO will spend most of the time just looking for executive sponsorship.

In practice, another common issue we observe is that traditional senior leaders with little digital experience tend to overestimate the IT component of the CDO role, and consequently, they decide to anchor the CDO role in the IT organization, reporting to the CIO. As a result, digital transformation initiatives are at risk of becoming "just another IT project" from the viewpoint of the rest of the organization.

Funding

Our research clearly shows that a CDO without a proper budget has a limited chance of success. CDOs without direct funding need to make a business case to directors/managers of business units for every initiative they want to undertake. Yet business leaders may rightfully ask why they should use their own budget for a digital initiative that may not pay off, or that might create benefits beyond their own units.

Consequently, it is important that leadership equips the CDO role with a digital "war chest" to ensure buy-in across the firm. Fred Herren, former CDO of SGS, explains that when it comes to digital transformation, there is "no choice between carrot and stick [to motivate people]. In digital, the stick never works. You need carrots, carrots, carrots . . ."

If you go in and you say, "Do this, and it's on your budget," the buy-in is limited. . . . It's much better to have your own war chest and to go around and to say, "This project is nice. Let me fund it." And then the people jump and follow you. It makes life much easier.

—FRED HERREN, FORMER CDO, SGS[7]

Jurisdiction

For most organizations, the chief digital officer is a relatively new role. As such, it's "the new kid on the block" and needs to be positioned within (and among) the existing structures and established roles, such as the chief marketing officer, chief technology officer, chief operating officer, and chief information officer. Studies have shown that this can be inherently difficult for organizations with a high level of internal politics, as it may lead to power struggles and dysfunctional behavior.

However, digital transformation is, by its nature, a cross-functional exercise that requires the involvement of people from all different functions of an organization. In terms of leadership and jurisdiction, CDOs need to find a space within the C-suite, and this might lead to conflict. Organizations that try to avoid this conflict by giving only limited jurisdiction to the CDO—or none at all—will set up the CDO for failure.

Similar to the need for their own funding, CDOs also require a certain "turf" that falls under their sole jurisdiction and control. Defining a clear mandate that is supported by the CEO and accepted by all other executives is a key element for a successful CDO role.

Decision Rights

Closely related to having a defined jurisdiction, CDOs require a certain set of decision rights that allows them to get the work done. Successful CDOs are given end-to-end responsibility in a certain area, even if it's limited at the outset, to carry out projects from inception to rollout and demonstrate their ability to produce results. To succeed in companywide transformations, CDOs must be able to bring onboard the business unit directors/managers. Beyond interpersonal skills, the best way to do this is by demonstrating real results and quick wins from digital initiatives. When results, and trust, have been established, it's easier to increase the scope of the CDO's role.

Mark Klein, CDO of Germany's ERGO Insurance Group, observes that the CDO can be successful only if he or she is given a real chance to make a difference and create results, without having to ask everyone else for permission: "So even if the other colleagues say, 'well, I don't want to do digitalization,' I can implement that end to end in my area, show that it's working and then bring it to my colleagues."[8]

Hacker's Toolbox

Define clear responsibilities and goals for the CDO role.
Before introducing the CDO role, make sure that the senior
leadership team has formulated clear expectations and goals.
Only then can you move forward to actually define the role's
details, its responsibilities and authority, that are required to
fulfill the stated goals. A good way to get started is to take
inspiration from successful CDOs in similar companies or
industries: What helped them to achieve their goals? How
was their role defined? While every organization's digital
journey is unique, it never hurts to learn from others' mistakes
and successes. Once the role is properly defined, take your
time to hire the right CDO for your organization by matching
role responsibilities with candidates. Executive search
agencies might be helpful to find a candidate that has the
right mix of digital competencies and transformation skills to
fit your specific needs.

Make sure to get executive consensus. Clearly define
the meaning of success (and failure) for the CDO role.
Even if digital transformation requires agility and moving
targets, be sure to discuss everyone's expectations and
find common ground. Be open and transparent about
shifting responsibilities, especially when it means to take
away authority from already existing roles. Define common
goals and collaboration processes, so that the CDO is well
embedded in the information flow and functioning of your
organization and not the odd one out.

A powerful mandate will lead to more tangible outcomes.
The more important the digital transformation is for your
organization, the higher the CDO role should be anchored
within the management hierarchy. For CDOs that are
in charge of a clearly defined task, for example digital
marketing, a functional mandate and anchoring are often
sufficient. However, for CDOs that are hired to transform
the whole organization across functions and hierarchies, a

powerful mandate is a key element of success. Make sure to align authority, funding, and decision rights with senior leaderships expectations, so that the CDO truly *can* do what she or he *should* do.

Self-Reflection Questions

Have you clearly defined the CDO role in terms of success expectations?

Is your CDO starting to become a self-marketer rather than delivering real results?

Does your CDO have the competence and credibility to be successful?

Is your organization prepared to undergo a real digital transformation and provide the necessary resources and authority for the CDO role?

RELATED CHAPTERS

Aligning the Top Team to Drive Transformation Success (Chapter 3)

How to Get Your Board Onboard (Chapter 7)

How to Make Digital and IT Work Together (Chapter 9)

How Digital Leaders Can Establish and Maintain Credibility (Chapter 22)

HOW BEST TO DEVELOP DIGITAL SKILLS WITHIN YOUR ORGANIZATION

Learning new digital tools, technologies, and business models presents a short-term challenge and a longer-term challenge. The short-term challenge? To upskill the workforce on digital developments that impact the business *today*. Often, digital skills and knowledge must be ramped up quickly through in-house training, external education, and recruitment of external talent.

Upskilling existing talent should employ a variety of approaches, so people can learn in ways that fit their individual learning styles. In addition to identifying information gaps prior to the training, digital leaders should test employees, post-training, to determine their proficiency with the new knowledge, and they should also ensure that training is reinforced until the new skills are mastered.

The longer-term challenge is to create a culture of self-directed learning. Rather than simply pushing out new learning content, digital leaders must also nurture a culture of lifelong learning—a workforce that learns how to continually learn on its own.

WHY IT MATTERS

Disruptions—digital and nondigital (such as COVID-19)—are materializing ever more frequently. As a result, organizations that default to "business as usual" will struggle to cope with these continual "shocks of the new." Thus, it's increasingly important that the workforce become as well informed and up to date as possible. According to a Gartner study, 67 percent of business leaders agreed that if their employees did not become significantly upskilled on digital by 2020, their companies would no longer be competitive.[1]

But what, exactly, does it mean to become "significantly upskilled on digital"?

Digital skills and knowledge fall into four general categories: technology, data, processes, and change management.[2] Technology covers new digital tools such as IoT, AI, augmented reality, blockchain, and the like. Data refers to the ability to understand and work with different types of data and extract key insights from it. The processes category includes understanding digital stakeholder journeys (customers, employees, etc.) and translating these journeys into new or augmented processes such as digital marketing and cybersecurity. Change management requires an understanding of how digitization differs from digital transformation, as well as the ability to navigate a transformation agenda.

Obviously, different employees will begin their skills-acquisition journeys from different starting lines. When it comes to digital competence, most organizations comprise three types of people: digital natives, digital immigrants, and digital ignorants. Digital natives grew up with digital technologies and are very comfortable using them. When a new tool is introduced, they have little trouble adopting it. However, they may not be well versed with the challenges of digital change management. Digital immigrants didn't grow up with digital technologies or data, and though they are never fully comfortable with them, they are willing to learn and adapt.[3] For digital ignorants, digital technologies are foreign and frustrating, even scary. These people may be natural Luddites, or they may have had negative experiences with new technologies.

The reality for most companies is that all three groups are important. Digital ignorants may not know much about new technologies, but they know a great deal about other important aspects of the business. And while many are willing to learn new skills or completely retrain to improve their future employability, few feel they are given the time or opportunity to do so.[4]

BEST PRACTICES AND KEY INSIGHTS

Organizations should tailor their digital knowledge and competence to the characteristics, learning styles, and constraints faced by all three groups and develop both short-term and long-term solutions.

Short-Term Solutions: Upgrading Digital Skills and Knowledge

In the short term, the key to digitally upskilling the workforce is to use multiple concurrent strategies. Again, it's important to recognize that people have different learning styles.[5] Some people learn best by reading; others by watching videos. Some like an in-class experience, while others prefer a self-paced model. Expecting everyone to conform to a single training-delivery mode will severely compromise learning.

As well, because learning gaps are different, they should not be targeted in the same way. For example, digital natives may not need to pay as much attention to core technology knowledge, but they might benefit from acquiring new digital business skills. Digital immigrants often need to improve their knowledge of the digital tools and technologies impacting the business, while digital ignorants may only need to become comfortable with *relevant* digital technologies. For them, user adoption is more important than the depth of their technical expertise.

Take the example of the live webinar, which, thanks to COVID-19, has become a ubiquitous feature of company life. Digital natives don't need to be taught the advanced features of the technology, but they may need help adapting their presentation skills to the new format. Digital immigrants will need more help to become comfortable with the technology, as well as new presentation approaches. Digital ignorants can settle for merely familiarizing themselves with the process of attending live webinars, even if they never actively use them as a presentation tool.

As Axel Springer, a European digital publishing house, transitioned from a traditional print media company to a digital platform company, it needed to transform its workforce. Much of this transformation occurred through hiring, downsizing, divestitures, and acquisitions. However, thousands of legacy employees had to make the transition to a digital world, including members of senior management.

Alexander Schmid-Lossberg, former head of Human Resources at Axel Springer, noted: "We needed to set up easy-to-access formats, lively formats, where you can alert people, where you can motivate people to then invest in their own abilities. Then, they can become active by themselves."[6]

To meet the challenge, the company launched multiple learning initiatives across different channels and modes. Senior management, including the board and management team, went to Silicon Valley to learn new ways of doing things and, most important, to shift their mindsets. For middle managers and line employees, the company launched multiple training programs across different formats. These formats included in-class and online training, "early bird" breakfast events for early risers, lunch meetups, "pizza connection" events based on different technical topics, speed networking, best-practice clubs, mentoring, evening speaking and learning "cocktail" events, innovation sprints, and so on.[7] There are plenty of creative ways to implement digital education. The key is to provide sufficient diversity to suit all learning styles.

US-based telecommunications company AT&T took a different approach to retraining. When the organization realized that half its 250,000-person workforce lacked the necessary skills to keep the company competitive, it embarked on a $1 billion reskilling program to develop an internal talent pipeline. As Bill Blase, senior EVP of Human Resources, observed, "It's important to engage and retrain workers rather than constantly going to the street to hire."[8]

The multiyear effort, which began in 2013, included online courses, a career center that allowed employees to identify and train for jobs that the company needed in the future, and a job simulation tool. Five years later, half of its employees had completed 2.7 million online courses, and the time required to take new offerings from idea to implementation had been cut in half.[9]

Long-Term Solutions: Building a Learning Culture

To succeed in a world that is changing faster and less predictably than ever before, it's not enough to upskill employees with the latest digital skills and knowledge, because companies will always be playing "catch-up." Employees need to become proactive lifelong learners by first believing that they have opportunities (and an unlimited capacity) to learn and grow. Lifelong learners must be supported by organizations that encourage appropriate risk taking and that reward employees for lessons learned and self-development. Organizations need to support collaboration across organizational boundaries and make learning accessible and broadly available. When employees and organizations support each other in this endeavor, a learning culture is built.[10]

In the longer term, part of the solution is to hire people with a broad range of knowledge and skills and an interest in learning more. These "T" people have both depth and breadth of knowledge. The letter T is a reference to the fact that they have both knowledge depth (the stem of the letter T) and breadth (the cross of the letter T).

Today, many companies are full of "I" people—employees with deep expertise in one area, but little knowledge or interest in other areas. T people are generally better at learning new skills and knowledge than I people.[11] In fact, over time, T people (who tend to have acquired their knowledge at school) can become "M" people. Like T people, M people have a broad range of knowledge and skills, but they have developed multiple areas of competence over time.[12] For example, after working for a number of years in manufacturing, a mechanical engineer may get an MBA with a technology focus and then switch careers to work in high-tech sales. Later on, he or she may study Python programming courses and move into data analytics.

Of course, systems and process are required to promote active learning, even for T or M people. Therefore, many companies employ a variety of media and innovations to accommodate the different preferences of how employees choose to learn.

Singapore bank DBS launched a number of programs to find out what would inspire learning and curiosity among its employees. One notable success was a program called GANDALF, in which employees could apply to receive grants of $1,000 toward training on any work-related topic. The twist with the GANDALF program was that the employees had to agree to teach what they'd learned to at least 10 other people within the bank. As of early 2019, 120 grant recipients had trained 13,500 other employees.[13] Many GANDALF scholars report that the teaching component of the program was actually more satisfying than learning.

At agriculture firm Cargill, employees "microlearn" by studying concepts or small lessons that they have to immediately apply. They are then asked to fill out a field report describing the results, lessons learned, and questions raised, and must also show a sample of their product.[14]

Increasingly, organizations are also moving beyond content management to content curation to reduce information overload on employees. Consulting firm Accenture focuses on content curation by providing current insights on emerging technologies to help keep its consultants up to date. The firm identifies useful external content and then combines it with internal content developed in consultation with in-house subject-matter experts. As of early 2019, the subject-matter experts had created more than 2,500 learning topics that were delivered as on-demand learning modules.

Hacker's Toolbox

Hire more all-rounders. In an increasingly volatile and unpredictable world, a broad base of transferable skills is more valuable than deep skills in a single area. Thus, think about hiring digital talent that are M people rather than I people—all-rounders who can work with multiple types of digital technologies and operating environments. M people tend to also have a strong learning orientation, as they have shown a tendency to augment their skills and knowledge in the past.

Offer digital learning across multiple structures and formats. People learn in different ways, so offer a variety of learning options. These may include classroom learning, online learning, peer learning, video learning, and so on. Provide a detailed picture of learner segments and their preferences, and facilitate input into learning agendas. The process of demystifying digital is important to increase people's comfort levels with new tools and technologies.

Learn from learners. Assemble an advisory group comprising learners from various levels across the organization. The group's mandate is to keep the organization and its leaders informed about the latest technologies that might impact the business. Ensure that the group gets time on the leadership agenda to share its insights.

Incentivize learning. Provide inducements for learning to the greatest extent possible, such as resources to pursue learning, and for sharing that learning with others in the organization. Incentives might also include dedicated time for learning, set aside in the corporate agenda. The benefits of episodic learning are rarely sustainable—learning needs to be ongoing. Fortunately, digital learning options and supporting technologies have improved dramatically since the COVID-19 pandemic.

Self-Reflection Questions

Are you offering multiple learning formats for your employees?

Are you aware of the balance among digital natives, immigrants, and ignorants?

Are you incentivizing your employees to share their digital knowledge?

Do you have enough T people in your organization?

What skills are people excited to develop?

Does your organization make it easy for individuals to learn while on the job?

RELATED CHAPTERS

Building Hyperawareness into Your Organization (Chapter 12)

Implementing Open Innovation Effectively (Chapter 15)

How Digital Leaders Can Establish and Maintain Credibility (Chapter 22)

WORKING ACROSS SILOS

When implementing digital transformation programs, large traditional companies may be caught off guard by their organizational structure. One major stumbling block is siloed structures, which preempt collaboration across entities.[1] Because most digital initiatives require a high level of cross-functional cooperation and resource fluidity to succeed, business leaders must prioritize business alignment to ensure collaboration across all business units and levels of hierarchy.

WHY IT MATTERS

Working in silos is one of the most commonly mentioned obstacles to digital success.[2, 3] In fact, many organizations have learned the hard way that digital transformation is less about technology and more about people.[4] Research has shown that, in digitally mature organizations, leaders are more than twice as likely to effectively support cross-functional teams as they are in organizations in the early stages of a digital transformation. Digitally mature organizations tend to be less hierarchical: they drive decision making down and throughout the organization.[5] By contrast, some early warning signs of poor collaboration include a lack of top-team alignment and an unsupportive culture.[6] Organizations that struggle to break down silos often overlook the fact that transformation requires a systemic approach to change—one that takes into account the interrelated aspects that can drive (or inhibit) organizational change.[7]

BEST PRACTICES AND KEY INSIGHTS

Our research uncovered two factors that either drive or inhibit collaboration: formal structures and organizational culture.[8] Not surprisingly, many organizations focus on formal structures, trying to break down organizational silos by making changes in the organizational structure—e.g., by creating more cross-functional committees or by creating a matrix model for some core processes.

> The big moment for an organization is when they have embraced the fact that digital transformation isn't a technical issue, but a cultural change.
> —IAN RODGERS, FORMER CHIEF DIGITAL OFFICER, LVMH[9]

But reorganizing is not the way out. Fostering a culture of sharing information and "rallying around the same goal" is a much stronger predictor of success.[10] Our research and experience both point to three things that can help your organization increase its chances of becoming truly collaborative, with a shared sense of unity and ambition. They are incentivization, resource sharing, and agile ways of working.

Incentivize Collaboration

One commonly cited barrier to collaboration is a nonexistent or misaligned incentive system. When Guido Jouret started as CDO of industrial giant ABB, he faced the daunting task of setting up the digital governance system of a globally distributed organization. Although he was equipped with enough financial power to make things happen, he knew that the key for real digital transformation was to align the various business units in the same direction. At ABB, traditional incentive systems were almost purposefully designed to do the opposite—to prevent, rather than foster, collaboration: Which unit has sold more items? Which region outperformed another?

Jouret knew that collaboration was critical to digital success. Many of the most interesting projects were not viable within one business unit but required involvement from multiple groups across traditional boundaries. So Guido put his money where his mouth was, explaining: "I basically put funding behind collaboration incentives and prioritize projects where BUs work together. When that happens, one plus one really equals four: $1 comes from one BU, $1 from the other BU, and I match it with $2 more. So now, all of a sudden, you get $4 for this project when each BU individually would always get only one."[11] Digital leaders have to rethink existing incentive systems, making sure the incentives align with the objectives. To increase collaboration, carrots usually work better than sticks.[12]

Foster Knowledge Exchange and Resource Mobility

A common challenge faced by many organizations is how to set up the digital team. When organizations set up separate digital teams so that dedicated groups of experts can push the agenda forward, they run the risk of losing touch with the rest of the organization. Hence, when the digital leaders at Rabobank were setting up their Digital Hub, they took steps to mitigate this risk. First, the physical location of the new unit had to demonstrate integration rather than separation. Thus, the hub was located in the HQ, in the center of a round office tower, signaling transparency and openness on all sides. Second, the hub chose to improve specific customer journeys, a task that involved the relevant operational people from all over the organization and across different regional units. Employees were seconded (temporarily reassigned) from their original workplaces to form multifunctional teams in the hub. By borrowing people from different functional units to temporarily work in the central hub, the digital leaders at Rabobank created a shared sense of digital vision and ownership—one that would continually grow throughout the global organization after employees returned to their original workplaces.[13]

Support Agile Ways of Working

Many organizations are struggling to find new ways of organizing that recognize the need for both hierarchy and systematic reporting relationships and allow for an agile approach to customer-centric multifunctional teams. There are countless models for agile work practices, and it can be difficult for digital leaders to find the best solution. Therefore, instead of striving for a perfect fit from the get-go, digital leaders should focus on adapting whatever model they choose to their specific needs.[14]

Dutch bank ING, a pioneer in digital transformation, followed the so-called Spotify model[15] to systematically (rather than episodically) redesign its organizational structure and fully embrace its digital journey. ING launched this radical transformation at its HQ, to set an example, and then rolled it out to the rest of the business. Adopting this model proved highly successful: not only did it help ING achieve the intended customer-centricity and reduce time to market, but it also generated positive spillover effects, such as hikes in employee productivity and workplace engagement.[16]

• • •

Fostering collaboration across organizational silos is a core challenge for many organizations that embark on a digital journey. Successful digital leaders create a sense of unity that makes everyone pull in the same direction through three key elements: incentivization of collaborative efforts, systematic team and knowledge exchange, and implementation of agile ways of working.

Hacker's Toolbox

Create a shared sense of ownership. The key to achieving business unity is to ensure that everybody is pulling in the same direction. Instead of collaboration initiatives that exist on paper only, lead with concrete actions that show how serious you are about breaking down silos. A good start is to revisit the goals of departments and subunits. Are they fostering suboptimization, or are they well aligned with strategic customer-facing outcomes your organization wants to achieve? Make sure every single employee is working to achieve the shared purpose of the organization, instead of hitting some KPIs or sticking to a plan.

Adjust your incentives. To break down silos, it's crucial to revisit your organization's incentive system and make sure that it's not working against you. Remove incentives that prohibit collaboration and create competing goals among units or functional areas—for example, when the logistics departments are incentivized by product availability while the finance department is incentivized by cash flow. Most incentive systems have such unintended side effects that need to be considered. Make sure incentives are designed to foster collaboration, such as project financing schemes that reward collaborative applications from more than one business unit with higher acceptance rates or extra funding on top. The key is to look at the incentive system as a whole rather than at each unit separately.

Establish an "agile way of working." A core element of agility is the ability to overcome silos and functional/unit-based rivalries. Many agile methods exist that can help you get inspired, but be aware that whatever you choose needs to be adapted to your specific organizational context. There is no one right way to do agile. A good way to get started is to look at popular and widely reported examples like the Spotify model or Scrum. See which elements would fit your current organization and what changes are necessary to implement agile ways of working at scale.

Self-Reflection Questions

Are your employees collaborating across business units?

Reflect on the incentive system that is applied throughout your organization. Does it foster or hinder collaboration?

Are you relying on roles, processes, and organizational structures that perpetuate silos and functional boundaries?

Are you confident that employees are rallying around a common goal and sharing the same vision for the future of the organization?

RELATED CHAPTERS

Funding Your Digital Transformation Program (Chapter 6)

Choosing the Right Digital Governance Model (Chapter 8)

How to Make Digital and IT Work Together (Chapter 9)

Accelerating Digital Using Agile Methods (Chapter 10)

Scaling Digital Initiatives (Chapter 27)

Part Six
Hacking Digital Momentum
Anchoring and Sustaining Performance

If you really look closely,
most overnight successes took a long time.
—Steve Jobs

Part One focused on initiation, or building a solid foundation for digital transformation. Parts Two to Five covered the phases and challenges of execution. To return to our construction metaphor, they focused on the structural integrity, functionality, and aesthetics of each floor of the building. Part Six, the final section of this book, examines how to sustain the positive momentum created by transformation—in essence, how to create an organization that no longer needs digital transformation as a specific program. Indeed, at some point in the future, the organization will no longer talk about digital transformation. Digital technology will be so embedded within the organization that it will constitute the fabric of all operations.

Let's be clear: setting up a digital transformation is hard. Embedding it within the organization is even harder. And maintaining performance over time is perhaps the most challenging task of all. Small wins send positive signals, but converting smaller wins into larger ones, and sustaining them, is not easy.

To start, it's important to create a pipeline of digital initiatives that will survive beyond the digital transformation program. The focus of these initiatives should be on effectively scaling them from pilots into full-blown projects, and eventually into a "new normal" way of doing things. In our experience, however, many organizations unleash a parade of pilots and minimum viable products that struggle to scale and become widely adopted. The "startup to scale-up" challenge needs to be tackled head-on; this is where the value lies.

As the saying goes, "You get what you measure," but in digital transformation it's not that straightforward. A huge proportion of digital transformation programs struggle to achieve benefits. By our count, 87 percent of them fail to meet expectations.[1] At the same time, we know that most organizations struggle with measurement. This begs the question: How do organizations *know* that they have failed if they don't properly measure the transformation? It's a muddy field. Digital investments have different horizons or risk profiles, and must be measured and managed as such. Like all other investments, digital transformations need clear and effective measures and KPIs to ensure long-term performance.

A key part of sustaining performance is to be aware of what comes next, and to stay on top of new trends, especially around digital tools and technologies. Often these trends emerge in adjacent or different industries. A wide-angle lens is required to see not only what's happening locally, but what's happening farther afield—in other industries or other parts of the world.

Finally, you must be able to respond and adapt to change. Any predictions on how the world will look at the onset of a digital transformation should be regularly revisited as time passes. Large and impactful events, such as the COVID-19 pandemic, are next to impossible to predict. Others may be easier to foresee, but equally hard to respond to—such as a global recession or natural disaster. Identifying an opportunity or threat is good, but avoiding it (a threat) or capturing it (an opportunity) is even better. In today's volatile world, agility is not enough. You also need to build enough robustness to absorb unavoidable shocks, and enough responsiveness to bounce back faster than your competitors. Digital tools and technologies can help build that kind of organizational resilience.

SETTING UP A PIPELINE
OF DIGITAL INITIATIVES

The way digital initiatives are selected and implemented, as well as the choice of decision-making authority, sets the stage for a company's digital transformation journey. To leverage the creativity of all stakeholders, internal and external, organizations must take a systematic approach. Companies that get this right recognize that while *ideation is best decentralized, evaluation and prioritization should be centrally coordinated.*

WHY IT MATTERS

When implementing digital transformations, most companies try to foster a culture of innovation, supported by digital entrepreneurship or intrapreneurship capabilities. Because ideas for digital initiatives can be generated by internal *and* external sources, it's important to cast the net wide. Encouraging ideation among all stakeholders is needed to create organizational hyper-awareness about potential digital threats and opportunities. A sufficient volume of internal and external ideas will also help the organization keep its pulse on digital developments. As Bart Leurs, chief digital and transformation officer of Rabobank, said: "If we want to have least 30 MVPs [minimum viable products] with real business potential every year, we need to process thousands of ideas at the ideation stage."[1] To scale the most promising ideas, many leaders emphasize the need for centralized decision-making authorities that will evaluate new ideas against strategic priorities.

BEST PRACTICES AND KEY INSIGHTS

To establish and maintain a pipeline of digital initiatives, firms need to manage two distinct phases: (1) ideation and (2) evaluation and prioritization. Together, these two phases form a funnel that drives continual innovation.

Ideation Best Practices

For the ideation phase, companies use different tools and systems to encourage and leverage creativity across all stakeholder groups—employees, customers, suppliers, etc. In this stage, the main goal is to create an ideation network that's as broad and heterogeneous as possible—i.e., everybody should be given a voice.[2] Internally, organizations may facilitate the crowdsourcing of ideas through ideation tools that are visible across the organization.

Food giant Nestlé, for example, launched the "InGenius" program in 2014 to leverage the creativity of its 300,000+ employees worldwide. Employees can pitch their ideas on a software ideation platform and get feedback and votes from other Nestlé employees. In the past five years, the InGenius program has spawned 48 commercialized ideas, ranging from using drones in warehouses to providing open-source hardware and software for small-scale farmers to help save water and increase income.[3]

Dutch financial services company Rabobank followed a more targeted approach. The company established innovation leads for its business lines, whose role was to source ideas within predefined innovation themes. "We don't have the bandwidth of big companies to freely ideate and filter ideas that pop up," said Bart Leurs. "We steer the innovation ideas already based on an innovation thesis."[4]

At some organizations, campaigns focus on certain innovation topics or themes to help increase the number and relevance of the ideas. Global testing services company SGS organized quarterly innovation campaigns rather than creating a generic ideation platform. Fred Herren, former CDO of SGS, said: "We have dedicated ideation champions, and their role is to promote the campaign at the region or the business level, and also to collect all the proposals to make sure that they are completed."[5]

Innovation platforms can also be used to stimulate and collect ideas from an external network of suppliers, partners, and customers. Many large organizations have benefited from such open innovation approaches,[6] including

Danish toy manufacturer Lego. In 2014, Lego launched "Lego Ideas" to access the creativity of engaged customers in a systematic way. Using the web-based platform, customers can easily share their ideas with other customers and propose new product designs directly to Lego. These range from new models based on existing packages to various "tweaks"—such as adding a motorized function to a formerly static product.[7]

> Innovation has nothing to do with how many R&D dollars you have. When Apple came up with the Mac, IBM was spending at least 100 times more on R&D. It's not about money. It's about the people you have, how you're led, and how much you get it.
> —STEVE JOBS, APPLE COMPUTER[8]

For Lego, this approach represents a radical strategic turnaround. Whereas creative customers were once considered threats (as users who were "hacking" the company's copyright-protected products), they are now actively encouraged to submit new product proposals and design innovations.[9]

Evaluation and Prioritization Best Practices

In this stage, organizations efficiently evaluate and prioritize the ideas. To accomplish this, innovation leaders employ a systematic "filter"—a dedicated decision-making authority or "digital innovation committee"—to evaluate new ideas against digital transformation priorities. The committee can be led by the CDO or other senior executive and include members from different business units.

At media conglomerate Thomson Reuters, a steering committee comprising stakeholders in businesses, digital, product, and marketing prioritizes the initiatives. Joe Miranda, CDO, emphasizes the need for transparency in the process: "We make sure that there's full transparency around where our focus is, why our focus is there, what we get out of that focus, and how that looks over a multiyear horizon or multiyear program."[10]

Although many organizations understand the need to filter innovation ideas, they often struggle with what criteria to use for prioritization. Initiatives need to be evaluated against two dimensions: value potential and feasibility. In addition, the digital innovation governance body should strive to create a balanced portfolio of initiatives—one composed of quick wins, cross-enterprise transformation initiatives, and business model shifts.[11] Once value potential and feasibility have been assessed, the initiatives should be continually reassessed according to KPIs that measure their intended business impact.

When evaluating and prioritizing ideas, it's important to use a clear assessment process and apply transparent criteria in order to ensure strategic alignment and buy-in. For some organizations, keeping the idea originator in charge (to push the idea forward to implementation) has proved useful. As Eberhard Ruess, former head of Nestlé's CIO office, explains: "The concept of InGenius was that you [who voice the idea] become the CEO for your idea. You develop it up to a minimum viable prototype, and then you are invited to pitch your product in front of the CEO and the CIO. It works very well."[12] Putting the idea originator in charge leads to a clear accountability and a strong feeling of ownership. In turn, this creates the necessary momentum and traction to push the idea forward.

Fred Herren of SGS understands the importance of giving recognition to the idea originator: "Whenever we have a successful project, we will obviously advertise it and make sure that the people are informed about it. The person who has submitted a proposal is praised, to encourage others to come forward with their ideas. This really helped us to gain momentum and traction."[13]

· · ·

Digital transformation can only be as good as the ideas that drive it. Thus, while creativity cannot be forced, organizations need to implement a systematic approach that allows them to capture and develop ideas from a broad range of sources. Leading digital organizations have set up structured processes that support ideation from initial concept toward a funnel of further development and continual evaluation. This way, they are less likely to overlook game-changing ideas while ensuring efficiency and return on investment.

Hacker's Toolbox

Cast your net wide. Great ideas may come from unexpected places. Make sure to put clear processes and practices in place to capture ideas from all stakeholders of your organizations, both internal and external. Research has shown that digital innovation often comes from heterogenous networks of people,[14] so try to facilitate the exchange and discussion of employees from various functions and departments on a regular basis. For example, organizing internal hackathons or idea contests can be a good way to get started.

Evaluate transparently and quickly. Speed and transparency are key aspects to foster ideation and innovation. On the one hand, making sure that the evaluation process is documented and accessible ensures fairness and continued involvement from ideators. On the other hand, being able to speedily separate the wheat from the chaff allows you to focus your resources on developing the most promising ideas further. Start by drawing up an ideation-to-innovation process that clearly outlines the key criteria and assessment procedures that your organization applies to new ideas. Such a funnel often includes a mix of crowdsourced criteria for early filtering, e.g., the number of likes that a proposed idea receives from employees, and later moves toward assessment by an expert committee or digital leadership group.

Keep the momentum. Facilitating and nurturing a culture of innovation and ideation is just as important as having a clear and commonly accepted process. The good news is that both things go hand in hand. When you set up the innovation process, a surefire way to maintain the momentum is to keep the originator involved, as either a key stakeholder or contributor or even as one leading the development. This way, ideators own their successes and failures and take direct accountability for the progress of development. In addition, broadcast success stories both internally and externally, so that future idea originators are encouraged to come forward.

Self-Reflection Questions

Are you tapping into the creativity of all stakeholders in your organization?

Do you make sure that no idea is overlooked, whether internally or externally sourced?

Do you have a clear and transparent process for idea evaluation and prioritization?

Are you leveraging the power of positive reinforcement by highlighting success stories internally and externally?

RELATED CHAPTERS

Taking an Inventory of Existing Digital Initiatives (Chapter 5)

Building and Managing Technology Infrastructure (Chapter 11)

Building Hyperawareness into Your Organization (Chapter 12)

Investing in Startups (Chapter 14)

Implementing Open Innovation Effectively (Chapter 15)

Moving from Product-Centricity to Services and Solutions (Chapter 17)

Scaling Digital Initiatives (Chapter 27)

Measuring the Performance of Digital Initiatives (Chapter 28)

SCALING DIGITAL INITIATIVES

Organizations focus significant attention on building and testing promising digital innovations and technologies. Often, this leads to successful pilots or proofs-of-concept. Yet these organizations struggle when it comes to generating real business value from digital initiatives at scale. This "startup to scale-up" challenge is one of the toughest elements of any digital transformation. The solution starts at the beginning: initiatives that scale successfully tend to be designed and developed with scaling in mind. However, planning for scale, by itself, is not enough to overcome the odds stacked against most digital initiatives. They need to be carefully and purposefully shepherded through different stages of growth using the approaches and strategies outlined below. Because business value is typically created only *after* a digital initiative is rolled out at scale, it's important to get it right.

WHY IT MATTERS

Digital projects often start as promising experiments. They are well funded, strongly supported by management, and staffed with smart and dedicated people. Under these conditions, they show great potential. However, most digital projects struggle, and ultimately fail, as they are expanded and replicated.[1] Those that survive often do so as pale shadows of their former selves, after being subjected to a multitude of cuts and compromises.

Scaling a digital initiative is about moving beyond the pilot stage to operationalize solutions that are sustainable and growth-creating.[2] A 2018 survey from analyst firm Gartner found that 83 percent of companies were in the planning, design, or tinkering stages of digital transformation, while only 17 percent had scaled their digital initiatives.[3] Another study, by Accenture, found that the largest contributor to digital transformation failure was an inability to effectively scale promising digital initiatives.[4]

BEST PRACTICES AND KEY INSIGHTS

Scaling digital initiatives is a task fraught with difficulty. And there is no one-size-fits-all approach. A number of factors need to be considered.

Align Scale with Ambition

The level of attention and activity should be in direct proportion to the ambition of the project. Digital projects that are small, discrete, or of limited duration often do not need to be scaled. For these types of initiatives—e.g., the development of a custom application for a small market—the focus can be tilted toward usability, functionality, and compliance.

More ambitious projects, however, must focus on scaling challenges from the get-go. Alignment with the prevailing IT landscape is often a necessary consideration, but it does not end there. Many digital projects fail to scale, not because of IT incompatibility, but because of organizational or cultural resistance.

Planning to Scale

There is a truism around scaling that states, "The longer a project goes without scaling, the harder it is to scale." Thus, scalability should be considered from the very beginning of a digital project. The following questions should form part of the planning process:

- How difficult will it be to integrate this initiative into existing processes and structures?

- What are the likely sources of resistance to this initiative?

- Will this initiative be compliant with existing rules and norms?

- Are there natural limits to the growth of this initiative?

Diego de Coen, former CDO of JTI, stressed the importance of regular scaling reviews for digital initiatives. He explained that as soon as it is clear that "there is value coming out of an idea, from that moment on we already start the IT processes. So we start already in parallel, with a different team looking at cybersecurity, another team looking if it is legally possible to roll that specific solution out in certain markets, and so on."[5]

Relying on scaling reviews of this kind can help leaders anticipate and avoid any challenges or bottlenecks along the critical path. Digital projects that are more radical need a "reality check" against the expected future payoffs.[6]

> What I continually say to my team is, "It's very easy to develop clever functionality and clever features. It's extremely hard to push it out at scale to our entire network of 23,000 banks. And so, unless you have a plan to get the features into 23,000 banks, I'm not interested."
> —JORN LAMBERT, EXECUTIVE VICE PRESIDENT DIGITAL SOLUTIONS, MASTERCARD[7]

Another way that organizations can plan for scale is to proactively anticipate the skill gaps that exist when moving from a pilot to full rollout. Very often, global companies will create country and regional pilots staffed with local development teams. When it comes to scaling, all the competencies (and budgets) are local. Hence, it becomes very difficult to shift the people with the right skills to extend the pilot further. The solution is to (1) create champions from the pilots, who can steward the project through a wider rollout, and (2) include people from other parts of the business in the pilot, so they can use their experience and newly acquired knowledge to help mitigate this problem.

Don't Fall into the Cut-and-Paste Trap

A common scaling mistake is to think that if a digital initiative works in one context, it will work well in other contexts. This assumption is almost universally false. Even very successful digital pilots need to be adapted to work at scale. Everything from apps to e-commerce sites to agile ways of working will invariably need to be adjusted to meet the needs of different parts of a business.

Rather than "cut and paste," we suggest "cut, adapt, paste, adjust." The first stage, "cut," consists of isolating a successful digital initiative. This initiative may be developed from scratch in a kind of greenfield environment, or it may be identified as working well in one part of an organization. The second stage, "adapt," consists of modifying the initiative to improve its portability across different parts of the organization. Activities at this stage might consist of feature standardization, IT compatibility checks, branding consistency, and legal and regulatory compliance. Once this stage is complete, the initiative is ready to be "pasted" (stage three).

However, although the initiative may be standardized and compliant, it will almost certainly *not* work effectively in all contexts. This brings us to the final stage, "adjust." Here, small changes are made to optimize the initiative to local conditions. These adjustments may include the addition of relevant local features, tweaks to the user experience, insertion of culture and language adjustments, and so on.

An example of "cut, adapt, paste, adjust" can be found in transactional websites. It makes little sense for large global retailers to develop unique transactional websites across countries or product lines. Thus, they tend to develop a standardized approach. However, there are major differences that need to be considered, including local languages, compliance rules, cultural norms, local application compatibility, etc. Therefore, global standards may be developed for transaction processing, product information and image libraries, customer databases, and so on. From there, adjustments are made regarding the look and feel, branding, language, and so on.

Make the Shift from Push to Pull

A main source of failure to scale is lack of buy-in from key stakeholders, such as executives, internal users, or customers. Digital initiatives may receive executive permission and funding to scale (they have push), but they typically fail unless they are sought after by relevant stakeholders (they do not have pull). Transitioning a digital initiative from the "push" to the "pull" stage is critical to successful scaling.

Often a push is necessary at the outset to encourage users to try the new initiative, but unless that push is translated into a pull, it will almost certainly fail. "If you scale an initiative by pushing it out actively, you will always need to continuously push it, and it will never grow organically by itself," explained Chetan Tolia of Swiss bank UBS.[8]

To create a pull effect, Sven Meier of German energy giant EnBW describes how he worked closely with a small number of business units, which focused on generating first results and demonstrating the value of the initiative. "Real results were generated. From that moment on, word spread quickly, and we had a hard time responding to the pull from the rest of the firm."[9]

Some companies have successfully created a "pull" effect by staffing the digital initiative from across the business units most likely to be impacted. In that way, specific business units' requirements are built in early, and the transfer of competence is made easier by redeploying the development team to its original business units to facilitate scaling.

Research has shown that there is no single way to generate pull: sometimes it's driven by rational, outcome-based factors. At other times, emotional factors are the key drivers.[10] In some cases, units are specifically built to create pull and facilitate the scaling of digital initiatives.

Randstad North America's CDO Alan Stukalsky noted that his company built a digital factory that is "responsible for taking great ideas, great concepts and products that have been built in a single location, like the U.S. or Mexico, or Japan—a product or technology or a process improvement that can 'travel'—and then packaging it up and putting it in such a way that other countries can easily implement it so they don't have to build it from scratch."[11]

For Large Initiatives, Find the Tipping Point

During large initiatives, there is often a tipping point at which it makes sense to transition a phased scaling approach to a big-bang implementation. This can occur in cases where there are strong network effects.

For example, during the early stages of the COVID-19 pandemic, many organizations were suddenly faced with the task of organizing remote working arrangements at scale. For many of these organizations, work-from-home arrangements had been dealt with on an ad hoc basis through a variety of different applications. The reality of moving from a small percentage of the workforce working from home to a majority required consolidation around a single technology.

At IMD Business School, we were using a variety of collaboration tools, including Cisco Webex, Adobe Connect, Skype, Facetime, and WhatsApp. After the pandemic arrived and more than 90 percent of staff started to work from home, and program delivery moved to virtual platforms, an institutional decision was made to adopt a single application: Zoom. After the decision was made, all other solutions were phased out.

Another tipping point can occur if attempts to scale meet cultural roadblocks. Dutch bank Rabobank built a Digital Hub in its head office for developing innovative new digital solutions for customer journeys, such as loan applications and the management of lost or stolen cards. The process Rabobank used to develop these solutions was based on agile ways of working, a methodology that was new to the bank. Although the Digital Hub was very successful, the bank encountered difficulties when it tried to scale the hub to other parts of the bank. There was a clash between the new agile approach and the traditional processes, culture, and incentives within the rest of the bank. It became difficult to maintain two distinct systems at the same time. For Rabobank, scaling the agile approach to digital innovation had hit a cultural wall.

The bank's leadership considered the benefits of the agile approach, along with the cultural challenges of scaling, and decided to make a wholesale, big-bang shift to agile methods across the entire retail bank. The agile methodology that was developed within its Digital Hub was modified for a widespread rollout, and within six months, it became the dominant approach for all product and service development and improvement activities.

Leverage a Common Challenge or Opportunity

As a rule, people are more willing to cooperate if they have something to gain. The same is true for scaling—e.g., responding to a shared problem or challenge, such as developing a common approach to attacking a key competitor. In other cases, cooperation can be fostered by finding new ways to capture opportunities, such as using the customer acquisition tools built into a CRM solution.

We have found that it can be extremely helpful to build scaling around an enterprisewide strategy or platform initiative. If different business units know that they need to align to an organizational strategy or platform, they tend to be more open to exploring options for scaling the relevant digital solutions.

Swiss industrial giant ABB has been operating for more than 100 years, and over that time, its four major business units developed a great deal of autonomy. This autonomy made scaling digital initiatives across business units extremely challenging. A key breakthrough came with the establishment of a companywide digital platform called "ABB Ability." This platform consisted of a suite of compatible protocols and technologies that was designed to work across the whole portfolio of connected products and services.

ABB's former CDO Guido Jouret explained how ABB Ability works: "This is essentially software that allows our business units to build connected robots more quickly or connected motors more quickly or offer new digital services to our customers. My team basically scouts the technology landscape, looking for promising companies and their technology. We then procure them and make them available to our business units."[12]

After ABB's business units were required to use the Ability platform, Jouret found it much easier to build and scale compatible digital initiatives.

• • •

The startup to scale-up challenge is one of the largest contributors to the high failure rate of digital transformation projects. Scaling challenges should be considered from the very beginning of a digital project. Technical obstacles to scaling are often significant, particularly with respect to IT compatibility and compliance, but they pale in comparison to organizational and cultural barriers.

Hacker's Toolbox

Plan to scale from the very beginning. Ask yourself if the systems that underpin the digital transformation, such as applications, programming resources, and systems hardware, can accommodate the growth required to scale. If the systems can't be scaled, redesign them or drop them. It may be helpful to involve as many potential blockers as possible early in an initiative's development, including IT, cybersecurity, legal, HR, and compliance. These people will help you to anticipate the potential scaling challenges in advance.

Do whatever you can to accelerate the transition of a digital initiative from push to pull. People will often resist a new digital initiative. An exception to this general rule was the move to working from home in response to the COVID-19 pandemic. People didn't resist very much for a simple reason—they had no choice. The push was external. If you can orchestrate a similar pressure for other digital initiatives, that can help. If not, then you need to create your own reasons to adopt (your own push), which often comes as a mandate from senior management. The pull typically occurs when other parts of the organization see the benefits of the initiative. Therefore, the more you can do to measure and then communicate the success of a digital project, the more likely it becomes that the push converts to a pull.

Scaling doesn't mean cut-and-paste. For each digital initiative, make a clear distinction between elements that are core and those that are modifiable. Core elements must be accepted as is—there is no negotiation.[13] Elements that fit into the core category may include cybersecurity and privacy policies, compatibility with existing data formats, connectivity with widely used systems and processes including cloud solutions, corporate branding, and so forth. Then there are elements that can, and often should, be adapted to local conditions. These elements may include local language support, cultural adaptations, general look and feel, and linkages to locally used applications, via APIs or other connective tools. Finding the right balance between core and modifiable elements for each digital initiative is critical.

Self-Reflection Questions

Is it likely that this initiative will need to be scaled in the future? If so, have you spent enough time thinking through potential scaling challenges or barriers?

Who are the people likely to be negatively impacted by scaling this initiative? (They may include people working on similar initiatives and/or IT and other implementation partners.)

Have you established the groundwork for selling the project internally to accelerate the shift from compliance-driven "push" to benefit-driven "pull"?

Is there a common vision, purpose, or platform to which you can link the initiative?

RELATED CHAPTERS

Building Organizational Momentum and Engagement (Chapter 4)

Choosing the Right Digital Governance Model (Chapter 8)

Building and Managing Technology Infrastructure (Chapter 11)

Setting Up a Pipeline of Digital Initiatives (Chapter 26)

How to Leverage Digital for Organizational Resilience (Chapter 30)

MEASURING THE PERFORMANCE OF DIGITAL INITIATIVES

Peter Drucker's mantra, "You can't manage what you don't measure," applies as much to digital transformation as it does to other business matters. But digital transformation presents a number of additional challenges. In some areas, such as digital marketing, there is a plethora of metrics. Here the challenge is to identify the *right* metrics. In most other areas, however, effective metrics are still emerging. This is why many executives have only a vague sense of how well their digital transformations are faring.

To effectively measure a transformation, it's important to first develop well-defined objectives. Without these, it's hard to know *what* to measure. There are four generic areas that will encompass most objectives: operational efficiency, customer engagement, employee engagement, and new value creation. Each has its own set of metrics. However, because it's often harder to measure the performance "forest" than the "trees," we recommend using digital scorecards (supported by dashboards) to visualize the overall performance of the transformation.

WHY IT MATTERS

Unlike areas such as finance, sales, and marketing, there are few widely agreed-upon metrics for assessing the performance of digital initiatives. Many managers with whom we've spoken have relied on relatively generic success measures, such as adoption rates of new digital tools, but failed to evaluate whether a tangible performance impact had been generated.

According to a 2020 study by BCG, only two out of five organizations have created measures to link digital tools and technologies to business impacts. The study also found that those that *did* create measures were much more likely to be associated with winning transformation programs.[1]

Many digital projects are inherently complex: they require a lot of cross-functional coordination, but are often subject to the same business-case processes as standard IT projects. Indeed, a 2020 study by consulting firm Gartner found that almost 50 percent of organizations had no specific metrics for measuring digital success.[2] As a result, digital projects are often labeled "failures" because they were established with false or unrealistic expectations.

BEST PRACTICES AND KEY INSIGHTS

Measuring progress on digital initiatives is challenging because they frequently do not produce results that can be directly quantified in a meaningful way. Rather than creating a complex algorithm, a better way to assess progress is to build a digital scorecard that captures real-time developments on all projects in an organization's digital portfolio and can be displayed in a dashboard format.

Begin with Clear Objectives

Elsewhere in this book, we have discussed the importance of establishing clear objectives for digital transformation—and these objectives must be consistently and effectively measured. Unfortunately, digital measures are sometimes poor proxies for the desired objectives. For example, the success of an app is often measured by downloads. The more an app is downloaded, the more it is seen as successful. However, app *usage* would be a far better measure of success because many apps are downloaded and rarely used.

> There is a huge amount of uncertainty on where you're moving, so the checks you do are different. It's more about checking your assumptions often so that you're able to stop projects quickly and don't get into big investments not knowing if it's going to be a real success.
> —BART LEURS, CHIEF DIGITAL TRANSFORMATION OFFICER OF RABOBANK[3]

Once a clear objective has been chosen, it must be converted into a format that can be measured. For example, Cisco's objective for digital transformation between 2015 and 2020, as described in an earlier chapter, was 40/40/2020, where 40 percent of total company revenue would come from recurring sources and 40 percent would come from software by the end of 2020.

In Cisco's case, it became necessary to create a clear distinction between revenues that accrued from one-time sales of products or services (such as a piece of networking equipment) and revenues that came from the sale of subscriptions (such as a renewable videoconferencing license). Similarly, the company needed to differentiate between software and hardware products and allocate the revenues of each separately—even in cases where they were bundled into a single offering.

Divide Digital Measures into Categories

We suggest dividing measures into four categories that directly link to how digital tools and technologies can positively impact business performance. They are:

1. Operational efficiency, or reduction of costs through improved operational speed and efficiency

2. Customer engagement, or improvement in customer satisfaction and interactivity

3. Employee engagement, or improvement in employee satisfaction and productivity

4. New value creation, or the creation of new sources of revenue and profit

See Table 28.1 for some examples of digital success metrics across these four categories.

Table 28.1 Examples of Digital Success Measures Across Four Categories

Digital Measurement Category	Operational Efficiency	Customer Engagement	Employee Engagement	New Source of Value Creation
High-level objective of the measures	To save costs and improve operational speed and efficiency	To improve customer satisfaction and engagement	To improve employee satisfaction and productivity	To find new sources of revenue and profit
Examples of measures	Time to market for digital products/services	Customer NPS on use of digital tools	Employee NPS on use of digital tools	Percentage of revenues from digital products/services
	Employee hours saved due to digital tools	Customer usage of digital tools (e.g., time on app or functions used)	Employee satisfaction with remote work	Percentage of revenues from digital channels (e.g., web, app)
	Cost savings due to digital tools (e.g., predictive maintenance)	Percentage lead conversion across digital channels	Employee usage of digital platforms (e.g., intranet, internal social networks)	Digital versus nondigital customer profitability
	Reduction in defects due to digital tools	Click-through rates and other digital marketing measures	New ideas generated via digital tools	New customer acquisition via digital channels
	Percentage of operations handled by digital means	Customer retention through digital channels	Degree of collaboration among employees across digital tools	
		Customer hours saved due to digital tools		
		Percentage of customers who are active or on a site or platform		

Operational Efficiency

Here, measurements are largely concerned with the use of digital tools and technologies to increase speed and reduce costs. Although objectives in this category may not be as exciting as customer-facing objectives, or those linked with new sources of value creation, they can add a lot of value. For example, predictive and preventative maintenance systems can significantly reduce defects and the costs of unnecessary equipment shutdowns. According to the US Department of Energy, predictive maintenance programs can result in a 25–30 percent reduction in maintenance costs and a 35–45 percent reduction in downtime.[4]

Other tools can reduce time to market for products and services by removing processes and other steps in a value chain. For example, after UK hospitality giant Mitchells & Butlers incorporated automation into how it handled paperwork, it saved more than 20,000 employee hours and more than 3 million pieces of paper.[5] It was also able to identify errors far sooner.

Customer Engagement

Perhaps the most mature area of digital measurement can be found in digital marketing, thanks to the rise of social media as an alternative channel for engaging with customers. These measures seek to assess marketing's effectiveness across different stages of a customer journey—from awareness of a product or service, to a specific action (such as clicking through to a website), to eventual purchase, adoption, and repurchase and advocacy.[6]

A number of measures have become key parts of any digital marketer's toolkit. These include traffic measurement, impressions, click-through rates, conversion rates, drop-offs, mentions, reposts, churn, and so on.

Beyond digital marketing tools, measures can be used to assess customer satisfaction through pulse surveys or NPS scores. Customer activity can be measured on a site or platform to ensure that customers' attention is being captured effectively. Another way that customer engagement can be measured is by time saved.

Netflix, Uber, Amazon, and other digital giants have effectively saved time by automating the process of watching, ordering transportation, and shopping. These time savings—such as the time it takes to find an answer to a question through an intelligent agent versus a call center—can be measured.

Singapore-based DBS Bank's digital transformation led to the development of the "customer hours" concept, which has since been adopted by other digital front-runners, including Google. The concept of customer hours (a unit of wait time for a customer) was born of a desire to make the customer's life better. Although the bank hoped to take 10 million customer hours out of the bank, it ended up taking out 250 million hours. And this helped generate a shared sense of purpose among DBS employees.[7]

Employee Engagement

Digital tools, like intranets, are often used to improve employee engagement, and the COVID-19 pandemic accelerated the use of these tools. Measures to assess how well digital tools are functioning could include the number of tasks that have become automated, revenue generation per employee, etc. It's important to measure tool adoption and use, including how many employees are using a tool, whether they are using all the tool's features, and how much time is saved by using the tool.

For example, McDonald's introduced gamification into its till-training exercises. Employees reported having a better understanding of the new system, and the corporation saw improved employee performance and engagement, as well as an increase in average order value.[8]

New Value Creation

In addition to operational efficiency and customer and employee engagement, it's important to determine whether digital tools and technologies have a positive impact on revenue and profitability through new forms of value creation. Value creation may come from new digital products, services, or business models. Examples of measures include the percentage of revenues and profits that come from digital products, services, or channels. Many organizations are offering their products and services through new channels, such as own-brand e-commerce, online marketplaces, and apps. The relative performance of these channels needs to be assessed.

Create a Visual Digital Scorecard

It's important to not only develop individual measures of success, but also establish an overall assessment of performance based on the objectives of the digital transformation. For example, Cisco might have dozens of measures to evaluate recurring revenue and software targets across R&D (e.g., new product development), manufacturing (e.g., production targets), marketing (e.g., awareness targets), and sales (e.g., revenue and profitability targets). Only after these measures have been consolidated would it be possible to assess whether the 40/40/2020 target had been met.

The algorithm or scorecard used to consolidate the individual measures into an omnibus assessment must be determined by each organization. We recommend collecting the measures in as close to real time as possible and presenting them as a visual dashboard. Dashboards can be created from almost all databases and data analytics tools.

When Danish sportswear company Hummel decided to put omnichannel retailing at the core of its digital transformation, it faced the challenge of tracking various indicators across different sales channels. It responded by creating customized, real-time dashboard tracking indicators (such as follower counts) across various social media platforms, unique page views and visits, e-commerce transactions, etc.[9] The most effective dashboards are visually appealing, up to date, and configurable, so that individual managers can modify the dashboard to fit their particular needs.

Hacker's Toolbox

Be mindful to have clear objectives since they make for better measures. It's hard to develop appropriate measures to track your digital initiatives. It's even harder if your objectives are unclear. First, clarify what you want to achieve; then ensure that your measures are consistent with your objectives.

Be careful with proxy measures. You can't always measure exactly what you want to achieve, so proxy measures are inevitable. Some proxy measures are better than others. (Recall the example of how app downloads are a poor proxy for app performance.) Likewise, cost reduction can be a relevant measure for improved efficiency, but because costs can be allocated in so many ways, it's often hard to specify the impact of particular digital solutions on the overall cost picture. A better metric for efficiency may be *hours saved*, which can usually be measured quite precisely (for employees or customers), and can thus provide a strong proxy for efficiency.

Create an intuitive, real-time overview. With a broad portfolio of initiatives and associated measures, an overall assessment of your digital transformation status may be hard to achieve. Usually, the best way forward is not to develop a complicated algorithm that combines all the KPIs into one number, but to create a digital transformation scorecard (supported by intuitive visualizations) that captures the real-time situation across the digital portfolio. Business intelligence tools like Tableau can create customized dashboards, which can then be adjusted for different stakeholder groups.

Self-Reflection Questions

Do you have clear measures for all initiatives in your digital portfolio?

Are metrics and targets clearly communicated and documented?

Who's in charge of establishing, controlling, and regularly updating measures for digital initiatives? Is there agreement across all stakeholders on the metrics and targets?

How easy is it for you to give an overview of the current state of your organization's digital transformation? What could make it easier?

RELATED CHAPTERS

Creating a Clear and Powerful Transformation Objective (Chapter 1)

Funding Your Digital Transformation Program (Chapter 6)

Building a Balanced Portfolio of Digital Initiatives (Chapter 20)

Scaling Digital Initiatives (Chapter 27)

How to Leverage Digital for Organizational Resilience (Chapter 30)

STAYING ON TOP OF
NEW TECHNOLOGIES

The ability to find, source, and experiment with new technologies is vital to many digital success stories. A Forrester report concluded that 86 percent of digitally mature companies view technology as a critical driver of business strategy.[1] But trying to keep pace with new developments can feel like "drinking from a digital fire hose" because technological innovation occurs so fast. So how do digital leaders determine what technology is potentially disruptive and what is merely a shiny object? How can they systematically place their bets on the emerging winners?

In today's environment, the best course of action is a "real option approach." This entails making many small bets, rather than a few big ones, to reduce innovation risk and ensure a broad range of options for future investments. Similarly, leveraging an ecosystem of innovation partners increases the odds of finding the next big thing. From there, it's all about moving fast—testing, prototyping, and then scaling or killing.

WHY IT MATTERS

History books are filled with postmortem tales of organizations that failed to spot, or react fast enough to, emerging technologies that would soon dominate their industries—and companies like Kodak,[2] Nokia,[3] and Blockbuster[4] are their tragic heroes. Timing is everything. Research indicates that emerging technology evolves slowly at first and then accelerates to widespread adoption, profoundly disrupting companies and whole industries in the process.[5] Jumping on every technological bandwagon to be on the safe side is a bad (and costly) strategy, especially at a time when new technologies are developed faster than ever before.[6] To sort the wheat from the chaff, organizations need to implement a systematic approach to identify, scope, and experiment with emerging technologies. Although uncertainty can't be eliminated, it *can* be managed.

BEST PRACTICES AND KEY INSIGHTS

Digital transformation and emerging technologies go hand in hand. In large corporations, CTOs and CIOs should make it their mission to identify technologies that may provide future value to their organizations. But they shouldn't stop there. They must also make the whole executive team aware of the potential business impact and timing of these technologies. This requires skillful communication, experiential learning, and persuasive powers, because nurturing an emerging technology is an up-front investment with a very uncertain return. For this reason, organizations should adopt a systematic approach, based on informed decision making, to identify, scope, and experiment with new technologies.

Cast Your Net Wide

There are many sources of new technologies, from in-house R&D departments to research centers, universities, and startups, to vendors and government labs (among others). In addition, technology innovation takes different forms—from basic research in materials science, to smart software applications, to advanced machine learning algorithms. Thus, it's important to put more focus on the areas that could directly impact the business or advance the digital transformation.

Establishing internal processes is a sensible first step. Promoting constant communication among R&D, engineering leaders, and the executive team is critical. But as technology penetrates every part of the organization, the firm's nontechnical functions also have a role to play. For example, we have seen new roles, such as CTO of marketing or CTO of HR, tasked with filtering through all the emerging technologies that could impact the firm at the functional level.

However, the bulk of the effort will occur outside the organization's traditional boundaries. Therefore, digital leaders should be alert to any media and stakeholders that might help them uncover new technology sources—or at least point them in the right direction. These include everything from social media and technology forums to conferences and universities, as well as regulatory and standards bodies. If this seems like a time-consuming effort, that's because it *is*.

> These big trends are not that hard to spot (they get talked and written about a lot), but they can be strangely hard for large organizations to embrace. We're in the middle of an obvious one right now: machine learning and artificial intelligence.
>
> —JEFF BEZOS, CEO, AMAZON[7]

The good news is that some companies have developed innovative practices to manage these complex external linkages—e.g., external technology advisory councils whose job is to report on promising new technologies and their potential impact. We've also seen CEOs allocate different emerging technology fields to each executive committee member. Each member is then tasked with externally researching and assessing the technology's potential and reporting back to the leadership team via structured workshops. This not only provides accountability, but also increases top-team awareness and promotes healthy debates on impact and timing to support the technology strategy.

Create Many Options Instead of Relying on One Big Bet

Constantly confronted with exciting new technologies, executives may feel obliged to lock in big investments in the early days of development. Doing this, however, severely limits the freedom for future decisions and creates sunk costs, something to be avoided in areas with high levels of uncertainty. Toyota was very late to the electric vehicle party because it focused instead on hydrogen-cell technology (a promising but ultimately disappointing solution) and non-plug-in hybrids.[8]

Tendayi Viki, partner at Strategyzer, explains: "The problem with the business case in the early stages of an innovation project is that the document will be filled with assumptions and very little knowledge. Leaders then have to decide whether they believe the story in the business case or not."[9]

A better strategy is to focus on creating future options, rather than narrowing one's degree of freedom, by placing many small bets instead of a few big ones.[10] The legendary founder of HP, Bill Hewlett, was well known for preferring to make "small bets to uncover unpredictable opportunities."[11] Making small commitments across a broad portfolio of promising technology innovations allows digital leaders to increase their investments once the payoffs become clearer, and minimize their losses in case of failures.

How should digital leaders determine which "small bets" to make? Two popular sources of intel on new technologies include Gartner's Hype Cycle[12] and Deloitte's annual "Tech Trends" report.[13] Another good starting point is ThoughtWorks Technology Radar, which provides both a generic overview and an assessment of new technologies. This resource also enables leaders to build their own radar and rank new developments into four areas: hold, assess, trial, and adopt.[14] Digital front-runners, like Cisco and Zalando, are using this approach, and they even publish their own radars.[15] Ultimately, however, there are no guarantees when it comes to evaluating the likely business impact and utility of a new technology.

Manage Hypothesis-Driven Experimentation

Once a promising new technology is identified, organizations should pursue a systematic approach to assessment and evaluation—often by formulating hypotheses and testing with experiments. Digital leaders, like global travel giant Booking.com, have embraced experimentation to the extent that it's become part of their regular business operations. After hiring a dedicated director of experimentation, Booking.com now runs more than 1,000 concurrent experiments on any given day.

Most large organizations have in-house capabilities to test and experiment with new tech. But with many new technologies, finding a use case that works can be just as difficult as developing the hardware and software. Moreover, in today's connected world, it's increasingly unlikely that a single organization can move an impactful new technology from idea to market all by itself. This has enhanced the importance of innovation networks and partner ecosystems, which, together, can generate, develop, and deliver technological innovations.

To ensure a clear value proposition for new technologies, successful innovators follow a portfolio approach that includes internalization, using practices like in-house test beds equipped with anonymized customer data, combined with an incubator or accelerator program, to capture best practices and new knowledge from the startup ecosystem. Some organizations also pursue joint research programs with other companies, universities, or research institutions.[16]

But how do you orchestrate a distributed approach to hypothesizing, testing, and experimentation? One example is ADAMOS,[17] a consortium (strategic alliance) of industrial manufacturing and engineering companies that aims to develop a technological platform for the industrial internet of things and Industry 4.0. Whereas each company would separately struggle to develop a competitive proposition in this fast-moving arena, ADAMOS allows all its members to benefit from a shared approach to technology scoping, experimentation, and development.

In the digital age, very few organizations have the capacities and capabilities to pioneer technological innovations by themselves. Thus, most organizations, small and large, will benefit from collaborative innovation strategies that leverage the power of networks.[18]

• • •

Although digital transformation is about people, organizations that want to lead the digital revolution must be experts in scoping, evaluating, and implementing new technologies into value-adding business propositions faster than their competition.

Hacker's Toolbox

Leverage curiosity and create a tech buzz. Creating a buzz around new technology in your organization is a great way to encourage everybody's involvement in the search for new technologies. Participate in (or sponsor) innovation events like hackathons, accelerators, or incubators to engage with the startup ecosystem and internalize new technologies. Make sure to capture new ideas via collaborative or social communication media, like an internal blog or tools like Slack or Discord. Avoid early judgment and invite everyone to participate, regardless of technological background knowledge or job role. Some companies create dedicated communication channels where "exciting new tech" can be discussed.

Focus on small bets to hedge your chances. Follow a real options approach of placing "many small bets instead of a few big bets" to keep your future options open. Technological innovation is inherently high risk, so the key is to leave the door open for future investments rather than taking a chance with early developments. Don't go all in until the technology has been matured, tested, and put into the real-world context in market situations that are similar to yours.

Build experimentation into your organization's DNA. It's not enough to just keep your eyes open and discuss new ideas. Establish a concrete pathway for new technology ideas to enter your organization in the form of experiments, so that you can make quick decisions about their fit and potential. If you have digital customer touchpoints, this will be easier to do. To get started, walk the talk and find out how experimentation can be formally integrated into your current business processes, so that it becomes part of your organization's DNA.

Self-Reflection Questions

How long has it been since you last discussed new technological opportunities for your organization?

Who's in charge of scouting new technologies for your organization? Is there a dedicated role or process in place?

When someone brings up technology innovations, does the organization focus on finding positive aspects and a "fit," or on reasons why it would never work here?

Have you hedged your bets across potential breakthrough technologies, or are all your eggs in one basket?

RELATED CHAPTERS

Building Hyperawareness into Your Organization (Chapter 12)

Managing Partnerships and Ecosystems (Chapter 13)

Investing in Startups (Chapter 14)

Implementing Open Innovation Effectively (Chapter 15)

Building a Balanced Portfolio of Digital Initiatives (Chapter 20)

HOW TO LEVERAGE DIGITAL FOR ORGANIZATIONAL RESILIENCE

I n recent years, resilience has become an important priority as organizations face disruptions of increasing frequency and intensity. Resilient organizations are able to bounce back, grow, and prosper in a new reality. With many organizations dependent on data, analytics, digital tools, and automation for their processes, digital technologies now constitute a critical element of business continuity and organizational resilience to sudden external shocks. In short, resilience is now an important ingredient in any digital transformation. If done correctly, digital transformation can be leveraged not only to build long-term organizational resilience, but also to deliver short-term gains such as top line growth and reduced cost.

WHY IT MATTERS

Some organizations outperform their peers during downturns. Others lose ground or don't survive. In fact, only one in seven companies increased both sales growth and profit margins during recent downturns.[1] Following major external shocks (such as the terrorist attacks on September 11, 2001, or the COVID-19 pandemic), short-term behavior prevailed. During the COVID-19 pandemic, for example, a quarter of organizations abandoned their investments in innovation projects[2] as economic uncertainty pushed them into survival mode.

By contrast, resilient organizations continue to invest and quickly deploy resources toward existing or new sources of value, rather than reducing their cost structure. During the COVID-19 crisis, apparel maker Levi Strauss reaped the benefits of its investments in e-commerce infrastructure and technology. In a matter of days, it was able to fulfill online orders from both its distribution and retail centers. It also launched digitally connected services such as curbside pickup and product customization, and leveraged AI to analyze and drive promotions, which enabled it to sell six times more inventory.[3]

American Express, which faced rising default rates and failing consumer demand, used the 2008 financial crisis as an opportunity to invest. Although the company initially sought to reduce costs, it quickly refocused to invest in early-stage technology startups that would accelerate its transition into digital commerce.[4] A decade later, American Express remains the undisputed leader in the market with a $92 billion market value, even as new technology startups have emerged to challenge it.[5]

BEST PRACTICES AND KEY INSIGHTS

Like many corporate buzzwords, such as "agility" and "digital transformation," "resilience" is often used but rarely defined. For us, an organization can be truly resilient only if it displays the following three traits of nimbleness, robustness, and responsiveness. *Nimbleness* is the ability to avoid threats. Nimble organizations have the ability to sense danger and move quickly to avoid damage. However, even the nimblest organizations cannot avoid every setback. Pandemics, natural disasters, and recessions tend to strike indiscriminately, and so *robustness*—the ability to absorb shocks—is a crucial organizational attribute, as is *responsiveness*—the ability to bounce back quickly and effectively from the shocks. Each of these resilience components can be enhanced through digital tools and technologies.

How Can Digital Enhance Nimbleness?

Before an organization can respond to threats, it needs to be able to *sense the environment* and see the threats coming. Thus, a strong *early warning* capability is a key to being nimble. Digital tools can improve an organization's ability to sense its environment in a number of ways. For example, social listening can act as an early warning system for detecting negative feedback or product/ service issues. In addition, anonymous employee feedback mechanisms can alert management to problems that would otherwise remain hidden.

Moving Quickly to Avoid Threats

Sensing is one thing, but responding is another. Because organizations are often handicapped by slow decision making, they are unable to react in time— even when they know what they need to do. Business intelligence software (such as dashboards) can help present data that will facilitate quick decision making, as can analytics tools that support decision making by rapidly suggesting alternatives. Meanwhile, collaboration tools can ensure that data and information are captured and shared across an entire organization, so that the people who need it can get it at speed. Finally, virtualization technologies can ensure that businesses continue to function even if key sites are compromised.

How Can Digital Enhance Robustness?

Robustness is the ability to absorb blows. Fragmented or spaghetti systems often contain potential failure points, many of which are hidden. Thus, it is important to build digital tools on top of a *stable technology infrastructure*. The importance of rapidly integrating new digital initiatives with existing IT rules, systems, and capabilities is often underestimated, even in normal times. Digital transformation is an end-to-end process—one closely intertwined with back-end business processes and systems. Unsurprisingly, therefore, the successful cases of transformation that we identified were often accompanied by a standardized approach to infrastructure.

> Bad companies are destroyed by crises;
> good companies survive them;
> great companies are improved by them.
> —ANDREW GROVE, COFOUNDER OF INTEL CORPORATION[6]

In organizations composed of several business units, a core digital infrastructure consolidates shared digital capabilities into a single platform to support different business processes. Take the example of global consumer goods company Nestlé, a company with products and services spread across different industries and markets. After the onset of the COVID-19 pandemic, Nestlé retooled its approach to data to respond to shifting consumer preferences. It set up tools to predict supply chain shifts and rethought how its factories should operate to cope with travel restrictions. "We wanted to prevent out-of-stock situations at retailers," said former CIO Filippo Catalano.[7]

A dedicated internal team built a dashboard to track COVID-19 outbreaks down to individual zip codes and to correlate this data with internal manufacturing and supply chain data to maintain product supply. The success of this initiative was partly due to Nestlé's GLOBE (Global Business Excellence) program, first introduced in 2000 with the aim of assessing and consolidating the different IT systems used by Nestlé and all its subsidiaries. As Eberhard Ruess, former head of Nestlé's CIO office, noted, "Without this common infrastructure, our distributed data structure would have been difficult to implement and scale."[8] For Nestlé, acquiring core data that was interoperable, accessible, and reusable across the company, and leveraging it with new AI techniques, made all the difference.

Setting Up Cybersecurity Prevention and Containment Measures

When organizations are under acute pressure, they can become prime targets for socially engineered attacks, such as phishing attempts or malware. Palo Alto Networks identified more than 40,000 malicious domains using coronavirus-related names during the first six months of the COVID-19 pandemic.[9]

Some cyberattacks can be avoided, or their impact reduced, by strong prevention and containment measures. But at some point, it's likely that an organization will be hit hard. A strong cybersecurity response plan will ensure that the firm is back up and running quickly. For example, many organizations are following a 3-2-1 approach to data backups. This means that all critical data is backed up in three separate locations, on at least two different storage media, and one storage location is remote and offline.

When Maersk was hit by the NotPetya computer virus in 2017, it knocked much of the company offline, because even though data was backed up in real time, all the backups were connected. As a result, the infection extended to all the backups at the same time. Luckily, one server in Africa was offline, due to a power cut in the area, and the company was able to recover much of its lost data.[10]

Several surveys have revealed a lack of involvement by security teams in their organization's digital transformation process.[11] As organizations undergo digital transformation, it is critical to implement a secure cloud environment, strict safeguards to protect the sharing and use of data essential to operations, security of IoT devices, and the protection of high-value assets. Thus, an organization's IT security teams should be involved in digital transformation planning from the outset.

Another key stakeholder to engage is senior management. In a study conducted by the Ponemon Institute, organizations in which senior management recognizes the importance of a secure digital transformation process were more likely to have both mature cybersecurity and digital transformation programs in place. The two initiatives work hand in hand.[12]

How Can Digital Enhance Responsiveness?

It is inevitable that organizations today will be impacted by disruption. Our exploration into the impact of COVID-19 on digital transformations underscores the importance of an organization's digital maturity level as it relates to how the organization responds to crises. We found that digitally mature organizations maintained their investments in innovative digital initiatives and *leveraged existing digital investments* to grow in markets where the need arose.[13]

SGS, a global testing and certification company, began its digital transformation in 2016 to enhance productivity through remote inspections and to develop new digital service offerings. During the COVID-19 pandemic, the company started offering video audits using a mobile application, as its inspectors could not travel on-site. Through the mobile application, customers could be guided in performing the inspection themselves. While the service itself was new, the mobile technology already existed in the company's ongoing digital initiatives. As Fred Herren, former head of Digital and Innovation, explains: "For business continuity, we didn't have time to launch something totally new. It was about using existing tools in new ways."[14] For SGS, the crisis accelerated the adoption of existing digital tools, which may have previously been considered as nice to have, but were soon deemed essential to satisfying the customer in the throes of a crisis.

Building Visibility into Your Supply Chain

Although there is plenty of discussion about how digital technologies are transforming organizations' business models and customer-facing activities, less widely discussed is the impact of these technologies on transforming supply chains. This is unfortunate, given that securing supply chain distribution is a high priority for many organizations when natural disasters, industrial accidents, or pandemics strike.

The advantages of digital supply chain management include increases in product availability, faster responses times, and better working-capital reductions.[15] While digital supply chains may mean different things to different organizations, ensuring supply chain visibility and control is especially helpful during a crisis.

After Hurricane Sandy took down Procter & Gamble's plant in Avenel, New Jersey, in 2012, the company made a conscious decision to become more proactive in its crisis response. In 2016, it invested in a cloud-based software that maintains a digital map of P&G's supply chain, along with the bill of materials for every product. By incorporating data from the company's ERP system as well as external data, such as weather forecasts, P&G can run scenarios to try to avoid disruptions in the most cost-effective manner.[16]

Leaders can stay a step ahead of supply chain disruptions by making informed decisions with real-time data. Teams can react quickly to insights to help them develop recovery actions to help their organizations navigate smoothly in times of disruption.

• • •

Given the importance of digital technologies, we recommend that digital leaders design their digital transformation with sufficient digital resilience, meaning that their transformation supports nimbleness, robustness, and responsiveness. Although financial reserves help to buffer an organization against losses, digital resilience enables organizations to mitigate their risks and quickly adjust to new realities following disruptions.

Hacker's Toolbox

Fix performance gaps. When prioritizing where to start, we recommend focusing on fixing performance gaps. Leading organizations often apply digital technologies to problems that are too cumbersome to fix with conventional methods. Real-time visibility of goods in a warehouse, though difficult to achieve with traditional ERP systems, can be relatively automatic using digital technologies. Data analytics is often used to help organizations with product replenishment and inventory planning.

Use technology to augment decision making. The default position is to use digital technologies to replace, rather than enhance, existing processes and operations. But leaders need to make rapid decisions under great uncertainty during times of disruption. Leveraging technology to better augment decision making in the areas of data analytics and scenario analysis is a good place to start. Machine learning and artificial intelligence methods were leveraged to improve supply chain planning, model disease progression, and assist clinical decision making during COVID-19. It's an area with immediate and direct benefit to key decision makers.

Leverage the central team as a source of real-time digital practices. In the event of a major disruption, real-time information about what works becomes crucial. Organizations, especially those that are highly decentralized, often discover that a centralized team is best positioned to gather and disseminate digital practices across the enterprise. Consider the example of Roche Diagnostics, where the central digital team actively assumed the role of the go-to source for digital best practices during COVID-19. The team listened for issues occurring in one country or business unit, quickly searched for digital solutions developed in other parts of the organization, and then disseminated them.[17]

Avoid single-source vendors where possible. Often, poor resilience is not directly the fault of an organization but is caused by the failure of a key supplier. Digital tools and technologies that are sole-sourced from a single vendor can pose a significant operational risk. Working with multiple vendors for critical, but nonproprietary, systems may add some additional cost, but it can pay back the investment multiple times in the event of a service interruption.

Self-Reflection Questions

How would you rate your organization's capabilities in the areas of nimbleness, robustness, and responsiveness?

Have you integrated resilience as a key element of your digital transformation?

Which ongoing digital initiatives would you accelerate to build your organization's resilience? What new initiatives would you propose?

Are you strongly aligned with key stakeholders, such as IT and security teams, to build a nimble, robust, and responsive digital infrastructure?

RELATED CHAPTERS

How to Make Digital and IT Work Together (Chapter 9)

Accelerating Digital Using Agile Methods (Chapter 10)

Building Hyperawareness into Your Organization (Chapter 12)

Building a Balanced Portfolio of Digital Initiatives (Chapter 20)

CONCLUSION

Beyond Digital Transformation

The Road to Becoming a Digital Organization

> *There are no shortcuts to any place worth going.*
> —Beverly Sills

One corporate leitmotiv states that "digital transformation is not a project but a journey." Point taken. But the *Oxford Learner's Dictionary* defines a journey as "an act of traveling from one place to another, especially when they are far apart."[1] By now, we've been digitally transforming our organizations for over a decade, so we get the "far apart" bit. But what about the destination? Is there an end to this journey?

Our answer is probably not.

Why? Because the relentless pace of technology innovation will not slow anytime soon. On the contrary, it will probably accelerate, continuing to radically impact the way we operate and manage every corner of our organizations. Research firm IDC predicts that by 2023 global spending by businesses on the technologies and services that enable digital transformation will reach $2.3 trillion. By 2024, more than half of all IT spending is expected to go toward digital transformation and innovation.[2]

We've seen many large firms struggle and ultimately overcome the first two stages of digital transformation: initiation and execution. They discovered ways to use digital technologies to change the way they relate to customers, improve operational performance, and enable their employees to work more effectively.

But digitizing the existing business has become mere table stakes today. We've seen far fewer firms graduating through the anchoring stage of digital transformation. This stage requires them to shift to new business models, fully connecting and automating their operations or augmenting employees' capabilities through human-machine collaboration.

There's no question that digital technology has triggered a seismic shift in the performance of our organizations, of individuals, and of entire societies. But what's next?

Many executives, academics, and consultants are seeking the holy grail of the post-digital world—or a "third shift" from industrial to digital to something else. All too often, the answer to "What's next?" is another shiny technology or a more advanced algorithm, such as quantum computing, cognitive computing, distributed ledgers, or more "intelligent" artificial intelligence. Most analysts, or self-proclaimed futurists, revert to technology as the central framing mechanism for future transformations.

As much as progress in technology is critical, we believe this forecast is wrong.

HACKING YOUR WAY TO A DIGITAL ORGANIZATION

The coming years will witness digitally driven changes in the business world that make everything we've experienced in the early days of digital transformation look like the opening act. And beyond technological development, organizational innovation will represent the biggest change for our businesses and our people.

The main business challenge has been, is, and will be the ability of our organizations to adapt fast enough to new technological possibilities and changing competitive situations. In other words, the "transformation thing." The holy grail will indeed be organizational—more specifically, the ability of corporations to make the "act" of digital transformation second nature.

We've written *Hacking Digital* to help make the process of graduating from digital transformation to a digital organization somewhat easier to navigate. We've addressed the main challenges and execution pain points that we've heard again and again in our consulting, teaching, and research work over the last decade. What we've learned is that both the main accelerators and the main hurdles of digital transformation are not about technology but about leadership, people, organizational structures, culture, or internal politics. It's the softer, but harder (i.e., more difficult) side of the equation that will propel organizations to the ultimate stage of digital transformation, that of *becoming a digital organization.*

When digital transformation becomes business as usual for your organization, people, and customers, you'll be there. In other words, digital will become transparent in the way you run your organization, manage your people, or leverage new waves of technological innovation. By this, we don't mean that you will cease to work with physical assets or people. We mean that your business and operating models will be built on a foundational layer of digital processes and data.

For example, a digital bank may still have branches, but behind the scenes, you'll find a set of digitally enabled operating procedures ensuring that the customer experience will be consistent across all channels. It's about a new organizational DNA anchored around digital mindsets, practices, capabilities, and behaviors. Throughout the book, we've covered best practices for building this organizational DNA. But as we've shown, there are no silver bullets for becoming a digital organization. It's hard work, but luckily, we have a few pointers.

ON BECOMING A DIGITAL ORGANIZATION

Powerful digital technologies, ubiquitous data, and advanced algorithms offer new strategic choices for products, services, and business models. At the same time, these technologies also present new organizational choices for designing, coordinating, and managing people and work. The narrative on digital transformation, to date, has focused relatively little attention on the organizational challenge of executing our chosen digital strategies.

Business leaders get bombarded with advice such as "Act like a startup" or "Uberize yourself." But how useful is this advice when you run a large, complex organization? Although we have a better understanding of the characteristics of digital companies, leaders have to develop an authentic version of their own organizations. Culture, leadership, organizational structure, complexity, and globality matter in how you blaze your trail to becoming a digital organization. Most organizations aren't known for being nimble and agile. So how can they develop the corporate agility required to become a digital organization and compete effectively and sustainably?

Previous research shows that becoming a digital organization is about developing a sustainable ability to rapidly adapt and self-organize to deliver value through emerging technologies.[3] It requires a rethinking about how to organize, as well as how to operate, in new and productive ways. It also requires an adaptive workforce. Becoming a digital organization remains an aspiration for most firms. Research shows that most organizations are in a state of transition: even among traditional firms that are knee-deep in the execution stage, only 7 percent are close to passing through the anchoring stage.[4] There's no off-the-shelf answer, but there *is* a blueprint.

Reaching this destination is more a marathon than a sprint, and at times, the journey can be uncomfortable. It requires tenacity and resilience. Foremost, it requires strong leadership to steer the course and keep the organization focused on the end goal. But it's worth the effort. Digital organizations are able to adapt to narrow windows of opportunity or respond to significant external events quickly. By this point, digital transformation, as an orchestrated process, will no longer be required.

The cadre of companies that have achieved *digital organization* status exhibit a number of common characteristics: a "digital-first" mindset, a digitally savvy and technologically augmented workforce, data-driven decision making, and an ability to self-organize and orchestrate work at scale (see Figure C.1). A tall order.

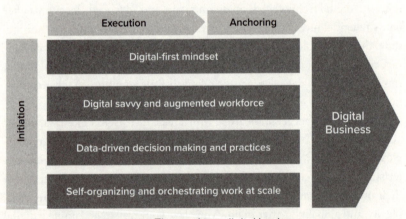

Figure C.1 The road to a digital business

Digital-first mindset. Digital transformation has intrinsically linked business transformation with technology. A positive and proactive attitude toward digital possibilities is particularly important. In digital organizations, an instinctive digital-first mindset is evidenced by how people throughout the firm explore digital solutions before traditional process-based ones, systematically using digital tools and data analytics. This mindset favors technology and a zero-based approach to solving problems, automating tasks to the extent possible, and encouraging digital experimentation and innovation.

Throughout this book, we've discussed what it takes to build a digital-first mindset. Excelling at open innovation, building hyperawareness, and becoming an agile organization are some of the ways to get there. As Capital One CEO Richard Fairbank noted: "Digital is who we are and how we do business. We need to make digital how we do business not only with our customers, but also how we operate the company."[5] As employees experience and publicize successes with this approach, positive attitudes cascade and spread through the larger organization.

Digitally savvy and augmented workforces. Raising digital IQ and developing key skills in an organization have been key challenges in digital transformation. These become a must-have when operating as a digital organization. And it's not a one-off. The need for continual learning becomes greater, not smaller. Digital organizations demonstrate an elevated capability to use tools and data to dynamically deploy and reconfigure, at speed, both human work and capital resources.

Then there is automation. As a rule, digital organizations default to automating core processes, especially repetitive and unproductive tasks. But the bulk of existing jobs are not displaced. They are augmented. Automation eliminates many of the tasks that used to bog down workflows, leaving humans to focus on more fulfilling and relevant tasks.

Human-machine collaboration becomes greater than the sum of the parts. Robin Bordoli, CEO of machine-learning company Figure Eight, described the potential: "It's not about machines replacing humans, but machines augmenting humans. Humans and machines have different relative strengths and weaknesses, and . . . the combination of these . . . will allow human intents and business process to scale 10X, 100X, and beyond that in the coming years."[6] For example, in radiology, computer-based algorithms have increased the productivity of diagnosing simple cases and, more importantly, have assisted medical professionals so they can concentrate on the most complex diagnoses. A better outcome.

Data-driven decision making. During digital transformations, people often wax lyrical about big data and the power of analytics to support strategic decisions. Truth is, most of us believe strongly in our own powers of intuition. And this is not a bad thing. Human judgment still matters in digital organizations. Jeff Bezos, founder and CEO of Amazon, identified two types of decisions: "There are decisions that can be made by analysis. These are the best kind of decisions. They are fact-based decisions that overrule the hierarchy. Unfortunately, there's this whole other set of decisions you can't boil down to a math problem."[7]

That said, in digital organizations, the default mindset is fact-based—from customer to operational to people decisions. This mindset even extends to the way you innovate and conduct experiments. Of course, to become data driven in your decision making, you need access to quality data: timely, accurate, and complete data.

Good data aids employees in improving internal business operations and responding effectively to customer demands. To truly leverage the investment in digitization, organizations must use their accumulated data in systematic analyses that drive important strategic decisions, as well as monitor and refine internal processes. Data enables digital organizations to be more tightly orchestrated and controlled than ever before. And paradoxically, this is a prerequisite to more employee autonomy. As employees and management realize the benefits of data-driven outcomes, they use fact-based approaches more consistently, creating a virtuous cycle.

Self-organizing agility. Organizational design is not a perfect science. Over time, regardless of how you organize, silos will still exist. Of course, the first trick is to organize so as not to entrench silos along reporting lines or functional domains. But to be successful, digital initiatives must cut through your organizational construct. Digital organizations display team and work fluidity based on *collaborative learning*. They use teamwork and partnering to solve problems without regard to discipline, geography, ownership, or other traditional parameters, ensuring that insights and solutions move rapidly and readily across boundaries.

Organizational leaders help by setting clear goals, encouraging boundary-spanning collaboration, providing liberal access to relevant information, and trusting their employees to bring their best expertise to bear for each challenge. Is this just about agile programs? No. It goes way beyond agile processes and tools. In digital organizations, agility and nimbleness are embedded in the DNA of how work is performed and how people come together, interact, and collaborate. With tighter synchronization and control through data and analytics, digital organizations can confidently grant more autonomy to their people. It's the shift to higher levels of *self-organization*.

Chinese company Haier, the world's largest appliance maker, took digital transformation a step further by innovating its organizational model to mimic the architecture of the internet. The company is organized around 200 customer-facing microenterprises and over 3,500 service and support microenterprises. It took Haier the best part of 10 years to redesign its core workflows and change workforce mindsets. But the effort has paid off.

Haier chairman and CEO Zhang Ruimin explains what drives the success of microenterprises:

> Successful micro-enterprises have three characteristics. First, they are very entrepreneurial and very good at identifying, developing and seizing new market opportunities, so that they can develop those markets and seize the opportunities. Secondly, they are very well self-organized. They are also very open to inviting people from outside their organization to join them in their research and development. The third characteristic is that these successful micro-enterprises are self-driven and very motivated. They are always looking for the next opportunity to grow.[8]

Reaching the level of a digital organization has two important corollaries. First, digital organizations have porous boundaries. They have an ability to quickly access external talent—be they machine-learning experts from a top university, software solution innovators from startups, or coders from the gig economy. Second, digital organizations are able to deploy internal resources and expertise flexibly to wherever customer or operational opportunities exist—beyond organizational boundaries, P/Ls, or budget cycles. When such digital dexterity is attained, workforce engagement and intrapreneurship become the outcomes.

So it's time to ask yourself:

- How far do you think your organization is from having a digital-first mindset?

- How digitally savvy is your workforce? Are you thinking about how automation can augment the value-added work within your organization?

- Do you have the data and the mindset needed to be data driven in your decision making?

- What is the ability of your workforce to self-organize across traditional boundaries?

If by now you're feeling depressed by the size of the challenge you're facing, don't be. You're not alone. Most firms are transitioning toward a digital organization, but few are there yet. What's important is the ability to gauge progress. There are clear signals that can help you know whether your organization is moving closer.

For instance, when collaboration and sharing take over from managerial coordination, there is no more need for digital governance. Airbus, having developed a community of 12,000 digitally savvy employees, decided it was mature enough to embed digital capabilities into the mainstream activities of the business. Hence, the company decided to disband its Digital Transformation Office, the main governance mechanism that underpinned Airbus's digital transformation.[9]

What's important is the aspiration and the drive to steer your company ever closer to becoming a true digital organization. It's about leadership. However, leaders cannot mandate the development of values and norms such as collaboration, self-organization, and fact-based decision making. But they *can* cultivate the conditions that encourage new mindsets and practices by, for instance, being role models, and by encouraging cross-silo collaboration or requiring data-driven decision making, together with the right level of organizational surgery to make it work.

At each stage of digital transformation, a new challenge presents itself. Some challenges are related to technology, but more often than not, the barriers to successful transformation are organizational. They concern people, organizational structure, culture, incentives, governance, vision, and a host of other thorny issues. After a decade of digital transformation experience, we have captured best practices from practitioners to help others hack their way through these difficult transformations.

We hope that *Hacking Digital* will help you move faster—from being a practitioner of digital transformation to becoming an architect of your own digital organization.

ACKNOWLEDGMENTS

They say it takes a village to raise a child. Well, it takes a city to write a book on digital transformation! There are a great many people who contributed to the ideas, examples, and prescriptions provided in these pages, and we would like to thank them all.

None of the best practices or insights described in *Hacking Digital* would have been possible without the hundreds of digital leaders who generously shared their time and experiences. Collectively, they have inspired, challenged and pushed our thinking on digital transformation, and showed great patience as we tested, revised, retested, and refined each recommendation. Without the openness and insight of these executives struggling daily with the challenges of digital transformation, nothing in this book would have been possible. Their names may not be on the jacket, but the hundreds of executives we interacted with on a regular basis are co-creators of this work, and their wisdom is at its heart. They are the real heroes of digital transformation.

At IMD, our colleagues at the Global Center for Digital Business Transformation—Jialu Shan, Elizabeth Teracino and Remy Assir, provided invaluable intellectual support and feedback that helped to clarify our thoughts and direction. A big thank you also goes to Lawrence Tempel, who helped with operational support. Anand Narasimhan and Natalija Gersak offered important and valuable oversight, while IMD President Jean-Francois Manzoni provided air cover where needed as well as financial support for many of our activities. We took inspiration from faculty colleagues operating in digital areas, including Goutam Challagalla, Carlos Cordon, Mark Greeven, Öykü Isik, Jennifer Jordan, Amit Joshi, Misiek Piskorski, and Howard Yu.

The Digital Vortex and Orchestrating Transformation teams from Cisco, including James Macaulay, Andy Noronha, Joel Barbier, and Jeff Loucks, helped to lay the intellectual foundations upon which this book has been built. Our editor, Pete Gerardo, provided conscientious and incisive criticism on our draft iterations. Our literary agent, Esmond Harmsworth, was a constant presence behind the scenes, expertly navigating the murky world of business publishing.

The highly professional team at McGraw Hill has been invaluable in helping us get this book over the finishing line. Stephen Isaacs, Judith Newlin, Scott Kurtz, Patricia Wallenburg, Kevin Commins, and Scott Sewell were trusted partners and advisors all the way. Thank you for your confidence and trust in this book.

NOTES

INTRODUCTION

1. Wade, M., and J. Shan. "Covid-19 Has Accelerated Digital Transformation, but May Have Made It Harder Not Easier." *MIS Quarterly Executive*, Vol. 19, No. 3, pp. 213–220, 2020.
2. Wade, M., and N. Obwegeser. "How to Choose the Right Digital Leader for Your Company." *MIT Sloan Management Review*, May 14, 2019. https://sloanreview.mit .edu/article/how-to-choose-the-right-digital-leader-for-your-company/.

CHAPTER 1

1. McIntyre, Alan, Julian Skan, and Francesca Caminiti. "Beyond North Star Gazing: How Our Four Winning Bank Models Map to Actual Market Evolution." Accenture, 2018. https://www.accenture.com/_acnmedia/PDF-85/Accenture-Banking-Beyond -North-Star-.pdf.
2. Obwegeser, Nikolaus, Tomoko Yokoi, Michael Wade, and Tom Voskes. "7 Key Principles to Govern Digital Initiatives." *MIT Sloan Management Review*, April 1, 2020. https://Sloanreview.mit.edu/Article/7-Key-Principles-to-Govern-Digital -Initiatives/.
3. "Digital Transformation Readiness Survey Summary." Center for Creative Leadership, 2018. https://www.ccl.org/wp-content/uploads/2018/04/Digital -Transformation-Survey-Report.pdf.
4. Wade, Michael J., James Macaulay, Andy Noronha, and Joel Barbier. Orchestrating Transformation: How to Deliver Winning Performance with a Connected Approach to Change. Lausanne: IMD, 2019.
5. Ibid.
6. Fitzgerald, Michael. "Inside Renault's Digital Factory." MIT Sloan Management Review (blog), January 10, 2014. https://sloanreview.mit.edu/article/inside-renaults -digital-factory/.
7. Editorial Board. "George H. W. Bush Had No Grand Dreams. His Competence and Restraint Were Enough." *Washington Post* (blog), December 1, 2018. https://

www.washingtonpost.com/opinions/george-hw-bush-wasnt-into-the-vision
-thing-but-he-skillfully-handled-historic-crises/2018/12/01/2b4b3512-4faf
-11e2-950a-7863a013264b_story.html.

CHAPTER 2

1. Kotter, John P. *A Sense of Urgency*. Boston: Harvard Business Press, 2010.
2. Gates, Bill, Nathan Myhrvold, and Peter Rinearson. *The Road Ahead*. New York: Viking, 1995.
3. Kattel, Rainer, and Ines Mergel. "Estonia's Digital Transformation: Mission Mystique and the Hiding Hand." Working paper. UCL Institute for Innovation and Public Purpose (IIPP), 2018. https://www.ucl.ac.uk/bartlett/public-purpose/publications/2018/sep/estonias-digital-transformation-mission-mystique-and-hiding-hand.
4. Price, Jonathan. *Transforming How We Transform*. BHP, 2019. https://www.bhp.com/media-and-insights/reports-and-presentations/2019/10/transforming-how-we-transform/.
5. Kaganer, Evegeny, Robert Wayne Gregory, and Catalin Codrean. "Driving Digital Transformation at the DBS Bank." *Harvard Business Review*, October 28, 2016.
6. Bloomberg, Jason. "How DBS Bank Became the Best Digital Bank in the World by Becoming Invisible." *Forbes* (blog), December 23, 2016. https://www.forbes.com/sites/jasonbloomberg/2016/12/23/how-dbs-bank-became-the-best-digital-bank-in-the-world-by-becoming-invisible/?sh=4b5665a73061.

CHAPTER 3

1. Sull, Donald, Charles Sull, and James Yoder. "No One Knows Your Strategy—Not Even Your Top Leaders." *MIT Sloan Management Review* (blog). Accessed February 12, 2018. https://sloanreview.mit.edu/article/no-one-knows-your-strategy-not-even-your-top-leaders/.
2. Sutcliff, Mike, Raghav Narsalay, and Aarohi Sen. "The Two Big Reasons That Digital Transformations Fail." *Harvard Business Review* (blog), October 18, 2019. https://hbr.org/2019/10/the-two-big-reasons-that-digital-transformations-fail.
3. Westerman, George, Didier Bonnet, and Andrew McAfee. *Leading Digital: Turning Technology into Business Transformation*. Boston: Harvard Business Review Press, 2014.
4. Nembhard, Ingrid M., and Amy C. Edmondson. "Making It Safe: The Effects of Leader Inclusiveness and Professional Status on Psychological Safety and Improvement Efforts in Health Care Teams." *Journal of Organizational Behavior*, November 2006. https://www.researchgate.net/publication/227521893_Making_It_Safe_The_Effects_of_Leader_Inclusiveness_and_Professional_Status_on_Psychological_Safety_and_Improvement_Efforts_in_Health_Care_Teams.
5. Silverberg, David. "Why You Need to Question Your Hippo Boss." *BBC News*. BBC, April 19, 2017. https://www.bbc.co.uk/news/business-39633499.
6. Hoffman, Reid. "Why Relationships Matter: I-to-the-We." LinkedIn, November 6, 2012. https://www.linkedin.com/pulse/20121106193412-1213-why-relationships

-matter-i-to-the-we/.

7. Sander, Peter. "An HR Lesson from Steve Jobs: If You Want Change Agents, Hire Pirates." *Fast Company* (blog), January 18, 2012. https://www.fastcompany .com/1665840/an-hr-lesson-from-steve-jobs-if-you-want-change-agents-hire-pirates.

8. Toegel, Ginka, and Jean-Louis Barsoux. "It's Time to Tackle Your Team's Undiscussables." *MIT Sloan Management Review* (blog), September 10, 2019. https:// sloanreview.mit.edu/article/its-time-to-tackle-your-teams-undiscussables/.

9. Anthony, Scott D., and Bernard C. Kümmerli. "A Simple Way to Get Your Leadership Team Aligned on Strategy." *Harvard Business Review* (blog), January 2, 2019. https:// hbr.org/2019/01/a-simple-way-to-get-your-leadership-team-aligned-on-strategy.

10. Toegel and Barsoux. "It's Time to Tackle Your Team's Undiscussables."

11. Jelassi, Tawfik. "In the Field with Accorhotels. How Can an Industry Incumbent Respond Strategically to Challenges from Digital Disruptors?" *IMD* (blog), November 2017. https://www.imd.org/research-knowledge/articles/a-strategic -response-to-digital-disruption-the-case-of-accorhotels/.

CHAPTER 4

1. "State of the Global Workplace." Gallup Inc., 2017. https://www.gallup.com/workplace/ 238079/state-global-workplace-2017.aspx.

2. Fitzgerald, Michael, Nina Kruschwitz, Didier Bonnet, and Michael Welch. "Embracing Digital Technology." *MIT Sloan Management Review*, October 7, 2013. https://sloanreview.mit.edu/projects/embracing-digital-technology/.

3. *Digital Transformation Review, Twelfth Edition: Taking Digital Transformation to the Next Level; Lessons from the Leaders.* Capgemini Research Institute, February 12, 2019. https://www.capgemini.com/wp-content/uploads/2019/02/Download-%E2 %80%93-Digital-Transformation-Review-12.pdf.

4. Cross, Rob, Thomas H. Davenport, and Peter Gray. "Collaborate Smarter, Not Harder." *MIT Sloan Management Review* (blog), September 10, 2019. https:// sloanreview.mit.edu/article/collaborate-smarter-not-harder/.

5. Ibid.

6. Hemp, Paul, and Thomas A. Stewart. "Leading Change When Business Is Good." *Harvard Business Review* (blog), December 2004. https://hbr.org/2004/12/leading -change-when-business-is-good.

7. Michelman, Paul, and Shantanu Narayen. "Key Words for Digital Transformation." *MIT Sloan Management Review* (blog), December 4, 2018. https://sloanreview.mit.edu/ article/key-words-for-digital-transformation/.

8. *Digital Transformation Review, Twelfth Edition.*

9. Westerman, George, Didier Bonner, and Andrew McAfee. *Leading Digital: Turning Technology into Business Transformation.* Boston: Harvard Business Review Press, 2014.

10. "Transform and Accelerate." Pernod-Ricard.com, December 18, 2019. https://www .pernod-ricard.com/en/media/press-releases/record-engagement-rate-pernod -ricard-employees/.

CHAPTER 5

1. Obwegeser, Nikolaus, Yokoi, Tomoko, Michael Wade, and Tom Voskes. "7 Key Principles to Govern Digital Initiatives." *MIT Sloan Management Review*, April 1, 2020.
2. Author interviews.
3. Frei, Frances X., and Anne Morriss. "Everything Starts with Trust." *Harvard Business Review* (blog), May–June 2020. https://hbr.org/2020/05/begin-with-trust.
4. Author interviews.
5. Bodson, Bertrand. "Inside View: Supercharging Our Digital Transformation." LinkedIn, September 25, 2019. https://www.linkedin.com/pulse/inside-view-supercharging-our-digital-transformation-bertrand-bodson/.
6. Author interviews.
7. *Covid-19 Digital Engagement Report*. Twilio, 2020.

CHAPTER 6

1. Carter, Philip, Lianfeng Wu, Dan Vesset, Eileen Smith, Craig Simpson, Swapnil Shende, Joseph C. Pucciarelli, et al. *IDC FutureScape: Worldwide Digital Transformation 2020 Predictions*, 2019.
2. Tabrizi, Benham, Ed Lam, Kirk Girard, and Vernon Irvin. "Digital Transformation Is Not About Technology." *Harvard Business Review* (blog), March 19, 2019. https://hbr.org/2019/03/digital-transformation-is-not-about-technology.
3. "Digital Leadership: An Interview with Angela Ahrendts, CEO of Burberry." Capgemini Consulting. August 16, 2012. https://www.capgemini.com/wp-content/uploads/2017/07/DIGITAL_LEADERSHIP__An_interview_with_Angela_Ahrendts.pdf.
4. Walker, Ron. "Think like a Venture Capitalist." KPMG LLP, August 20, 2019. https://advisory.kpmg.us/articles/2019/think-like-a-venture-capitalist.html.
5. Kelly, Brianna. "Mondelez Invests in Food Business Incubator the Hatchery." *Chicago Business* (blog), March 21, 2019. https://www.chicagobusiness.com/consumer-products/mondelez-backs-food-biz-incubator-hatchery.
6. *Digital Transformation Review, Twelfth Edition: Taking Digital Transformation to the Next Level; Lessons from the Leaders*. Capgemini Research Institute, February 12, 2019.
7. Adapted from Westerman, George, Didier Bonner, and Andrew McAfee. *Leading Digital: Turning Technology into Business Transformation*. Boston: Harvard Business Review Press, 2014.
8. Westerman, Bonner, and McAfee. *Leading Digital*.
9. Author interviews.

CHAPTER 7

1. Bonnet, Didier. "It's Time for Boards to Cross the Digital Divide." *Harvard Business Review*, July 9, 2014. https://hbr.org/2014/07/its-time-for-boards-to-cross-the-digital-divide.

2. Rickards, Tuck, and Rhys Grossman. "The Board Directors You Need for a Digital Transformation." *Harvard Business Review*, July 13, 2017. https://hbr.org/2017/07/the-board-directors-you-need-for-a-digital-transformation.

3. Weill, Peter, Thomas Apel, Stephanie L. Woerner, and Jennifer S. Banner. "It Pays to Have a Digitally Savvy Board." *MIT Sloan Management Review*, March 12, 2019. https://sloanreview.mit.edu/article/it-pays-to-have-a-digitally-savvy-board/.

4. Larcker, David F., and Brian Tayan. "Netflix Approach to Governance: Genuine Transparency with the Board." Stanford Graduate School of Business, May 2018. https://www.gsb.stanford.edu/faculty-research/publications/netflix-approach-governance-genuine-transparency-board.

5. Deloitte. "Bridging the Boardroom's Technology Gap," June 29, 2017. https://www2.deloitte.com/us/en/insights/focus/cio-insider-business-insights/bridging-boardroom-technology-gap.html.

6. Ibid.

7. Sarrazin, Hugo, and Paul Willmott. "Adapting Your Board to the Digital Age." McKinsey, June 13, 2016. https://www.mckinsey.com/business-functions/mckinsey-digital/our-insights/adapting-your-board-to-the-digital-age#.

8. Larcker and Tayan. "Netflix Approach to Governance."

9. Jordan, Jennifer, and Michael Sorell. "Why You Should Create a 'Shadow Board' of Younger Employee." *Harvard Business Review*, June 4, 2019. https://hbr.org/2019/06/why-you-should-create-a-shadow-board-of-younger-employees?ab=hero-main-text4.

10. Weill, Apel, Woerner, and Banner. "It Pays to Have a Digitally Savvy Board."

CHAPTER 8

1. Wade, Michael J., James Macaulay, Andy Noronha, and Joel Barbier. *Orchestrating Transformation: How to Deliver Winning Performance with a Connected Approach to Change*. Lausanne: IMD, 2019.

2. Passerini, Filippo. "Transforming the Way of Doing Business via Digitization." Slideshare.com, May 21, 2012.

3. Wade, Macaulay, Noronha, and Barbier. *Orchestrating Transformation*.

4. Author interviews.

5. Jenkins, Patrick. "Orange Bank: Is a Phone Company the Future of Fintech?" Financial Times, January 22, 2018. https://www.ft.com/content/6bd8ac00-f7c4-11e7-88f7-5465a6ce1a00.

6. "Digital Ambassadors." Radiall, August 2017, https://www.radiall.com/insights/digitalambassadors.

7. Moazed, Alex. "Why GE Digital Failed." *Inc.*, January 8, 2018. https://www.inc.com/alex-moazed/why-ge-digital-didnt-make-it-big.html.

8. Author interviews.

9. Author interviews.

10. Author interviews.

11. *Digital Transformation Review, Twelfth Edition: Taking Digital Transformation to the Next Level; Lessons from the Leaders.* Capgemini Research Institute, February 12, 2019. https://www.capgemini.com/wp-content/uploads/2019/02/Download-%E2%80%93-Digital-Transformation-Review-12.pdf.

CHAPTER 9

1. "The Digital Culture Challenge: Closing the Employee-Leadership Gap." Capgemini, Digital Transformation Institute, 2017. https://www.capgemini.com/wp-content/uploads/2017/12/dti_digitalculture_report.pdf.

2. McDonald, Mark P. "Digital Strategy Does Not Equal IT Strategy." *Harvard Business Review*, November 19, 2012. https://hbr.org/2012/11/digital-strategy-does-not-equa.

3. Yoo, Youngjin, Ola Henfridsson, and Kalle Lyytinen. "Research Commentary: The New Organizing Logic of Digital Innovation: An Agenda for Information Systems Research." *JSTOR*, December 2010. https://www.jstor.org/stable/23015640?seq=1.

4. Hess, Thomas, Christian Matt, Alexander Benlian, and Florian Wiesböck. "Options for Formulating a Digital Transformation Strategy." *MIS Quarterly Executive*, June 2016.

5. Brotman, Adam, Curt Garner, and Michael Fitzgerald. "How Starbucks Has Gone Digital." *MIT Sloan Management Review*, April 4, 2013.

6. Deloitte. "Postdigital Partners: CIOs and Chief Digital Officers," May 9, 2013. https://deloitte.wsj.com/cio/2013/05/09/postdigital-partners-cios-and-chief-digital-officers/.

7. Fuchs, Christoph, Philipp Barthel, and Matthias Berger. "Characterizing Approaches to Digital Transformation: Development of a Taxonomy of Digital Units." 14th International Conference on Wirtschaftsinformatik. Siegen, Germany, April 2019.

8. Brotman, Adam, Curt Garner, and Michael Fitzgerald. "How Starbucks Has Gone Digital." *MIT Sloan Management Review*, April 4, 2013.

CHAPTER 10

1. "Agile Transformation from Agile Experiments to Operating Model Transformation: How Do You Compare to Others?" KPMG, 2019.

2. Denning, Stephen. *The Age of Agile: How Smart Companies Are Transforming the Way Work Gets Done.* New York: AMACOM, 2018.

3. Forth, Patrick, Tom Reichert, Romain de Laubier, and Saibal Chakraborty. "Flipping the Odds of Digital Transformation Success." *BCG*, October 29, 2020. https://www.bcg.com/publications/2020/increasing-odds-of-success-in-digital-transformation#factor4.

4. To learn more about Scrum and Extreme Programming, please see these introductory references: https://www.scrum.org/resources/what-is-scrum and http://www.extremeprogramming.org/.

5. Dikert, Kim, Maria Paasivaara, and Casper Lassenius. "Challenges and Success Factors for Large-Scale Agile Transformations: A Systematic Literature Review." *Journal of Systems and Software*, Vol. 119, pp. 87–108, September 2016. https://www.sciencedirect.com/science/article/pii/S0164121216300826.

6. Bohem, Barry, and Richard Turner. "Management Challenges to Implementing Agile Processes in Traditional Development Organizations." IEEE Software, October 2015. https://www.researchgate.net/publication/3248286_Management_Challenges_to_Implementing_Agile_Processes_in_Traditional_Development_Organizations.

7. Denning. *The Age of Agile*.

8. Howard, Annie. "Case Study: Bosch Embracing Agility." Bosch, September 2020. https://www.scrumatscale.com/wp-content/uploads/2020/09/Annie-Howard-Bosch-Slides.pdf.

9. Wade, Michael J., James Macaulay, Andy Noronha, and Joel Barbier. *Orchestrating Transformation: How to Deliver Winning Performance with a Connected Approach to Change*. Lausanne: IMD, 2019.

10. Gardner, Heidi K. "When Senior Managers Won't Collaborate." *Harvard Business Review*, March 2015. https://hbr.org/2015/03/when-senior-managers-wont-collaborate.

11. Esbensen, Bo Krag, Klemens Hjartar, David Pralong, and Olli Salo. "A Tale of Two Agile Paths: How a Pair of Operators Set Up Their Organizational Transformations." McKinsey, February 4, 2019. https://www.mckinsey.com/industries/technology-media-and-telecommunications/our-insights/a-tale-of-two-agile-paths-how-a-pair-of-operators-set-up-their-organizational-transformations.

12. Loucks, J., Macaulay, J., Noronha, A., Wade, M. *Digital Vortex: How Today's Market Leaders Can Beat Disruptive Competitors at Their Own Game*. Lausanne: IMD, 2016.

13. Chen, Roger Ronxin, Ramya Ravichandar, and Don Proctor. "Managing the Transition to the New Agile Business and Product Development Model: Lessons from Cisco Systems." *Business Horizons*, Vol. 59, No. 6, pp. 635–644, November–December 2016.

14. Paasivaara, Maria, and Casper Lassenius. "Empower Your Agile Organization: Community-Based Decision Making in Large-Scale Agile Development at Ericsson." IEEE, February 21, 2019. https://ieeexplore.ieee.org/document/8648263.

15. Ibid.

16. Dikert, Paasivaara, and Lassenius. "Challenges and Success Factors for Large-Scale Agile Transformations"; Denning, *The Age of Agile*.

17. Denning, Steve. "Why and How Volvo Embraces Agile at Scale." *Forbes,* January 26, 2020. https://www.forbes.com/sites/stevedenning/2020/01/26/how-volvo-embraces-agile-at-scale/?sh=46619f4d4cf0.

18. Hayward, Simon. *The Agile Leader: How to Create an Agile Business in the Digital Age*. London: Kogan Page, 2021.

19. Denning, Stephen. *The Leader's Guide to Radical Management: Reinventing the Workplace for the 21st Century*. San Francisco: Jossey-Bass, 2010.

20. Alqudah, Mashal, and Rozilawati Razali. "A Review of Scaling Agile Methods in Large Software Development." *International Journal on Advanced Science Engineering and Information Technology*, Vol. 6, No. 6, December 2016. http://insightsociety.org/ojaseit/index.php/ijaseit/article/view/1374.

21. Dikert, Paasivaara, and Lassenius. "Challenges and Success Factors for Large-Scale Agile Transformations."

22. Author interviews.

CHAPTER 11

1. Mayor, Tracy. "5 Building Blocks of Digital Transformation." MIT Management Sloan School, June 27, 2019. https://mitsloan.mit.edu/ideas-made-to-matter/5 -building-blocks-digital-transformation.

2. "Fitzgerald, Michael, Nina Kruschwitz, Didier Bonnet, and Michael Welch. "Embracing Digital Technology: A New Strategic Imperative." *MIT Sloan Management Review*, October 7, 2013. https://sloanreview.mit.edu/projects/ embracing-digital-technology/.

3. Forth, Patrick, Tom Reichert, Romain de Laubier, and Saibal Chakraborty. "Flipping the Odds of Digital Transformation Success." *BCG*, October 29, 2020. https://www.bcg.com/publications/2020/increasing-odds-of-success-in-digital -transformation#factor4.

4. Davenport, Thomas H., and George Westerman. "Why So Many High-Profile Digital Transformations Fail." *Harvard Business Review*, March 9, 2018. https://hbr .org/2018/03/why-so-many-high-profile-digital-transformations-fail.

5. Bonnet, Didier, and George Westerman. "The New Elements of Digital Transformation." *MIT Sloan Management Review*, November 19, 2020. https:// sloanreview.mit.edu/article/the-new-elements-of-digital-transformation/.

6. Dynatrance. "76% of CIOs Say It Could Become Impossible to Manage Digital Performance, as IT Complexity Soars." *Businesswire*, January 31, 2018. https://www .businesswire.com/news/home/20180131005240/en/76-CIOs-Impossible-Manage -Digital-Performance-Complexity.

7. High, Peter. "The First Ever CIO of $16 Billion Micron Technology." *Forbes*, January 11, 2016. https://www.forbes.com/sites/peterhigh/2016/01/11/the-first-ever-cio-of -16-billion-micron-technology/?sh=1af69b88519e.

8. Joshi, Amit, and Michael Wade. "The Building Blocks of an AI Strategy." *MIT Sloan Management Review*, August 10, 2020. https://sloanreview.mit.edu/article/the -building-blocks-of-an-ai-strategy/.

9. Bonnet and Westerman. "The New Elements of Digital Transformation."

10. Office of Inspector General. "Undeliverable as Addressed Mail." US Postal Service, 2014. https://www.uspsoig.gov/sites/default/files/document-library-files/2015/ ms-ar-14-006.pdf.

11. "5 Digital Marketing Best Practices for 2021 and Beyond." *Stirista*, December 2, 2020. https://www.stirista.com/digital-marketing-best-practices.

12. Nagle, Tadhg, Thomas C. Redman, and David Sammon. "Only 3% of Companies' Data Meets Basic Quality Standards." *Harvard Business Review*, September 11, 2017. https://hbr.org/2017/09/only-3-of-companies-data-meets-basic-quality-standards.

13. "What Is a Data Quality Audit? Ensuring Your Data Integrity." *DataOpsZone*, November 26, 2019. https://www.dataopszone.com/what-is-a-data-quality-audit/.

14. Bonnet and Westerman. "The New Elements of Digital Transformation."

15. "Big Data and AI Executive Survey 2019 Executive Summary of Findings." NewVantage Partners LLC, 2019. https://www.tcs.com/content/dam/tcs-bts/pdf/insights/Big-Data-Executive-Survey-2019-Findings-Updated-010219-1.pdf.

CHAPTER 12

1. Ferguson, Jamie, and Nate Anderson. "Step by Step Building a Digital Strategy." World Economic Forum Annual Meeting, January 10, 2018. https://www.weforum.org/agenda/2018/01/step-by-step-building-a-digital-strategy/.

2. Anthony, Scott D., Patrick S. Viguerie, Evan I. Schwartz, and John Van Landeghem. "2018 Corporate Longevity Forecast: Creative Destruction Is Accelerating." *Innosight*, 2018. https://www.innosight.com/wp-content/uploads/2017/11/Innosight-Corporate-Longevity-2018.pdf.

3. Yokoi, Tomoko, Jialu Shan, Michael R. Wade, and James Macaulay. "Digital Vortex 2019: Continuous and Connected Change." IMD (report), Global Center for Digital Business Transformation, May 2019.

4. Wade, Michael, Jialu Shan, and Didier Bonnet. "Lifting the Lid on Disruption Fever." *Journal of Strategy and Management*, Vol. 3, No. 4, 2020. https://www.researchgate.net/publication/343191542_Lifting_the_lid_on_disruption_fever.

5. McGrath, Rita. *Seeing Around Corners: How to Spot Inflection Points in Business Before They Happen.* Boston/New York: Houghton Mifflin Harcourt, 2019.

6. Loucks, Jeff, James Macaulay, Andy Noronha, and Michael Wade. *Digital Vortex: How Today's Market Leaders Can Beat Disruptive Competitors at Their Own Game.* Lausanne: IMD, 2016.

7. Ibid.

8. Jordan, Jennifer, and Michael Sorell. "Why Reverse Mentoring Works and How to Do It Right." *Harvard Busines Review*, October 3, 2019. https://hbr.org/2019/10/why-reverse-mentoring-works-and-how-to-do-it-right.

9. Wade, Michael, and Jialu Shan. "How China Is Rebooting Retail." IMD (article), March 2018. https://www.imd.org/research-knowledge/articles/how-china-is-rebooting-retail/.

10. Boler-Davis, Alicia. "How GM Uses Social Media to Improve Cars and Customer Service." *Harvard Business Review*, February 12, 2016. https://hbr.org/2016/02/how-gm-uses-social-media-to-improve-cars-and-customer-service.

11. Author interviews.

12. Loucks, Macaulay, Noronha, and Wade. *Digital Vortex*.

13. Ibid.

14. Ibid.

15. McGrath, *Seeing Around Corners*.

16. Venkatraman, Venkat. "How to Read and Respond to Weak Digital Signals." *MIT Sloan Management Review*, February 22, 2019. https://sloanreview.mit.edu/article/how-to-read-and-respond-to-weak-digital-signals/.

CHAPTER 13

1. Auerbach, Jonathan. "Why Partnership Is the Business Trend to Watch." World Economic Forum Annual Meeting, January 16, 2018. https://www.weforum.org/agenda/2018/01/why-partnership-is-the-business-trend-to-watch/.

2. Barreira, Teresa. "Choosing the Right Partner for Your Business's Digital Transformation." *Forbes India*, March 26, 2019. https://www.forbesindia.com/blog/digital-navigator/choosing-the-right-partner-for-your-digital-business-transformation/.

3. Rear, Andrew. "Partnership as a Digital Enabler at Munich Re." Bain (web log), August 30, 2018. bain.com/insights/partnership-as-a-digital-enabler-at-munich-re-video/.

4. Obwegeser, Nikolaus, Amalie C. Dam, Kim H. Fenger, Karine Arenfeldt, and Johan V. Silkjaer. "Aligning Drivers, Contractual Governance, and Relationship Management of IT-Outsourcing Initiatives." *Journal of Information Technology Case and Application Research*, Vol. 22, No. 1, 2020. https://doi.org/10.1080/15228053.2020.1786265.

5. Hinings, Bob, Thomas Gegenhuber, and Royston Greenwood. "Digital Innovation and Transformation: An Institutional Perspective." *Information & Organization*, Vol. 28, No. 1, 2018. https://doi.org/10.1016/j.infoandorg.2018.02.004.

6. Relihan, T. "In the Age of Digital Everything, Is It Time to Eliminate IT?" MIT Management Sloan School, February 13, 2019. https://mitsloan.mit.edu/ideas-made-to-matter/age-digital-everything-it-time-to-eliminate-it.

7. De Backer, R., and E. K. Rinaudo. "Improving the Management of Complex Business Partnerships." McKinsey, 2019. https://www.mckinsey.com/business-functions/strategy-and-corporate-finance/our-insights/improving-the-management-of-complex-business-partnerships.

8. Fenwick, N. "How to Pick the Right Partners to Accelerate True Digital Transformation." *Forrester* (blog), September 12. 2019. https://go.forrester.com/blogs/accelerate-digital-transformation-2/.

9. Hale, Conor. "Novartis' Sandoz Drops out of Prescription App Deal with Pear Therapeutics." *Fierce Biotech*, October 16, 2019. https://www.fiercebiotech.com/medtech/novartis-sandoz-drops-out-prescription-app-deal-pear-therapeutics.

10. Kane, Gerald C., Doug Palmer, Anh Nguyen Phillips, David Kiron, and Natasha Buckley. "Accelerating Digital Innovation Inside and Out." *MIT Sloan Management Review* and Deloitte Insights, June 2019. https://www2.deloitte.com/content/dam/Deloitte/lu/Documents/deloitte-digital/lu-accelerating-digital-innovation.pdf.

11. The Economist Intelligence Unit. *Connecting Companies: Strategic Partnerships for the Digital Age*. Telstra, 2015. http://connectingcompanies.cope.economist.com/wp-content/uploads/sites/4/2015/09/Connecting-Companies-Whitepaper_final.pdf.pdf.

12. Kannan, Anand. "3 Points to Consider While Choosing a Digital Transformation Partner." *Hakuna Matata* (blog), October 1, 2020. https://www.hakunamatatatech.com/our-resources/blog/3-points-to-consider-while-choosing-a-digital-transformation-partner/.

13. *The Digital Enterprise: Moving from Experimentation to Transformation.* World Economic Forum, 2020. http://www3.weforum.org/docs/Media/47538_Digital%20Enterprise _Moving_Experimentation_Transformation_report_2018%20-%20final%20(2).pdf.

14. Marchand, Donald A., Michael R. Wade, and Fang Li. "Digital Business Transformation." IMD (article), December 2014. https://www.imd.org/research -knowledge/articles/digital-business-transformation/.

15. Hoffman, William, Raphael Bick, Austin Boral, Nicolaus Henke, Didunoluwa Olukoya, Khaled Rifai, Marcus Roth, and Tom Youldon. "Collaborating for the Common Good: Navigating Public-Private Data Partnerships." McKinsey, May 30, 2019. https://www.mckinsey.com/business-functions/mckinsey-analytics/our -insights/collaborating-for-the-common-good.

16. Sears, Joshua B., Michael S. McLeod, Robert E. Evert, and G. Tyge Payne. "Alleviating Concerns of Misappropriation in Corporate Venture Capital: Creating Credible Commitments and Calculative Trust." *Strategic Organization*, June 10, 2020. https:// doi.org/10.1177/1476127020926174.

17. Spooner, Nick. "How to Establish a Successful Digital Partnership." *Digital Pulse*, March 7, 2016. https://www.digitalpulse.pwc.com.au/establish-successful-digital -partnership/.

18. Riccio, John. "Meeting of Minds: How Strategic Partnerships Are Shaping Today's Business Model." *Digital Pulse*, November 16, 2015. https://www.digitalpulse.pwc .com.au/strategic-partnerships-shaping-todays-business-models/.

CHAPTER 14

1. Flesner, Patrick, Michael Wade, and Nikolaus Obwegeser. "Making Corporate Venture Capital Work." *MIT Sloan Management Review*, June 18, 2019. https:// sloanreview.mit.edu/article/making-corporate-venture-capital-work/.

2. Kane, Gerald C., Doug Palmer, Anh Nguyen Phillips, David Kiron, and Natasha Buckley. "Accelerating Digital Innovation Inside and Out." *MIT Sloan Management Review* and Deloitte Insights, June, 2019. https://www2.deloitte.com/content/dam/ Deloitte/lu/Documents/deloitte-digital/lu-accelerating-digital-innovation.pdf.

3. *Open Innovation: Building, Scaling and Consolidating Your Firm's Corporate Venturing Unit.* IESE Business School and Oppino, 2018. https://media.iese.edu/research/pdfs/ ST-0478-E.pdf.

4. Brigl, Michael, Stefan Gross-Selbeck, Nico Denhert, Florian Schmieg, and Steffen Simon. "After the Honeymoon Ends: Making Corporate-Startup Relationships Work." *BCG*, June 13, 2019. https://www.bcg.com/en-ch/publications/2019/corporate -startup-relationships-work-after-honeymoon-ends.

5. Gaba, Vibha, and Gina Dokko. "Learning to Let Go: Social Influence, Learning, and the Abandonment of Corporate Venture Capital Practices." *Strategic Management Journal*, May 26, 2015.

6. Graham, Luke. "Samsung to Back European Start-Ups with $150 Million Investment Fund." *CNBC*, July 12, 2017. https://www.cnbc.com/2017/07/12/samsung-next -backs-european-start-ups-150-million-investment-fund-venture-capital.html.

7. Ibid.
8. Flesner, Wade, and Obwegeser. "Making Corporate Venture Capital Work."
9. Ibid.
10. Brigl, Gross-Selbeck, Denhert, Schmieg, and Simon. "After the Honeymoon Ends."
11. Orn, Scott, and Bill Growney. "How to Approach (and Work with) the 3 Types of Corporate VCs." *TechCrunch*, May 26, 2020. https://techcrunch.com/2020/05/26/how-to-approach-and-work-with-the-3-types-of-corporate-vcs/.
12. Brigl, Gross-Selbeck, Denhert, Schmieg, and Simon. "After the Honeymoon Ends."

CHAPTER 15

1. Chesbrough, Henry W. *Open Innovation: The New Imperative for Creating and Profiting from Technology*. Boston: Harvard Business School Press, 2003.
2. Brigl, Michael, Alexander Roos, Florian Schmieg, Xinyi Wu, and Max Hong. "Corporate Venturing Shifts Gears." *BCG*, April 25, 2016. https://www.bcg.com/en-ch/publications/2016/innovation-growth-corporate-venturing-shifts-gears-how-largest-companies-apply-tools-innovation.
3. Thompson, Neil C., Didier Bonnet, and Yun Ye. "Why Innovation's Future Isn't (Just) Open." *MIT Sloan Management Review*, May 11, 2020. https://sloanreview.mit.edu/article/why-innovations-future-isnt-just-open/.
4. Zynga, Andy, Kathleen Diener, Christoph Ihl, Dirk Lüttgens, Frank Piller & Bruno Scherb. "Making Open Innovation Stick: A Study of Open Innovation Implementation in 756 Global Organizations." *Research-Technology Management*. Vol. 61, No. 4. 2018.
5. Thompson, Bonnet, and Ye. "Why Innovation's Future Isn't (Just) Open."
6. Brunswicker, Sabine, and Henry Chesbrough. "The Adoption of Open Innovation in Large Firms." *Research-Technology Management*, Vol. 61, No. 1, 2018. https://doi.org/10.1080/08956308.2018.1399022.
7. Zynga, Andy, Kathleen Diener, Christoph Ihl, Dirk Lüttgens, Frank Piller & Bruno Scherb. "Making Open Innovation Stick: A Study of Open Innovation Implementation in 756 Global Organizations." *Research-Technology Management*. Vol. 61, No. 4. 2018.
8. Bauer, Stefan, Nikolaus Obwegeser, and Zlato Avdagic. "Corporate Accelerators: Transferring Technology Innovation to Incumbent Companies." *MCIS Conference Proceedings*, 2016. https://www.researchgate.net/publication/310766520_Corporate_Accelerators_Transferring_Technology_Innovation_to_Incumbent_Companies.
9. Lockhart, Campbell, and Tomas Lackner. "Open Innovation—an Integrated Tool in Siemens." *InnovationManagement.se* (interview), September 5, 2013. https://innovationmanagement.se/2013/09/05/open-innovation-an-integrated-tool-in-siemens/.
10. Lakhani, Karim R., Katja Hutter, Stephanie H. Pokrywa, and Johann Fuller. *Open Innovation at Siemens*. Case 613-100. Harvard Business School, 2013. https://www.hbs.edu/faculty/Pages/item.aspx?num=44999.

11. Lifshitz-Assaf, Hila. "Dismantling Knowledge Boundaries at NASA: The Critical Role of Professional Identity in Open Innovation." *Administrative Science Quarterly*. Vol. 63, No. 4, pp. 746–782, December 2018. https://www.hbs.edu/faculty/Pages/item.aspx?num=56512.

12. Author interviews.

13. Thompson, Bonnet, and Ye. "Why Innovation's Future Isn't (Just) Open."

14. Shipilov, Andrew. "A Better Way to Manage Corporate Alliances." *Harvard Business Review*, December 2, 2014. https://hbr.org/2014/12/a-better-way-to-manage-corporate-alliances.

15. Barrett, Brian. "McDonald's Bites on Big Data with $300 Million Acquisition." *Wired*, March 25, 2019. https://www.wired.com/story/mcdonalds-big-data-dynamic-yield-acquisition/.

16. Light, David, Jitendra Kavathekar, and Raghav Narsalay. "A Hands-Off Approach to Open Innovation Doesn't Work." *Harvard Business Review*, May 3, 2016. https://store.hbr.org/product/a-hands-off-approach-to-open-innovation-doesn-t-work/H02UYX.

17. Thompson, Bonnet, and Ye. "Why Innovation's Future Isn't (Just) Open."

18. Brunswicker and Chesbrough. "The Adoption of Open Innovation in Large Firms."

CHAPTER 16

1. "Tay (bot)." Wikipedia. https://en.wikipedia.org/wiki/Tay_(bot).

2. Leonhardt, Meghan. "Equifax to Pay $700 Million for Massive Data Breach. Here's What You Need to Know About Getting a Cut." *CNBC*, July 22, 2019. https://www.cnbc.com/2019/07/22/what-you-need-to-know-equifax-data-breach-700-million-settlement.html.

3. Lobschat, Lara, Benjamin Mueller, Felix Eggers, Laura Brandimarte, Sarah Diefenbach, Mirja Kroschke, and Jochen Wirtz. "Corporate Digital Responsibility." *Journal of Business Research*, Vol. 122, pp. 875–888, January 2021. https://doi.org/10.1016/j.jbusres.2019.10.006.

4. Elias, Howard. "Diversity Is the Bridge on Which We Can Cross the Skills Gap." World Economic Forum Annual Meeting, January 16, 2020. https://www.weforum.org/agenda/2020/01/diversity-tech-skills-gap-4ir-digital-revolution/.

5. Salinas, Sara. "Zuckerberg on Cambridge Analytica: 'We Have a Responsibility to Protect Your Data, and If We Can't Then We Don't Deserve to Serve You.'" *CNBC*, March 21, 2018. https://www.cnbc.com/2018/03/21/zuckerberg-statement-on-cambridge-analytica.html.

6. Elks, Sonia. "Gig Economy Is 'Extreme Exploitation' Says British Film Director Ken Loach." *Thomson Reuters Foundation News*, October 21, 2019. https://news.trust.org/item/20191021154702-2qrbp.

7. Buolamwini, Joy. "Artificial Intelligence Has a Problem with Gender and Racial Bias. Here's How to Solve It." *Time*, February 7, 2019. https://time.com/5520558/artificial-intelligence-racial-gender-bias/.

8. Edelman, Gilad. "Facebook's Deepfake Ban Is a Solution to a Distant Problem." *Wired*, July 1, 2020. https://www.wired.com/story/facebook-deepfake-ban-disinformation/.

9. "Data Protection and Valorisation—Unipol Data Vision." Unipol Gruppo. http://www.unipol.it/en/sustainability/integrated-approach/data-protection-and-valorisation-unipol-data-vision.

10. Conger, Kate, and Daisuke Wakabayashi. "Google Employees Protest Secret Work on Censored Search Engine for China." *New York Times,* August 16, 2018. https://www.nytimes.com/2018/08/16/technology/google-employees-protest-search-censored-china.html. Also Captain, Sean. "How Tech Workers Became Activists, Leading a Resistance Movement That Is Shaking Up Silicon Valley." *Fast Company,* October 15, 2018. https://www.fastcompany.com/90244860/silicon-valleys-new-playbook-for-tech-worker-led-resistance.

11. Aston, Ben. "Write a Project Charter: How-to Guide, Examples & Template." *Digital Project Manager*, July 5, 2019. https://thedigitalprojectmanager.com/project-charter/.

12. An example of an ethics checklist for data scientists is provided at https://deon.drivendata.org/.

CHAPTER 17

1. "Is Servitization Helping Your Business Rise Up the Value Chain?" *The Manufacturer*, June 14, 2017. https://www.themanufacturer.com/articles/servitization-helping-business-rise-value-chain/.

2. Chambers, John, and Diane Brady. *Connecting the Dots: Lessons for Leadership in a Start-Up World*. London: HarperCollins Publishers, 2018.

3. Ruh, William, "Industry Leaders Perspectives." *Digital Transformation Review, Twelfth Edition: Taking Digital Transformation to the Next Level; Lessons from the Leaders*. Capgemini Research Institute, February 12, 2019. https://www.capgemini.com/wp-content/uploads/2019/02/Download-%E2%80%93-Digital-Transformation-Review-12th-Edition.pdf.

CHAPTER 18

1. Sawers, Paul. "Kone Monetizes Connected Elevators with Alexa, Music-Streaming, and Digital Displays." *Venturebeat*, November 30, 2019. https://venturebeat.com/2019/11/30/kone-monetizes-connected-elevators-with-alexa-spotify-and-digital-displays/.

2. Ulaga, Wolfgang, and Stefan Michel. "Bill It, Kill It, or Keep It Free?." *MIT Sloan Management Review*, October 30, 2018. https://sloanreview.mit.edu/article/bill-it-kill-it-or-keep-it-free/.

3. Paul, Kari. "Zoom Releases Security Updates in Response to 'Zoom-Bombings.'" *The Guardian*, April 23, 2020. https://www.theguardian.com/technology/2020/apr/23/zoom-update-security-encryption-bombing.

CHAPTER 19

1. Cusumano, Michael A., David B. Yoffie, and Annabelle Gawer. "The Future of Platforms." *MIT Sloan Management Review*, February 11, 2020. https://sloanreview .mit.edu/article/the-future-of-platforms/.

2. Matveeva, Sophia. "How New Platforms Solve the Chicken or the Egg Dilemma." *Forbes*, May 30, 2019. https://www.forbes.com/sites/sophiamatveeva/2019/05/30/ how-new-platforms-solve-the-chicken-or-the-egg-dilemma/?sh=135598d75cef.

3. Shah, Semil. *Transcript: @Chamath at StrictlyVC's Insider Series*. Haystack, 2015. https://semilshah.com/2015/09/17/transcript-chamath-at-strictlyvcs-insider-series/.

4. Nath, Trevir. "How Airbnb Makes Money." *Investopedia*, December 10, 2020. https:// www.investopedia.com/articles/investing/112414/how-airbnb-makes-money.asp.

5. Adapted from Cusumano, Michael A., Annabelle Gawer, and David B. Yoffie. *The Business of Platforms: Strategy in the Age of Digital Competition, Innovation, and Power*. New York: Harper Business, 2019.

6. "Etsy Market Cap 2013–2020: ETSY." Macrotrends, n.d. https://www.macrotrends. net/stocks/charts/Etsy/etsy/market-cap.

7. "Klöckner: Trailblazing the Steel Industry." World Economic Forum, 2019. https:// reports.weforum.org/digital-transformation/klockner/.

8. Roy, Prasanto K. "Why Did Walmart Buy India's Flipkart?" *BBC News*, May 11, 2018. https://www.bbc.com/news/world-asia-india-44064337.

9. Schultz, Abby. "Sotheby's Buys Online Antique and Vintage Furniture Retailer Viyet." *Barron's*, February 13, 2018. https://www.barrons.com/articles/sothebys-buys -online-antique-and-vintage-furniture-retailer-viyet-1518556570.

10. "Richemont to Buy Watchfinder as Pre-Owned Watch Market Heats Up." *Reuters*, June 1, 2018. https://www.reuters.com/article/us-watchfinder-m-a-richemont/ richemont-to-buy-watchfinder-as-pre-owned-watch-market-heats-up-idUSKCN 1IX5HQ.

11. Holt, Siobhan. "Watchfinder & Co Opens Second Store in Paris." *Retail Jeweller*, October 15, 2020. https://www.retail-jeweller.com/retail/watchfinder-co-opens -second-store-in-paris-15-10-2020/.

12. "Chinese Tech Giants Alibaba and JD.com Have Won Over Luxury Brands." *Retail Insight Network*, April 9, 2019.

13. Liu, Alex, and Jenny Hsu. "Tmall Luxury Connects High-End Brands with China's 'New Luxury' Gen Z Consumers." *Businesswire*, August 25, 2020. https://www .businesswire.com/news/home/20200824005678/en/Tmall-Luxury-Connects-High -End-Brands-with-China%E2%80%99s.

14. Schaller, Andreas, and Mathias Christen. "ADAMOS IIoT Platform Is Growing: Five Further Mechanical Engineering Firms Have Joined." *Dürr*, January 23, 2019. https://www.durr.com/en/media/news/news-detail/view/adamos-iiot-platform-is -growing-five-further-mechanical-engineering-firms-have-joined-2422.

15. Parker, Geoffrey, Marshall Van Alstyne, and Sangeet P. Choudary. *Platform Revolution: How Networked Markets Are Transforming the Economy—and How*

to Make Them Work for You. New York: W. W. Norton, 2016. See also Cusumano, Gawer, and Yoffie. *The Business of Platforms.*

CHAPTER 20

1. Bonnet, Didier. "A Portfolio Strategy to Execute Your Digital Transformation." Capgemini Consulting White Paper, 2016. https://www.capgemini.com/consulting/wp-content/uploads/sites/30/2016/08/portfolio_strategy-didier-bonnet.pdf.
2. Lakhani, Karim R., Marco Iansiti, and Kerry Herman. *GE and the Industrial Internet.* Harvard Business School Faculty & Research, 2015. https://www.hbs.edu/faculty/Pages/item.aspx?num=47272.
3. Bonnet, Didier, and George Westerman. "The Best Digital Business Model Put Evolution Before Revolution." *Harvard Business Review*, January 20, 2015. https://hbr.org/2015/01/the-best-digital-business-models-put-evolution-before-revolution.
4. Bonnet. "A Portfolio Strategy to Execute Your Digital Transformation."
5. Lakhani, Iansiti, and Herman. *GE and the Industrial Internet.*
6. Bonnet. "A Portfolio Strategy to Execute Your Digital Transformation."
7. Ibid.
8. Etherington, Darrel. "Banking Startup Simple Acquired for $117M, Will Continue to Operate Separately." *TechCrunch*, February 20, 2014. https://techcrunch.com/2014/02/20/simple-acquired-for-117m-will-continue-to-operate-separately-under-its-own-brand/.
9. Ulaga, Wolfgang, Franck Estoquié, Heiko Gebauer, Erik Grab, Stephan März, Patrick Soler, Hans van der Velden, Chloe Renault, Athanasios Kondis, and Lindsay McTeague. "From Product to Service: Navigating the Transition." IMD (article), 2013. https://www.imd.org/contentassets/9a2c2d15c4194e139a79da4b2ab936d6/26.-from-product-to-service-final-22-07-13.pdf.
10. Obwegeser, Nikolaus, Tomoko Yokoi, Michael Wade, and Tom Voskes. "7 Key Principles to Govern Digital Initiatives." *MIT Sloan Management Review*, April 1, 2020. https://sloanreview.mit.edu/article/7-key-principles-to-govern-digital-initiatives/.

CHAPTER 21

1. Wade, Michael, Jennifer Jordan, and Elizabeth Teracino. "Every Leader Needs to Navigate These 7 Tensions." *Harvard Business Review*, February 20, 2020. https://hbr.org/2020/02/every-leader-needs-to-navigate-these-7-tensions.
2. Glazer, Robert. "'Command and Control' Leadership Is Dead. Here's What's Taking Its Place." *Inc.*, August 12, 2019. https://www.inc.com/robert-glazer/command-control-leadership-is-dead-heres-whats-taking-its-place.html.
3. Mangelsdorf, Martha E. "From the Editor: Decision Making in the Digital Age." *MIT Sloan Management Review*, December 19, 2013. https://sloanreview.mit.edu/article/from-the-editor-decision-making-in-the-digital-age/.
4. Majdan, Krzysztof and Michal Wasowski. "We sat down with Microsoft's CEO to discuss the past, present and future of the company." *Business Insider*. April 20,

2017. https://www.businessinsider.com/satya-nadella-microsoft-ceo-qa-2017
-4?r=US&IR=T.

5. Ifeanyi, KC. "'Pandora Broke My Heart': Tim Westergren, Digital Radio Pioneer, Returns to Break the Music Industrial Complex." *Fast Company*, April 30, 2020. https://www.fastcompany.com/90494948/pandora-broke-my-heart-tim -westergren-digital-radio-pioneer-returns-to-break-the-music-industrial-complex.

6. Weiner, Yitzi. "Red Hat CEO Jim Whitehurst on Why It's So Important for a Leader to Be Humble." *Medium*, January 31, 2019. https://medium.com/authority-magazine/ red-hat-ceo-jim-whitehurst-on-why-its-so-important-for-a-leader-to-be-humble -3128113c3a36.

7. Shaywitz, David. "Novartis CEO Who Wanted to Bring Tech into Pharma Now Explains Why It's So Hard." *Forbes*, January 16, 2019. https://www.forbes.com/sites/ davidshaywitz/2019/01/16/novartis-ceo-who-wanted-to-bring-tech-into-pharma -now-explains-why-its-so-hard/?sh=5edf3d197fc4.

8. Amed, Imran. "CEO Talk: Angela Ahrendts on Burberry's Connected Culture." *The Business of Fashion*, September 3, 2013. https://www.businessoffashion.com/articles/ ceo-talk/burberry-angela-ahrendts.

9. Jordan, Jennifer, and Michael Sorell. "Why You Should Create a 'Shadow Board' of Younger Employees." *Harvard Business Review*, January 4, 2019. https://hbr .org/2019/06/why-you-should-create-a-shadow-board-of-younger-employees.

10. Author interviews.

11. Author interviews.

12. Hogan Assessments. *Hogan Agile Leader*. https://www.performanceprograms.com/ shop/hogan-agile-leader-report/.

CHAPTER 22

1. Péladeau, Pierre, and Olaf Acker. "Have We Reached 'Peak' Chief Digital Officer?" *Strategy+Business* (blog), March 26, 2019. https://www.strategy-business.com/blog/ Have-we-reached-peak-chief-digital-officer?gko=2443a.

2. Wade, Michael. "From Dazzling to Departed—Why Chief Digital Officers Are Doomed to Fail." World Economic Forum, February 12, 2020. https://www .weforum.org/agenda/2020/02/chief-digital-officer-cdo-skills-tenure-fail/.

3. Wade, Michael, and Nikolaus Obwegeser. "How to Choose the Right Digital Leader for Your Company." *MIT Sloan Management Review*, May 14, 2019. https:// sloanreview.mit.edu/article/how-to-choose-the-right-digital-leader-for-your -company/.

4. *Digital Leadership: Unilever: Consumer-First Approach Accelerates Digital Transformation. An Interview with Rahul Welde, Unilever.* Capgemini Research Institute, 2019. https://www.capgemini.com/ch-en/wp-content/uploads/sites/43/ 2019/02/Download-%E2%80%93-DTR-12_Unilever_Web.pdf.

5. Chng, Daniel Han Ming, Tae-Yeol Kim, Brad Gilbreath, and Lynne Andersson. "Why People Believe in Their Leaders—or Not." *MIT Sloan Management Review*,

August 17, 2018. https://sloanreview.mit.edu/article/why-people-believe-in-their-leaders-or-not/.

6. *Digital Transformation Review, Twelfth Edition. Taking Digital Transformation to the Next Level; Lessons from the Leaders.* Capgemini Research Institute, February 12, 2019. https://www.capgemini.com/wp-content/uploads/2019/02/Download-%E2%80%93-Digital-Transformation-Review-12.pdf.

7. Chng, Kim, Gilbreath, and Andersson. "Why People Believe in Their Leaders—or Not."

8. Author interviews.

9. Author interviews.

10. Wade and Obwegeser. "How to Choose the Right Digital Leader for Your Company."

11. Hamel, Gary, and C. K. Prahalad. "Strategic Intent." *Harvard Business Review*, July–August 2005. https://hbr.org/2005/07/strategic-intent.

CHAPTER 23

1. Horlacher, Anna, and Thomas Hess. "What Does a Chief Digital Officer Do? Managerial Tasks and Roles of a New C-Level Position in the Context of Digital Transformation." *Proceedings of the 49th Hawaii International Conference on System Sciences*, 2016. DOI: 10.1109/HICSS.2016.634.

2. Wade, Michael, and Nikolaus Obwegeser. "How to Choose the Right Digital Leader for Your Company." *MIT Sloan Management Review*, May 14, 2019. https://sloanreview.mit.edu/article/how-to-choose-the-right-digital-leader-for-your-company/.

3. Walchshofer, Manuela, and René Riedl. "Der Chief Digital Officer (CDO): Eine Empirische Untersuchung." *HMD Praxis der Wirtschaftsinformatiked*, 2017. DOI: 10.1365/s40702-017-0320-7.

4. Tumbas, Sanja, Nicholas Berente, and Jan vom Brocke. "Digital Innovation and Institutional Entrepreneurship: Chief Digital Officer Perspectives of Their Emerging Role." *Journal of Information Technology*, Vol. 33, no. 3, 2018. DOI: 10.1057/s41265-018-0055-0.

5. Singh, Anna, Patricia Klarner, and Thomas Hess. "How Do Chief Digital Officers Pursue Digital Transformation Activities? The Role of Organization Design Parameters." *Long Range Planning*, Vol. 53, No. 3, 2019. https://doi.org/10.1016/j.lrp.2019.07.001.

6. Singh, Anna, and Thomas Hess. "How Chief Digital Officers Promote the Digital Transformation of Their Companies." *MIS Quarterly Executive*, Vol. 16, 2017. https://www.researchgate.net/publication/316629795_How_Chief_Digital_Officers_Promote_the_Digital_Transformation_of_their_Companies.

7. Author interviews.

8. Author interviews.

CHAPTER 24

1. Wiles, Jackie. "Foster Innovation to Drive Digital Transformation." *Gartner*, April 1, 2019. https://www.gartner.com/smarterwithgartner/foster-innovation-to-drive-digital-transformation/.

2. Davenport, Thomas H., and Thomas C. Redman. "Digital Transformation Comes Down to Talent in 4 Key Areas." *Harvard Business Review*, May 21, 2020. https://hbr.org/2020/05/digital-transformation-comes-down-to-talent-in-4-key-areas.

3. Wang, Qian (Emily), Michael D. Myers, and David Sundaram. "Digital Natives and Digital Immigrants," *Business & Information Systems Engineering*, Vol. 5, pp. 409–419, November 8, 2013. https://link.springer.com/article/10.1007/s12599-013-0296-y#:~:text=The%20article%20looks%20at%20the,stage%20during%20their%20adult%20life.

4. See *PwC 23rd Annual Global CEO Survey: Navigating the Rising Tide of Uncertainty*. http://www.ceosurvey.pwc. See also Fuller, Joseph B., Judith K. Wallenstein, Manjari Raman, and Alice de Chalendar. "Your Workforce Is More Adaptable Than You Think." *Harvard Business Review*, May 1, 2019. https://hbr.org/2019/05/your-workforce-is-more-adaptable-than-you-think.

5. Pashler, Harold, Mark McDaniel, Doug Rohrer, and Robert Bjork. "Learning Styles: Concepts and Evidence." *PubMed*, December 1, 2009. https://journals.sagepub.com/doi/full/10.1111/j.1539-6053.2009.01038.x?casa_token=Dn8qaRIkmq4AAAAA%3AgPyPJ3xb9quzsRXFPuGngk9miRicgs2NRqOxFeSs-KiwGofm5ue8WTHNUkWBE9GMHc5frzGRzbsS. https://doi.org/10.1111/j.1539-6053.2009.01038.x.

6. Piskorski, Mikolaj J., and Ivy Buche. "Digital Transformation at Axel Springer." IMD, 2016. Case Study Reference No. IMD-7-1733.

7. Ibid.

8. Caminiti, Susan. "AT&T's $1 Billion Gambit: Retraining Nearly Half Its Workforce for Jobs of the Future." *CNBC*, March 13, 2018. https://www.cnbc.com/2018/03/13/atts-1-billion-gambit-retraining-nearly-half-its-workforce.html.

9. Donovan, John, and Cathy Benko. "AT&T's Talent Overhaul." *Harvard Business Review*, October 1, 2016. https://hbr.org/2016/10/atts-talent-overhaul.

10. Bersin, Josh, and Marc Zao-Sanders. "Making Learning a Part of Everyday Work." *Harvard Business Review*, February 19, 2019. https://hbr.org/2019/02/making-learning-a-part-of-everyday-work.

11. Boynton, Andy. "Are You an 'I' or a 'T'?" *Forbes*, October 18, 2011. https://www.forbes.com/sites/andyboynton/2011/10/18/are-you-an-i-or-a-t/?sh=6f33fba46e88.

12. Brassey, Jacqueline, Katie Coates, and Nick van Dam. "Seven Essential Elements of a Lifelong-Learning Mind-Set." McKinsey & Company, 2019. https://www.mckinsey.com/~/media/McKinsey/Business%20Functions/Organization/Our%20Insights/Seven%20essential%20elements%20of%20a%20lifelong%20learning%20mind%20set/Seven-essential-elements-of-a-liefelong-learning-mind-set.pdf.

13. Lundberg, Abbie, and George Westerman. "The Transformer CLO." *Harvard Business Review*, January 1, 2020. https://hbr.org/2020/01/the-transformer-clo.

14. Ibid.

CHAPTER 25

1. Altschuler, Max. "How Managers Can Support Business Unity." *MIT Sloan Management Review*, April 7, 2020. https://sloanreview.mit.edu/article/how -managers-can-support-business-unity/.

2. Goran, Julie, Laura LaBerge, and Ramesh Srinivasan. "Culture for a Digital Age." McKinsey, June 20, 2017. https://www.mckinsey.com/business-functions/mckinsey -digital/our-insights/culture-for-a-digital-age.

3. Obwegeser, Nikolaus, Tomoko Yokoi, Michael Wade, and Tom Voskes. "7 Key Principles to Govern Digital Initiatives." *MIT Sloan Management Review*, April 1, 2020. https://sloanreview.mit.edu/article/7-key-principles-to-govern-digital-initiatives.

4. Kane, Gerald C., Anh Nguyen Philips, Jonathan R. Copulsky, and Garth R. Andrus. *The Technology Fallacy: How People Are the Real Key to Digital Transformation.* Cambridge, MA: MIT Press, 2019. https://mitpress.mit.edu/books/technology-fallacy.

5. Kane, Gerald C., Anh N. Phillips, David Kiron, and Natasha Buckley. *Accelerating Digital Innovation Inside and Out.* Deloitte, 2019. https://www2.deloitte.com/us/ en/insights/focus/digital-maturity/digital-innovation-ecosystems-organizational -agility.html.

6. Kappelman, Leon, Russell Torres, Ephraim McLean, Chris Mauer, Vess Johnson, and Kevin Kim. "The 2018 SIM IT Issues and Trends Study." *MIS Quarterly Executive*, Vol. 18, No. 1, March 2019.

7. Wade, Michael R., James Macaulay, Andy Noronha, and Joel Barbier. *Orchestrating Transformation: How to Deliver Winning Performance with a Connected Approach to Change.* Lausanne: IMD, 2019.

8. Ibid.

9. "Ian Rogers, LVMH; When Luxury Goes Digital." Capgemini. https://www .capgemini.com/ian-rogers-lvmh/.

10. "How to Create & Cultivate a Digital Culture in Your Organization." Digital Marketing Institute, January 9, 2018. https://digitalmarketinginstitute.com/blog/ how-to-create-and-cultivate-a-digital-culture-in-your-organization.

11. Author interviews.

12. Harvard University. "Carrots Are Better Than Sticks for Building Human Cooperation, Study Finds." *ScienceDaily*, September 4, 2019. http://www .sciencedaily.com/releases/2009/09/090903163550.htm.

13. Wade, Michael R., and Lisa Duke. "Rabobank: Building Digital Agility at Scale." IMD (case study), October 2019. https://www.imd.org/research-knowledge/for -educators/case-studies/Rabobank-Building-digital-agility-at-scale/. Reference No. IMD-7-2020.

14. Hron, Michal, and Nikolaus Obwegeser. "Scrum in Practice: An Overview of Scrum Adaptations." *Proceedings of the 51st Hawaii International Conference on System Sciences*, 2018. DOI: 10.24251/HICSS.2018.679.

15. Cruth, Mark. "Discover the Spotify Model: What the Most Popular Music Technology Company Can Teach Us About Scaling Agile." *Atlassian*, 2020. https:// www.atlassian.com/agile/agile-at-scale/spotify.

16. Schlatmann, Bart. "ING's Agile Transformation." *McKinsey Quarterly*, January 10, 2017. https://www.mckinsey.com/industries/financial-services/our-insights/ings -agile-transformation.

PART SIX

1. Wade, Michael, and Jialu Shan. "Covid-19 Has Accelerated Digital Transformation, but May Have Made It Harder Not Easier." *MIS Quarterly Executive*, Vol. 19, No. 3, 2020.

CHAPTER 26

1. Author interviews.
2. Yoo, Youngjin, Richard J. Boland, Kalle Lyytinen, and Ann Majchrzak. "Organizing for Innovation in the Digitized World." *Organization Science*, pp. 1398–1408, September 2012.
3. InGenius: Nestlé's Employee Innovation Accelerator. Accessed February 16, 2021. https://ingenius-accelerator.nestle.com/.
4. Author interviews.
5. Author interviews.
6. Chesbrough, Henry W., and Melissa M. Appleyard. "Open Innovation and Strategy." *California Review Management*, Vol. 50, Fall 2007. https://doi.org/10.2307/41166416.
7. LEGO Ideas. Accessed February 16, 2021. https://ideas.lego.com/.
8. Schlender, Brent and Steve Jobs. "The Three Faces of Steve." *Fortune Magazine.* November 9, 1998. https://archive.fortune.com/magazines/fortune/fortune_archive/ 1998/11/09/250880/index.htm.
9. Harwood, Roland. "Unleashing Customer Innovation with LEGO Ideas." *100%Open*, April 30, 2014. https://www.100open.com/unleashing-customer-innovation-with -lego-ideas/.
10. Author interviews.
11. Obwegeser, Nikolaus, Tomoko Yokoi, Michael Wade, and Tom Voskes. "7 Key Principles to Govern Digital Initiatives." *MIT Sloan Management Review*, April 1, 2020. https://sloanreview.mit.edu/article/7-key-principles-to-govern-digital-initiatives.
12. Author interviews.
13. Author interviews.
14. Müller, Sune D., Nikolaus Obwegeser, Jakob V. Glud, and Gunnar Johildarson. "Digital Innovation and Organizational Culture: The Case of a Danish Media Company." *Scandinavian Journal of Information Systems*, Vol. 31, No. 2, 2019.

CHAPTER 27

1. Mattes, Frank. "Scaling-Up: The Framework." *The Digital Transformation People*, May 17, 2019. https://www.thedigitaltransformationpeople.com/channels/strategy -and-innovation/scaling-up-the-framework/.
2. "The Secrets to Scaling Digital." Hitachi Consulting, 2019. https://www.hitachi vantara.com/en-us/pdf/hcc/point-of-view/hitachi-scaling-digital-pov.pdf.

3. Moyer, Kristin, and Ian Cox. "Digital Business Transformation: Closing the Gap Between Ambition and Reality." Gartner Research, June 18, 2018. https://www.gartner .com/en/documents/3879565/digital-business-transformation-closing-the-gap -between-.

4. Abood, David, Aidan Quilligan, Raghav Narsalay, and Aarohi Sen. Accenture, 2019. https://www.accenture.com/_acnmedia/Thought-Leadership-Assets/PDF/ Accenture-IXO-HannoverMesse-report.pdf.

5. Author interviews.

6. Obwegeser, Nikolaus, Tomoko Yokoi, Michael Wade, and Tom Voskes. "7 Key Principles to Govern Digital Initiatives." MIT Sloan Management Review, April 1, 2020. https://sloanreview.mit.edu/article/7-key-principles-to-govern-digital-initiatives/.

7. Wade, Michael, James Macaulay, Andy Noronha, and Joel Barbier. Orchestrating Transformation: How to Deliver Winning Performance with a Connected Approach to Change. Lausanne: IMD, 2019.

8. Author interviews.

9. Author interviews.

10. Salzman, Marian L., Ira Matathia, and Ann O'Reilly. Buzz: Harness the Power of Influence and Create Demand. Hoboken, NJ: John Wiley & Sons, 2005.

11. Author interviews.

12. Author interviews.

13. Büchel, Bettina, and Michael R. Wade. "Anchored Agility: The Holy Grail of Competitiveness." IMD (article), June 2013. https://www.imd.org/research -knowledge/articles/anchored-agility-the-holy-grail-of--competitiveness/.

CHAPTER 28

1. Forth, Patrick, Tom Reichert, Romain de Laubier, and Saibal Chakraborty. "Flipping the Odds of Digital Transformation Success." BCG, October 29, 2020. https://www.bcg .com/en-ch/publications/2020/increasing-odds-of-success-in-digital-transformation.

2. Moore, Susan. "How to Measure Digital Transformation Progress." Gartner, September 30, 2019. https://www.gartner.com/smarterwithgartner/how-to-measure -digital-transformation-progress/.

3. Interview with authors.

4. US Department of Energy. "Types of Maintenance Programs." Operations & Maintenance Best Practices Guide: Release 3.0, Chapter 5, 2013. https://www1.eere .energy.gov/femp/pdfs/OM_5.pdf.

5. Duguid, Ryan. "How Automation Is Transforming the Supply Chain Process." Manufacturing.net, September 7, 2018. https://www.manufacturing.net/automation/ article/13245800/how-automation-is-transforming-the-supply-chain-process.

6. Gregory, Sonia. "19 Important Digital Marketing Metrics for Measuring Success." FreshSparks, August 13, 2019. https://freshsparks.com/digital-marketing-success/.

7. Sia, Siew Kien, Christina Soh, and Peter Weill. "How DBS Bank Pursued a Digital Business Strategy." MIS Quarterly Executive, Vol. 15, No. 2, 2016. https://aisel.aisnet .org/misqe/vol15/iss2/4/.

8. "How to Use Digital Learning to Increase Employee Engagement." *Profiles Asia Pacific*, May 5, 2020. https://www.profilesasiapacific.com/2020/05/05/digital-learning -employee-engagement/.

9. Hansen, Rina, and Sia Siew Kien. "Hummel's Digital Transformation Toward Omnichannel Retailing: Key Lessons Learned." *MIS Quarterly Executive*, Vol. 4, No. 2, 2015. https://aisel.aisnet.org/misqe/vol14/iss2/3/.

CHAPTER 29

1. Fenwick, Nigel. "The State of Digital Business 2018: Top Technologies." *Forrester* (blog), March 2, 2018. https://go.forrester.com/blogs/digital-business-top-tech/.

2. Lucas Jr., Henry C., and Jie Mein Goh. "Disruptive Technology: How Kodak Missed the Digital Photography Revolution." *Journal of Strategic Information Systems*, Vol. 18, No. 1, pp. 46–55, March 2009. https://www.sciencedirect.com/science/article/ abs/pii/S0963868709000043. https://doi.org/10.1016/j.jsis.2009.01.002.

3. Aspara, Jaakko, Juha-Antti Lamberg, Arjo Laukia, and Henrikki Tikkanen. "Strategic Management of Business Model Transformation: Lessons from Nokia." *Management Decision*, Vol. 49, No. 4, May 2011. https://www.research-gate.net/publication/244085692_Strategic_management_of_business_model _transformation_Lessons_from_Nokia.

4. Davis, Todd, and John Higgins. "A Blockbuster Failure: How an Outdated Business Model Destroyed a Giant." *Chapter 11 Bankruptcy Case Studies*, 2013. https://trace .tennessee.edu/utk_studlawbankruptcy/11.

5. McGrath, Rita. *Seeing Around Corners: How to Spot Inflection Points in Business Before They Happen*. Boston: Houghton Mifflin Harcourt, 2019.

6. Kane, Gerald C., Anh Nguyen Phillips, Jonathan R. Copulsky, and Garth R. Andrus. *The Technology Fallacy: How People Are the Real Key to Digital Transformation*. Cambridge, MA: MIT Press, 2019.

7. *Entrepreneur* Staff. "Read Jeff Bezos's Inspiring Letter to Shareholders on Why He Keeps Amazon at 'Day 1.'" *Entrepreneur*, April 12, 2017. https://www.entrepreneur .com/article/292797.

8. Loveday, Steven. "Toyota Won't Make a Proper EV Because Dealers Say It Won't Sell." *InsideEVs*, December 7, 2018. https://insideevs.com/news/341448/toyota-wont -make-a-proper-ev-because-dealers-say-it-wont-sell/.

9. Viki, Tendayi. "How Making Small Bets Can Help Leaders Accept Innovation Failure." *Forbes*, June 11, 2020. https://www.forbes.com/sites/tendayiviki/ 2020/06/11/how-making-small-bets-can-help-leaders-accept-innovation-failure/ ?sh=315d633d2c10.

10. McGrath. *Seeing Around Corners*.

11. Sims, Peter. *Little Bets: How Breakthrough Ideas Emerge from Small Discoveries*. New York: Simon & Schuster, 2011, p. 21.

12. "Gartner Hype Cycle." Gartner, 2020. https://www.gartner.com/en/research/ methodologies/gartner-hype-cycle.

13. Deloitte. "Tech Trends 2020," https://www2.deloitte.com/content/campaigns/za/ Tech-Trends-2020/Tech-Trends-2020/Tech-Trends-2020.html.

14. ThoughtWorks. *Technology Radar: An Opinionated Guide to Technology Frontiers*, Vol. 23, 2020. https://www.thoughtworks.com/radar.

15. Zalando Tech Radar—2020. https://opensource.zalando.com/tech-radar/.

16. McAfee, Andrew, and Erik Brynjolfsson. "Investing in the IT That Makes a Competitive Difference." *Harvard Business Review*, July 1, 2008. https://hbr.org/ 2008/07/investing-in-the-it-that-makes-a-competitive-difference.

17. ADAMOS. https://www.adamos.com/.

18. "Collaborative Innovation: Transforming Business, Driving Growth." World Economic Forum, August 2015. http://www3.weforum.org/docs/WEF _Collaborative_Innovation_report_2015.pdf.

CHAPTER 30

1. Reeves, Martin, David Rhodes, Christian Ketels, and Kevin Whitaker. "Advantage in Adversity: Winning the Next Downturn." BCG Henderson Institute, January 18, 2019. https://bcghendersoninstitute.com/advantage-in-adversity-winning-the-next -downturn-5853b4425db1.

2. Palmer, Maija. "Pandemic Kills Corporate Innovation Plans." *Sifted*, June 9, 2020. https://sifted.eu/articles/pandemic-kills-corporate-innovation/.

3. Trentmann, Nina. "Covid-19 Forces Levi to Accelerate Its Consumer Strategy Shift." *Wall Street Journal*, August 1, 2020. https://www.wsj.com/articles/covid-19-forces -levi-to-accelerate-its-consumer-strategy-shift-11596223224.

4. Eaton, Kit. "Amex Invests $100 Million in Its Future: Digital Ecosystem, Not the Plastic Card." *Fast Company*, September 11, 2011. https://www.fastcompany.com/ 1793698/amex-invests-100-million-its-future-digital-ecosystem-not-plastic-card.

5. Verhage, Julie, Jenny Surane, and Bloomberg. "New Tech Startups Challenge AmEx in the Niche Corporate Card Market." *Fortune*, March 8, 2020. https://fortune. com/2020/03/08/new-tech-startups-want-to-remake-the-corporate-card/.

6. Takahashi, Dean. "Intel CEO: Bad companies are destroyed by crises . . . great companies are improved by them." Venturebeat.com. April 23, 2020. https://venturebeat. com/2020/04/23/intel-ceo-bad-companies-are-destroyed-by-crises-great-compa- nies-are-improved-by-them/.

7. "Technology Versus Pandemic." *Porsche Consulting Magazine*, July 23, 2020. https:// newsroom.porsche.com/en/2020/company/porsche-consulting-nestle-cio-filippo -catalano-21556.html.

8. Author interviews.

9. Olson, Ryan, "COVID-19: The Cybercrime Gold Rush of 2020." *Palo Alto Networks* (blog), July 21, 2020. https://blog.paloaltonetworks.com/2020/07/unit-42-cybercrime -gold-rush/.

10. Greenberg, Andy. "The Untold Story of NotPetya, the Most Devastating Cyberattack in History." *Wired*, August 22, 2018. https://www.wired.com/story/notpetya-cyberattack -ukraine-russia-code-crashed-the-world/.

11. See "Cyber Security in the Age of Digital Transformation." Nominet White Paper. https://nominetcyber.com/cyber-security-in-the-age-of-digital-transformation. And see Nofal, Hani. "The Unspoken Truth: The Role of Cybersecurity in Breaking the Digital Transformation Deadlock." *GBM 8th Annual Security Survey 2019*.

12. "Bridging the Digital Transformation Divide: Leaders Must Balance Risk & Growth." *Ponemon Institute Research Report*, March 2018. https://www.ibm.com/downloads/cas/ON8MVMXW.

13. Global Center for Digital Business Transformation. IMD Business School, 2020.

14. Author interviews, August 2020.

15. Gstettner, Stefan, Robert Roesgen, Amit Ganeriwalla, and Gideon Walter. "Three Paths to Advantage with Digital Supply Chains." *BCG*, February 1, 2016. https://www.bcg.com/en-ch/publications/2016/three-paths-to-advantage-with-digital-supply-chains.

16. Cosgrove, Emma. "How P&G Created a 'Ready for Anything' Supply Chain." *Supply Chain Dive* (newsletter), June 3, 2019. https://www.supplychaindive.com/news/pg-ready-for-anything-supply-chain-disaster-response/555945.

17. Author interviews.

CONCLUSION

1. McArthur, G., C. K. Wu, J. Hull, A. Kingston, and M. McIntosh. "Journey." In Oxford Learner's Dictionary. Oxford University Press, n.d. https://www.oxfordlearnersdictionaries.com/definition/american_english/journey_1.

2. *Worldwide Semi-Annual Digital Transformation Spending Guide*. International Data Corporation, 2019.

3. Soule, Deborah L., Akshita Puram, George F. Westerman, and Didier Bonnet. "Becoming a Digital Organization: The Journey to Digital Dexterity." *SSRN Electronic Journal*, December 2, 2015. https://doi.org/10.2139/ssrn.2697688.

4. Bonnet, Didier, Akshita Deora Puram, Jerome Buvat, Subrahmanyam KVJ, and Amol Khadikar. "Organizing for Digital: Why Digital Dexterity Matters." Capgemini Consulting (research paper), 2015.

5. Capital One Q4 2013 earnings call. http://investor.capitalone.com/static-files/8c0456aa-22d3-4fb9-b515-187783c1f015.

6. Johnson, Nick. Interview of Robin Bordoli: "How Artificial Intelligence Can Help You Get 100x More Work Done." *Salesforce Live*. Accessed February 17, 2021. https://www.salesforce.com/video/1718054/.

7. Girard, Bernard. *The Google Way: How One Company Is Revolutionizing Management as We Know It*. San Francisco: No Starch Press, 2009.

8. "For Haier's Zhang Ruimin, Success Means Creating the Future." *Knowledge@Wharton* (podcast), April 28, 2018. Accessed February 17, 2021. https://knowledge.wharton.upenn.edu/article/haiers-zhang-ruimin-success-means-creating-the-future/.

9. "Digital Transformation Becomes Mainstream: Airbus Digital Teams Join Engineering and Operations." Airbus, May 15, 2020. https://www.airbus.com/ newsroom/news/en/2020/05/digital-transformation-becomes-mainstream-airbus -digital-teams-join-engineering-and-operations.html.

INDEX

Page numbers followed by *f* and *t* refer to figures and tables, respectively.

ABOUT THE AUTHORS

Michael Wade

Michael Wade is a professor of innovation and strategy at IMD and directs IMD's Global Center for Digital Business Transformation, a research group focused on digital disruption and transformation. He has authored ten books on digital and technology topics. His academic research has appeared in *Harvard Business Review*, *MIT Sloan Management Review*, *Strategic Management Journal*, and *MIS Quarterly*, among others. He directs a number of executive programs at IMD on digital topics, including Leading Digital Business Transformation, Digital Disruption, Digital Execution, and Digital Transformation for Boards. Michael regularly comments on digital topics in the print and visual media, and has been named one of the top digital thought leaders in Switzerland three times by *Bilanz*, *Le Temps*, and *Handelszeitung*.

Didier Bonnet

Didier Bonnet is a professor of strategy and digital transformation at IMD Business School. He has more than 25 years' experience in strategy development, globalization, and business transformation for large corporations, and has worked in over 15 countries. Prior to IMD, Didier was a strategy consultant and EVP, Global Digital Transformation at Capgemini Invent. He is coauthor of the bestselling book *Leading Digital: Turning Technology into Business Transformation*. Didier's research has been published in *Harvard Business Review*, *MIT Sloan Management Review*, *R&D Management*, and *Business Strategy Review*, as well as the *Financial Times* and *Forbes*, among others. Didier is also a regular media commentator on digital transformation topics. He was named "Global Digital Leader—2018" by the CDO Conclave and was named in the top five global thought leaders and influencers on digital disruption in 2021 by Thinkers 360. He graduated with a degree in economics and obtained his Doctorate from New College, University of Oxford.

Tomoko Yokoi

Tomoko Yokoi is a researcher and writer at the Global Center for Digital Business Transformation at IMD. She is a *Forbes* contributor on topics related to digital transformation and innovation, and her articles have been published in numerous practitioner outlets such as *MIT Sloan Management Review* and *Quartz,* among others. Tomoko brings practitioner insights to her research, drawing from 20 years of experience as a senior executive in B2B and B2C industries ranging from industrial technologies and healthcare to enterprise software and educational services. As a part-time digital entrepreneur, she keeps her finger on the pulse of new technologies and trends, and provides advisory services in digital business transformations. She holds an MBA from IMD and an MALD from the Fletcher School of Law and Diplomacy.

Nikolaus Obwegeser

Nikolaus Obwegeser is a professor and director of the Institute for Digital Technology Management at the Bern University of Applied Sciences (BFH). His areas of expertise include digital business transformation and innovation. A scholar and author, Nikolaus has had his research published in numerous highly regarded academic and practitioner outlets, including *MIT Sloan Management Review*, *Technovation*, and the *Journal of Product Innovation Management*. Before joining BFH, Nikolaus was a research fellow at IMD and an associate professor of information systems at Aarhus University (Denmark). Apart from his research activities, Nikolaus regularly provides advisory and consulting services for public and private organizations in the area of digital business transformation.